WINNING THE RACE?

Religion, Hope, and Reshaping the Sport Enhancement Debate

Sports and Religion

A SERIES EDITED
BY JOSEPH L. PRICE

WINNING THE RACE?

Religion, Hope, and Reshaping the

Sport Enhancement Debate

Tracy J. Trothen

MERCER UNIVERSITY PRESS | *Macon, Georgia*

MUP/ P516

© 2015 by Mercer University Press
Published by Mercer University Press
1501 Mercer University Drive
Macon, Georgia 31207
All rights reserved

9 8 7 6 5 4 3 2 1

Books published by Mercer University Press are printed on acid-free paper
that meets the requirements of the American National Standard for
Information Sciences—Permanence of Paper for Printed Library Materials.

ISBN   978-0-88146-543-3
Cataloging-in-Publication Data is available from the Library of Congress

In loving memory of L and B, who accompanied me through much of my writing.

Contents

Acknowledgments

This research was made possible through the Lilly Theological Research Grants Program and supported by the Canadian Foundation for Spiritual Care/Fondation Canadienne de Soins Spirituels. (CFSC/FCSS). I am indebted to Queen's University, for sabbatical time during which I wrote most of these pages.

My research assistant in the summer of 2013, Nadine Abu-Ghazaleh, discovered valuable sources that helped inform this book. She also put together my bibliography, organizing numerous sources into proper style, which was no small feat.

I am very grateful for the careful editing and critical feedback by Sport and Religion Series editor Joe Price, Professor of Religious Studies at Whittier College. His thoughtful questions helped me write a clearer and more cogent book. My colleague Calvin Mercer generously reviewed portions of the manuscript; his comments added significantly to the last two chapters. Thanks also to numerous colleagues and friends who discussed the topics of this book with me. These conversations were stimulating and inspiring.

I also want to thank the people at Mercer University Press who helped move this book through the publishing process. In particular, thanks to Marsha Luttrell, Publishing Assistant, and Dr. Marc Jolley, Director of Mercer University Press. Any mistakes are mine alone.

Particular thanks goes to my husband, Ron, who always believed in the value of this book and encouraged me along the way. Appreciation also goes to other family members, including Allan, Curt, Susanne, Sophia, and Gwen for many spirited conversations about sport. Several friends and colleagues stimulated my thinking as I wrote. To them I am also very grateful. Special thanks goes to my friend Marie for helping me with the index.

Foreword

In recent years much of the scholarly work about sports and religion has focused on the origins of sports in religious rituals, the historical development of sports and their acceptance or rejection by established religious communities, and cultural issues related to the mythic resonance of sports with deeply held beliefs. Often the works have displayed evangelical sympathies while examining the testimonies of athletes, while others have utilized comparative methods to explore the personal, spiritual significance of sport (such as creating the prospect for "flow") or to analyze the religious power of sports to bind and direct groups of passionate followers.

In her distinct work Tracy Trothen takes a different tack (to use a sporting metaphor from sailing) by raising ethical and theological questions about the intersections of sports with techno-science. Repeatedly, she addresses foundational issues and questions related to human nature, the quest for perfection, and the basis for hope.

Among the fundamental questions that she asks is: What does it mean to be human? For instance, did the prosthetic legs of Oscar Pistorius, who competed in the 4x400 relay in the 2012 Summer Olympics, give him a technological advantage beyond those of human skeletal and muscular structure? And does simply raising questions about his fitness to compete belittle what it means to be human? Related questions also arise. Should humans—as humans—demand that contests and events be restricted to those who can compete without the aid of devices that restore human functions required for the events? Or should humans—as humans—enthusiastically celebrate the inclusiveness of participation that prosthetic devices might enable? And further, do prescribed drugs for asthmatic athletes provide them with a similar, though unseen, advantage for their competitions by improving their respiratory functions? Do enhanced devices and medical intervention enable performances that are beyond human potential?

In the human quest for excellence or what might be called a perfect performance, Trothen raises additional questions about the pursuit of records and the effects that improved equipment, nutritional awareness, and medical treatments might have on athletes pursuing record-setting performances. How can one argue, she wonders, that the best-ever human performance was swum by a record breaker in a polyurethane bodysuit than by the previous record holder since the suit itself was judged to provide a measureable reduction in time? The underlying question about technological enhancements of equipment available to multiple participants also can be applied to the improved design of heads on golf clubs or the dimpling of golf balls, both of which claim to improve the length and flight of a well-struck ball; or the difference in homerun production following the introduction of the live ball in baseball; or the dramatic increase in the cleared height for pole vaulters after the introduction of fiberglass poles. To what extent do the new distances reflect better human performance or simply improved equipment?

Trothen connects these issues about equipment improvement also to the possible diminution of hope, which comprises the spiritual core of the sports experience. If dramatically improved equipment shifts the prospects for victory or personal best performance from ability, discipline, and execution to the use of stellar equipment and performance enhancing supplements, then what effect will there be on the athlete's and fan's experiences of hope?

Not only does Trothen deal in depth with the multiple issues, she also explores criteria for considering what questions are responsible and how responses to probing questions should be proposed.

Deftly noting their boundaries and intersections, Trothen traverses the often discrete territories of theological ethics, sports history, technological innovations, and pharmaceutical effects to study their converged impact on the meaning derived from the experience of sport. In *Winning the Race?* Trothen adds new dimensions of sophisticated analysis to the growing interdisciplinary field of sports and religion.

—Joseph L. Price
Editor, Sports and Religion
A Series by Mercer University Press

Preface

What Might Religion Have to Do with Sport and the Enhancement Debate?

I have been a die-hard Toronto Maple Leafs fan since I was ten years old. I have yet to see them win a Stanley Cup. I get frustrated and blame everything from the rise of professionalism in sport to coaches, owners, referees, fans, and even a lack of heart in some players. Yet all it takes is a new season, a team that tries hard, a few wins and I'm back on board. After being asked by several people over the years why I persist in being a Leafs' fan or why I pour time into my own very modest sports efforts, I turned my mind more deeply to those questions.

Why is it that so many of us put so much time and emotional and physical energy into sport? More than 100 million people tuned into NASCAR programming in 2012. The London 2012 summer Olympics was the most-watched event in television history with 217.4 million viewers watching part or all of these Olympic games. Viewership is diverse, with men and women well represented,[1] and dedicated fans will use whatever technology they can to watch their teams or athletes: "avid sports fans are 52 per cent more likely to own a tablet [or smart phone and other devices] than non-avid fans" and "41 per cent of all television related tweets are about sports programming, although sport accounts only for 1.3 per cent of all television programming."[2] Is it simply that we have nothing better to do or is it that we are procrastinating, avoiding more meaningful and pressing concerns? While these reasons might be part of what drives so many of us fans, I am not convinced that is the whole story.

---

[1] Forty percent of the viewership was female in 2012. Takefive, "The Marketing Muscle of Sports," webinar, 13 March 2013 (speakers: John Miller, Stephen Master, Mike Wall), http://www.comcastspotlight.com/markets/spokane/6619/news/9285/take5-webcast-feature-the-marketing-muscle-of-sports.

[2] Takefive, 2013.

As I thought back to my Toronto Maple Leaf commitment, my time playing house league ice hockey or my more recent dedication to (very slow) distance running, I came up with many reasons, none of them fully capturing my experiences with sports: time to myself while running; adrenaline rushes as a fan and as a participant; relationships developed through sports; experiences of myself as other than an academic; the intensity of embodyment; being present in the moment; and so on.

Sport includes, and is more than, these pieces for many of us. Indeed, the closest descriptor that I can offer is that sport is like a religion in many ways and may even be called a secular religion. While many may chafe at that contention, I stand by it. Sport is *not* an organized mainstream religion. Yet, it *can* function similarly or complementarily to a religion in many respects. I suggest that the pursuit and embrace of hope are at the core of this religious-like phenomenon. What we hope for is connected to our worldviews, convictions, and values. And, as I will show, hope as it is found in sport, is affected by the increasing use of techno-science innovations.

Scholars from a variety of disciplines including religious studies, theology, kinesiology, sports studies, literature, history, philosophy, health studies, and psychology have addressed the relationship between sport and religion. Although not new, the topic has generated vigor of a different sort in the last decade. Previously, most scholars were interested in the ancient Olympia and/or muscular Christianity with some attention to muscular Judaism and Islamism. More recently, attention has broadened to the consideration of sport as a religion, although remarkably few religious studies scholars or theologians—with some very notable exceptions—have contributed to this discussion directly.

With the decline of organized mainstream Christianity in countries such as Canada, parts of the United States, and the United Kingdom, questions regarding life's meaning and human hopes have not gone away. Rather, on an experiential level, they are pursued elsewhere. For some, sport provides this venue.

The importance of technology and science to competitive sport is growing. The insatiable pursuit of better performances and broken records requires new techniques to keep improving athletic performances. Sport, an enhancing activity in itself, seems destined to be the frontier of the twice enhanced. As elite athletes use more technology and science to improve their performances, they are seeking to enhance what are already very enhanced bodies and athletic abilities. In other words, participation in sports, by definition, usually improves one's physical condition, and technology and science are being used to improve these physical improvements even further. Neither the implications of this doubling effect on the spiritual dimension of sport,[3] nor the relevance of this spiritual dimension to the shaping of the sport enhancement debate, have been considered in any depth. These two issues are the focus of this book.

The most competitive athletes hone their bodies to the highest degree possible, assisted by scientific tests, cutting edge equipment, rigorous training regimens, and other enhancing techniques. Indeed, enhancement use in sport has occurred throughout history. Ancient Olympians used bread soaked in opium and euphoria-inducing mushrooms to improve their performance.[4] Enhancing ourselves to become the "best" we can be has always been part of what it means to be human.

However, we then want to transcend the next obstacle; there is little lasting satisfaction in a broken record. The assumption that sports records are there to be broken indefinitely by "natural" athletes is problematic. Without new ways to enhance athletes and their performances, it becomes increasingly unlikely that records will continue to be broken. Because records have been broken in the past, we assume and infer that records will always be broken in the future. This is an inductive fallacy; so long as humans are the athletes, records cannot be broken forever since humans are limited. Innovations such as more effective running shoes and training regimens have allowed runners to post faster times but such improvements are not likely to continue to shorten running times indefinitely. However, if innovations in technology and science (what some, including myself, call "techno-science") continue to the point of moving humans beyond the human condition (to the transhuman or posthuman), then athletes and their performances can continue to be enhanced.

---

[3] I am indebted to Ron Cole-Turner for suggesting this phrase.

[4] M. R. King, "A League of their Own? Evaluating Justifications for the Division of Sport into 'Enhanced' and 'Unenhanced' Leagues," *Sport, Ethics and Philosophy* 6, no. 10 (2012): 34.

Because competition is so intense in elite sports, athletes and their coaches look hard for any possible edge. The intensity of the competition means that some athletes and coaches use banned means for the win. This has prompted sports regulating bodies such as the World Anti-Doping Agency (WADA), an International Olympic Committee (IOC) organization created in 1999, to develop increasingly more advanced scientific methods to screen for banned substances and technologies. This development of scientific testing is another complicated aspect of the intersection of techno-science with sport and religion.

South African middle-distance runner Caster Semenya is one example of how science is being used to uncover possible unfair advantages. Semenya was required to undergo gender testing since some thought she possessed too many masculine characteristics. But where it gets complicated is how the scientific results are evaluated. What makes someone female or male or in the middle? What is considered acceptable and what is not has a lot to do with our values and what we think humans should be. These values and ideas shape how we use science and technology, and how we decide what is fair and unfair in elite sports.

Increasingly we are faced with the technologically enhanced or trans-athlete (a shortened term for the transhuman athlete) and the questions that this raises. Is there a point at which we are no longer human but trans- or even post-human? What does it mean to be human? How much technology usage does it take to become transhuman? Who decides how far we go? What do these techno-science pursuits tell us about our values and hopes?

There is a wide body of work regarding enhancement technologies and humanity from both secular and religious perspectives. But explorations of the intersection of sport, techno-science and religion are largely absent. As I considered doping and the use of enhancements in sport, I found myself wondering about what the religious or spiritual dimension of sport might have to do with the enhancement issue. If sport functions as a religion for many people, how might this understanding of sport influence the way we understand the use of techno-science in sport, and how we decide what is an acceptable advantage?

A recurring theme in material written about sport and religion is hope. We hope for our teams to win—even when they haven't for decades sometimes. We hope that the Olympic athlete representing our country, even if they have recently sustained an injury, wins. We hope that the star athlete to whom we look as a role model deserves that status. And we hope that the underdog will defy all odds and come out on top. It seems that many fans and athletes hold on relentlessly to their sporting dreams, making sport—in my words—a location of hopes. These hopes are central to sport's religious function. So, if hope is important in elite sports, we need to ask how the increasing use of techno-science in sport might affect hope. And, as importantly, if we approach the enhancement debate beginning with the understanding that sport is a secular religion that is built around hope, how might this valuing of hope reshape the enhancement debate?

These are the ponderings that took form during my very slow runs. And this book is my attempt to begin a conversation about those questions.

Chapter 1

Introduction: It's Time to Complicate Things

In this book I consider the following: how elite sports function as a religion; the spiritual quality of hope in sport; how techno-science might affect and be affecting hope in sport; and, lastly, how an understanding of elite sports as a secular religion centered on hope might reshape the sport enhancement debate.

At this point, it is important to consider the broad concept of spirituality. Later, in chapter five, I will explore this concept as it relates to sport more thoroughly. For now, I will introduce a working definition. Based on empirical research, Kenneth I. Pargament, professor of psychology at Bowling Green University in Ohio, and an expert in the fields of religion and spirituality, understands spirituality as "a distinctive...human motivation, a yearning for the sacred." In short, he understands it as a "'search for the sacred,' the cornerstone of religion, and a natural and normal part of life."[1] This definition becomes more complicated as he wades into the meanings of search and sacred.

Pargament proposes that the sacred has both theistic and nontheistic meanings. For those who embrace a theistic faith, sacred can refer to "concepts of higher powers and God" whereas in "nontheistic sanctification, a significant object is assigned divine like qualities."[2] Further, both theists and nontheists "can perceive spiritual qualities in various aspects of life."[3] Hope is, I propose, a spiritual quality. And hope is a spiritual quality that many find in sport, be it as an athlete or a fan.

---

[1] Kenneth I. Pargament, "Searching for the Sacred: Toward a Non-Reductionist Theory of Spirituality," in *APA Handbooks in Psychology, Religion, and Spirituality: Vol. 1 Context, Theory, and Research*, ed. K. I. Pargament, J. J. Exline, and J. Jones, 257–74 (Washington, DC: American Psychological Association, 2013) 258.

[2] Ibid., 259.

[3] Ibid., 260.

Building on a literary review of fifty-five articles and thirty books from several disciplines regarding hope, pastoral theologian Pamela McCarroll—with Helen Cheung, who serves as a manager in mental health services—proposes a "descriptive definition" of hope that I will assume throughout this book: "*Hope is the experience of the opening of horizons of meaning and participation in relationship to time, other human and nonhuman being, and/or the transcendent.*"[4] Similar to Pargament's approach, this understanding of hope embraces theistic and nontheistic perspectives and is inclusive of secular and religious experiences. McCarroll explains that "horizons of meaning and participation" are important aspects of hope that were represented throughout the sources. The "opening" of these horizons suggests "a broadening of perspective" that is important to experiences of hope.[5]

What is meaningful varies according to context and person. Meaningfulness has a subjective quality that can be different for each individual and can vary throughout that individual's life. The identification of meaning as a horizon is meant to emphasize the contextual nature of meaning and to suggest that hope happens when one's perspective is shifted and "a vista opens up that had not been previously perceived." There is a transformative quality in hope; one sees things in a different way and this new perspective is part of hope.

Participation is identified as the other horizon to underscore the "ways meaning is embodied in the multivalent relationships in which we participate.... The emphasis on participation suggests that hope is related to discovering oneself as participating in a larger whole, connected to, engaged by, and in relationship with that within which one is already embedded but sees with new eyes."[6] To summarize, hope is about connection, relationship, and meaning. Hope has to do with the emergence of an awareness of the interconnectedness of life and the possibilities therein. It awakens us to a deeper truth that is already present but not always seen. Often, hope comes

---

[4]Pamela R. McCarroll, *The End of Hope—The Beginning: Narratives of Hope in the Face of Death and Trauma* (Minneapolis: Fortress Press, 2014) 48.
[5]Ibid., 49.
[6]Ibid., 49.

with a sense of awe that assists us in seeing "the interconnectivity of all things."[7]

Perhaps you are already thinking of examples of the hopes held and inspired by sports fans and players. As religion and sport scholar Joseph L. Price illustrates through the example of the Chicago Cubs' persistent pursuit of the pennant,[8] losing alone does not destroy hope. Fans and participants are tenacious. We do not often give up on that which is sacred to us even when our hope seems illogical to others. Even Nelson Mandela was convinced that "sport has the power to change the world. It has the power to inspire in a way that little else does.... Sport can create hope where once there was despair. It is more powerful than governments in breaking down barriers."[9]

Hope, as with other propositional attitudes such as belief, desire, and wonder,[10] can be damaged and can be rebuilt. Because spirituality is a *search* for the sacred, it is a dynamic process. This dynamism includes the reworking of spiritual qualities and their meanings when one is confronted by crisis or disappointment. The meaning of hope is not often critically examined until something disrupts us, threatening the foundation that our notion of hope has been built upon—our values, ideals, and worldviews. Pargament's research indicates that when hope, as a spiritual quality, is threatened, anxiety rises and coping efforts to reinforce the normative state activate.[11] So we often continue to believe what we want (witness the insistence that disgraced cyclist Lance Armstrong was innocent or that he was set-up or pressured) in the face of strong rational reasons to surrender these convictions.

Further, when we are confronted with the reality that elite athletes are not 100 percent natural or pure, we tend to resist this knowledge. The word

---

[7]Ibid., 50.

[8]Joseph L. Price, *Rounding the Bases: Baseball and Religion in America* (Macon, GA: Mercer University Press, 2006) 209.

[9]As quoted by Mark Householder in Mark Householder, Benjamin J. Chase, and Ted Kluck, "Are Sports the Problem? Three Views," *Christianity Today* 54, no. 2 (2010): 26.

[10]Randolph Feezell, *Sport, Philosophy, and Good Lives* (Lincoln: University of Nebraska Press, 2013) 50–51.

[11]Pargament, "Searching for the Sacred," 264.

"natural" implies that nothing is added to us. This is a difficult concept to imagine when we stop to consider that it is common in more privileged parts of the world to vaccinate against many diseases, supplement our diets with vitamins, take medications for illnesses, implant pacemakers, and wear corrective eyewear. These arguably "unnatural" interventions have become accepted as almost natural because they are used regularly. Most of us value notions of purity and naturalness, but because we also value winning and near-flawless athletic performances, we have a potential conflict. Technology and science are used in several ways to supplement the qualities and characteristics with which athletes are born. The question is, at what point, if any, does the use of enhancements affect our engagement with sport as a secular religion? Can techno-science usage threaten or enhance the hope that sport represents for so many? So far, apart from some individual cases, it seems that the elasticity and persistence of human hope has largely withstood any internal dissonance caused by techno-science challenges to the "natural" or purity ideal.

Sometimes what we hope for is not very life-sustaining. What we hope for and desire is built on values. These values often are assumed and unexamined; we absorb certain views and may not think too much about what values are informing those views or from where we acquire those values. The sources of authority that influence the values we hold include our families of origin, friendships, media, the law, science, education, and that thing many call gut, or intuition, or spirit. That our values are often not discussed is not surprising. Aside from, and in spite of, Scottish philosopher Alasdair MacIntyre's classic work *After Virtue: A Study in Moral Theory* (first appearing in 1981 with a third edition released in 2007),[12] even contemporary philosophers have not paid these questions much attention. As Oxford University professor Guy Kahane notes, "recent philosophy has neglected important questions about value ... about what attitude we should have to the world and our place in it. These are questions we must ask even if we are not religious believers."[13]

---

[12] Alasdair MacIntyre, *After Virtue: A Study in Moral Theory*, 3rd ed. (Notre Dame, IN: University of Notre Dame Press, 2007).

[13] Guy Kahane, "Mastery Without Mystery: Why There Is No Promethean Sin In Enhancement," *Journal of Applied Philosophy* 28, no. 4 (2011): 355. In elite sport,

Often, what most fans hope for in elite or professional sport is winning, which in turn surpasses other ethical goods such as strengthening community, developing skills, or inspiring others. Yet evidence suggests that an excessively high value placed on winning often results in unhappiness largely because a lot more teams or athletes lose than win. This desire to win at all costs needs to be expanded, adapted, or rebuilt on alternative values that yield more happiness and health.[14] Many facets of elite sports are geared towards winning alone. Even the ways in which the enhancement debate is approached reflect an almost exclusive focus on winning.

Enhancements tend to be evaluated based on whether they provide an unfair advantage; in other words, the central concern is with winning or attaining a personal best. While winning and personal bests are very important, there are additional goods in sport that also can be affected by enhancement use. It is commonplace to assume that in elite sports winning is the highest good. Other goods such as teamwork, altruism, the capacity to live in the present moment, and—yes—spirituality, are also goods that are found in sport. In particular, I am concerned with the value of sport's spiritual dimension and how this dimension might be affected by techno-science.

It is neither my intent, nor is it possible, to prove the ontological existence of spirituality in sport, or anywhere else for that matter. What is important for the purposes of this book is that people derive meaning from their experiences in sport that some consider spiritual in nature. The lack of

---

too, there is an absence of agreed upon values at least partly because of a failure to discuss values adequately. This lack of agreement and discussion is perhaps most evident in how banned enhancements are understood. For example, within the elite cyclist culture (Tour de France), the use of often-banned substances to enhance performance has been accepted by many cyclists, coaches, managers, and other "inner circlers" competing at the top levels for decades [see for example, Rob Beamish, *Steroids: A New Look at Performance-Enhancing Drugs* (Santa Barbara, CA: Praeger, 2011)]. Yet, this practice is not generally seen as acceptable among fans and sports regulating bodies.

[14]Feezell, *Sport, Philosophy, and Good Lives*, 56. Furthermore, Lowenthal found that hope is an important factor in the promotion of physical health [(K. M. Lowenthal, *Religion, Culture and Mental Health* (Cambridge, UK: Cambridge University Press, 2007)].

recognition of this spiritual dimension has hindered more complex ethical reflection on athletes' use of techno-science, and has not contributed to meaningful understandings of hope as it is experienced in sport.[15]

Techno-science and Sport: Super Swimsuits,
   Oscar Pistorius, and Caster Semenya

On a popular level, it seems that there is always a news story about a drug scandal or some other unfair advantage in sport. In 2013 it was Alex Rodriguez in the news accused of doping and, preceding him Lance Armstrong. But banned drugs are not the only means of enhancing athletes and their performances. The number of examples of performance-enhancing technologies seems to be growing. The following are sketches of three such cases to which I will refer throughout these pages: "super" swimsuits, Oscar Pistorius, and Caster Semenya.

Super Swimsuits

Referred to as "doping-on-a-hanger" or as "technological doping," full-body polyurethane swimsuits were launched with the introduction of the Speedo Fastskin at the 2000 Sydney Olympics. Initially this suit generated curiosity and only a little suspicion. Howver, after the 2000 Olympics, debate grew somewhat regarding the acceptability of the Fastskin swimming

---

[15] Important also is Pargament's finding that "spiritual coping methods are tailored to provide solutions to problems of human finitude and insufficiency" [Pargament "Searching for the Sacred: Toward a Non-Reductionist Theory of Spirituality," 264]. If indeed spirituality is the main human response to struggles related to finitude and insufficiency, and if sport has a spiritual dimension, then the intersection of sport with techno-science has significant implications for how we understand and address what it means to be human, particularly since the development of many enhancement technologies is geared towards either radical life extension or immortality. Some of these implications will be explored in the coming chapters. See Derek F. Maher and Calvin Mercer, eds., *Religion and the Implications of Radical Life Extension* (New York: Palgrave Macmillan, 2009); Ronald Cole-Turner, *Transhumanism and Transcendence: Christian Hope in an Age of Technological Enhancement* (Washington, DC: Georgetown University, 2011); and Calvin Mercer and Tracy J. Trothen, *Religion and Transhumanism: The Unknown Future of Human Enhancement* (Westport, CT: Praeger, 2015).

suit, as it was reputed to enhance performance by 3 percent.[16] Fairness was the critical issue. Did these suits merely "optimize" athletic performance—as elite swimmer Ian Thorpe insisted when asked about the Fastskin swimsuit he trialed for Adidas—or did they unfairly enhance performance?

Speedo's even more cutting edge 2008 Fastskin LZR greatly intensified the debate. Forty-three records were broken at the 2009 Fédération Internationale de Natalation (FINA) World Championship meet.[17] Concerns emerged regarding how these suits affected the basic test of swimming: Were the suits fair? And was swimming still the sport as we know it when the super swimsuits were used?[18]

Since the polyurethane material reduced drag and muscle oscillation, moving through the water became easier for swimmers.[19] On 1 January 2010 FINA banned the use of these swimsuits in competitions. The record wins stand but will, undoubtedly, be regarded as questionable since an enhancing swimsuit was worn.[20]

Oscar Pistorius: Cheetah Legs

Oscar Pistorius was born in 1986 without fibulae in his lower legs, but amputation at eleven months old gave him the possibility of mobility with the help of fitted prosthetics. Eventually carbon-fiber Cheetah Flex-Foot legs allowed Pistorius to run. After winning several races at the Paralympics, including record-breaking times in the 100, 200, and 400 meters, Pistorius

---

[16]Tara Magdalinski, "Performance Technologies: Drugs and Fastskin at the Sydney 2000 Olympics" *Media International Australia* 97 (2000): 59–69.

[17]Lanty M. O'Connor and John A. Vozenilek, "Is It the Athlete or the Equipment? An Analysis of the Top Swim Performances from 1990 to 2010," *Journal of Strength and Conditioning Research* 25, no. 12 (2011): 3239.

[18]Tara Magdalinski, *Sport, Technology and the Body: The Nature of Performance* (New York: Routledge, 2009) 109.

[19]M. Munro, "Dressing for Success at the Olympics; Is it 'Doping on a Hangar' or is it Just a Swimsuit? Either Way, Canada is Hoping that a Little Technology Will Lead to a Gold Strike in Beijing," *The Gazette*, 27 July 2008, http://search.proquest.com/docview/434667680?accountid=6180.

[20]Brad Partridge, "Fairness and Performance-Enhancing Swimsuits at the 2009 Swimming World Championships: the 'Asterisk' Championships," *Sport, Ethics and Philosophy* 5, no. 1 (2011): 63–74.

wanted to compete in the Olympic Games. In 2008, Pistorius was banned from International Association of Athletic Federations (IAAF) competitions because his prosthetics were determined to be a technical device that aid performance after test findings indicated that he used 25 percent less energy than an able-bodied athlete (IAAF rule 144.2, 2008).[21] However, the court of arbitration overturned this decision later that same year, since there was no clear evidence of an advantage, and the tests conducted to date had not taken into account all aspects of running.

On 23 March 2011, Pistorius made the Olympic qualifying time for the 400-meter race and the 400-meter relay.[22] Although Pistorius did not medal when he competed in the 2012 London Summer Olympics, his presence showed the world that technology can be used to bridge the gap in elite sports between abled and disabled athletes. Pistorius transgressed the boundary between the artificial and the natural; the human and the machine; and the Paralympics and the Olympics.

Pistorius's participation in the Olympic Games as a double-amputee athlete has helped raise questions around not only the issue of fairness but also the categorizing of athletes on the basis of ability and disability.[23] Disabled bodies are often devalued as imperfect and lacking. Pistorius has helped us question what we value and what makes an athlete strong and admirable.[24]

---

[21] Brendan Burkett, Mike McNamee ,and Wolfgang Potthast, "Shifting Boundaries in Sports Technology and Disability: Equal Rights or Unfair Advantage in the Case of Oscar Pistorius?" *Disability & Society* 26, no. 5 (2011): 643–54; Mark Sutcliffe, "Amputee Sprinter Treads Uneven Track," *The Ottawa Citizen*, 13 January 2008, http://www2.canada.com.

[22] Gareth A. Davies, "London 2012 Olympics: double amputee Oscar Pistorius makes 400m qualifying time," *London Telegraph*, 24 March 2011, www.telegraph.co.uk/sport/othersports/olympics/8403343/London-2012-Olympics-double-amputee-Oscar-Pistorius-makes-400m-qualifying-time.html.

[23] Leslie Swartz and Brian Watermeyer, "Cyborg Anxiety: Oscar Pistorius and the Boundaries of What it Means to be Human," *Disability & Society* 23, no. 2 (2008): 187–90.

[24] Pistorius later was arrested for the murder of girlfriend Reeva Steenkamp, and eventually found guilty of culpable homicide. In South Africa the media reported that he was regarded as "a hero by both blacks and whites, transcending the racial divide of the country" (Wire Services, Murder or Accident? *Kingston Whig*

Caster Semenya: Questions of Science, Sex, and Gender

The third example is middle-distance South African runner Caster Semenya. Winning the women's 800-meter race at the 2009 IAAF World Championships in Athletics by a pronounced margin of 2.45 seconds, Semenya's masculine features became cause for speculation. It was reported by the media that competitors and others expressed concern that she had an unfair advantage due to what was seen as her excessive muscularity. International Olympic Committee (IOC) policy allows for any suspicious-looking female competitor to be questioned and tested in order to prevent a possible unfair advantage.[25] However, other advantages such as height, superior eyesight, or better depth-perception are considered acceptable.

Semenya was subjected to gender testing and rumored to have "failed" these tests. After an eleven-month suspension, she was permitted to return to competition.[26] The results of the tests were not made public for reasons of confidentiality, and neither were possible requirements, such as hormone therapy if Semenya were found to have hormone levels outside of the normal range for women (hormone therapy affects muscle mass).[27]

Science has shown that there are variations in sex; not everyone possesses physiological and biological traits that define them clearly as male or female. Social theorist Debra Shogan, in her well-regarded book, *The Making of High-Performance Athletes: Discipline, Diversity, and Ethics*, tells us that medical science recognizes at least five sexes: male, intersexed male, true intersexed male, intersexed female, and female.[28] Even though Semenya's physiology and biology seem to be natural—that is, she has made no changes

---

Standard, 23 February 2013, 18). Sports stars ought not be automatically regarded as moral exemplars.

[25] Vicki Krane, "Gender, Identity and Ethics," paper presented at the International Convention on Science, Education and Medicine in Sport (Glasgow, United Kingdom, 21 July 2012).

[26] April Vannini and Barbara Fornssler, "Girl, Interrupted: Interpreting Semenya's Body, Gender Verification Testing, and Public Discourse," *Cultural Studies Critical Methodologies* 11, no. 3 (2010): 243–57.

[27] Krane, "Gender, Identity and Ethics," 2012.

[28] Debra Shogan, *The Making of High-Performance Athletics: Discipline, Diversity, and Ethics* (Toronto, ON: University of Toronto Press, 1999) 56–63.

to her birth sex—in Semenya's case natural may not have been considered a good thing.[29]

Semenya is not the first woman to be investigated for appearing too manly. In 1994, English bodybuilder Zoe Warwick took her own life after suffering from the effects of her steroid use in the late 1980s. Warwick was presented by the media as representative of the worst case of what doping could do: turn a woman into a monstrous unnatural man-woman.[30]

Semenya was pressured by the media to make herself look to fit accepted embodiment categories. Appearing on the cover of *You!* magazine, with the headline: "We turn South Africa's power girl into a glamour girl— and she loves it. Wow, look at Caster now,"[31] she was made to look glamorous and stereotypically feminine, with the message that it is much better to appear as *You!* presented her, rather than extremely muscular and strong.[32] In an interview with the *Sunday Times* newspaper two years later, she is reported as saying that she no longer found pleasure in her *You!* "makeover," asking: "'What makes you a lady? Does it mean if you are wearing skirts and dresses you are a lady?'"[33]

Semenya's case raises issues around narrow embodiment categories and the use of science to ensure conformity to social norms. Why some genetic anomalies that give an athlete a competitive advantage are acceptable while others are not should give us pause.

These three examples provide a quick look into some of the ways in which technology and science are being used in elite sports. They will be referred to from time to time in this book.

A Word About Method

I approach these questions about techno-science and how its usage affects the spiritual dimension of sport from a Christian theo-ethical

---

[29] Krane, "Gender, Identity and Ethics," 2012; Kutte Jönsson, "Who's Afraid of Stella Walsh? On Gender, 'Gene Cheaters', and the Promise of Cyborg Athletes," *Sport, Ethics and Philosophy* 1, no. 2 (2007): 239–62.

[30] Magdalinski, *Sport, Technology and the Body*, 91–107.

[31] As quoted in Kopano Ratele, "Looks: Subjectivity as Commodity," *Agenda* 90, no. 25 (2011): 97.

[32] Ratele, "Looks: Subjectivity as Commodity," 92–103.

[33] As quoted in Ratele, "Looks: Subjectivity as Commodity," 99.

perspective, drawing on postmodern and feminist insights. A Christian theological lens provides an example of how a recognized religious tradition can illuminate some of the hidden and implicit faith claims of sport.

Postmodernism

Postmodern insights are helpful in critically understanding some of the features of the secular religion of sport. In the following paragraphs I introduce a postmodern critique of universal claims, grand narratives, epistemological categories (or how we know and organize the world), and binary constructions such as male/female, abled/disabled, pure/impure, and good/bad. By considering these insights in dialogue with sport, the importance, as well as the limitations, of postmodern critique become clearer. Throughout this book I rely on these critiques to raise questions about the intersections of sport, religion, and techno-science, and the possible meanings of these intersections.

Universal claims and grand narratives are critiqued rightly in postmodern thought for failing to include the diversity of humanity, the world, and the cosmos. To say that elite athletes play only to win is reductionist; some do and many want to win *as well as achieve other goods* that can be experienced in sport. To group people together and claim that all are the same or share the same story is to deny the irreducibility (uniqueness) of each person. However, this critique of *universalisms* does not justify the rejection of *general* claims.

The outright rejection of grand narratives or universal values has a serious down side if these are confused with general narrative themes, or general binding values. It can mean the loss of group identity and political power gained through the assertion of group interests.[34] For instance, if one believed it was unjust for women to be excluded from Olympic competition, one would likely want to make the claim that this exclusion negatively affects *almost* all women and, in different ways, *almost* all men. It is important to name general narrative themes and to note that there will be exceptions.

---

[34]Lisa Edwards and Carwyn Jones, "Postmodernism, Queer Theory and Moral Judgment In Sport," *International Review for the Sociology of Sport* 44, no. 4 (2009): 334–35.

The postmodern caution that any critique of the status quo can become absorbed and appropriated, minimizing substantial change, is to be heeded. [35] For instance, women have gained acceptance in Olympic competition but in some Olympic sports continue to be seen as lesser athletes—at least by fans and, sometimes, by particular sports organizations. For instance, women's ice hockey became an Olympic-medal sport in 1998, but viewership of men's hockey greatly exceeds women's hockey. In the 2014 Olympics, more than 625,000 Canadians streamed the men's gold medal hockey final while only 325,000 streamed the women's gold medal win. [36] Although the Olympic rules changed, attitudes toward women's hockey have been shifting more gradually.

Taken to an extreme, postmodern critique can mean the rejection of normative ethics (e.g., the branch of ethics that is concerned with how we understand what is morally right and wrong[37]) and imply an ethical relativism in which anything is acceptable based only on individual preference or choice. For example, postmodern theorists usually embrace values of diversity and inclusion. [38] However, theoretically, these values cannot be imposed universally since this imposition may not respect a particular narrative. A way to acknowledge the possibility of an exception is to distinguish between universalisms and generalizations. Universalisms are absolute claims whereas generalizations are binding claims—true mostly, but not always and not forever.

The insights that no truth is absolute and no understanding perfect do not necessarily lead to the conclusion that normative claims are prohibitive but rather that these claims must be general and not absolute. They need to

---

[35]Gillian A. Walker, *Family Violence and the Women's Movement: the Conceptual Politics of Struggle* (Toronto, ON: University of Toronto Press, 1990).

[36]Bill Brioux, "TV Ratings for Olympics Down, Digital Viewing Soars," in *The* (Halifax) *Chronicle Herald*, 25 February, 2014, thechronicleherald.ca>News>Sochi 2014.

[37]Normative ethics is an umbrella term for different types of ethical theories including, most commonly, virtue ethics, deontological ethics, and consequentialist ethics.

[38]See, for example, the collection of essays in Pamela Dickey Young, Heather Shipley, and Tracy J. Trothen, eds, *Religion and Sexuality: Diversity and the Limits of Tolerance* (Vancouver, BC: UBC Press, 2015).

be binding and responsive to changing contexts and insights. As techno-science advances, there is an increasing need for ethical analyses and evaluations even though these will be partial and not once-and-for-all. Postmodern theory can help us understand that our response to the use of technology and science in sport may need to change as we are confronted with new developments. Speaking in generalities can be constructive as long as we understand that there will be exceptions. General claims have exceptions. Universal claims do not.[39]

Similarly, the postmodern rejection of binary thinking is valuable but to a point. Postmodern theory rightfully cautions against dividing the world into clear-cut binaries: male/female, white/black, abled/disabled, young/old, etc. Such categorical thinking excludes anyone who does not fall into either category and does not permit divergence from these categories. Furthermore, typically one element of the binary is valued at the expense of the other.

The intersection of sport and religion with techno-science has the potential to destabilize many of these embodiment categories. For example, highly effective prosthetic limbs are blurring the boundaries between that which has been considered therapeutic and that which has been considered enhancing. It has been argued that runner Oscar Pistorius's prosthetic Cheetah legs give him an unfair *advantage*. Pistorius's speed on his Cheetah legs has challenged the value-laden construction that able-bodied is better than disabled in sport and that everyone—universally—falls into clearly defined categories of either abled or disabled. Another is example is Caster Semenya. Scientific testing was used to determine where to locate her—as either male or female—and/or possibly to provide her with physiological therapy so that she could better fit into the female category. Postmodernist critique holds that there is no one "essence" of maleness or femaleness and that sex and gender are much more fluid than often thought.

But binary thinking is not all bad. Binaries can, paradoxically, help to both generate awareness of difference and to reinforce limiting categories. To insist that all binaries are bad and damaging is to fall into the binary trap (e.g., there is only binary thinking and non-binary thinking, and the former

---

[39] Leon Culbertson, "Pandora Logic: Rules, Moral Judgment and the Fundamental Principles of Olympism," *Sport, Ethics and Philosophy* 6, no. 2 (2012): 201.

is good and the latter bad). Sometimes binaries are ways of highlighting difference without necessarily imposing a value judgment. Pondering the potential for technology to blur the boundaries between human and machine, senior lecturer in theology and religious studies at the University of Glasgow, Heather Walton cautions against the wholesale demonizing of binaries, because "… I am uneasy about a significant problem that emerges if cyborg politics and theology encourage us to loosen our grasp upon notions of difference and alterity in order to embrace an indeterminacy that might too easily become manipulated by us."[40] While binaries tend to polarize and then marginalize those who do not fit, binaries also assist us in recognizing a degree of difference, if not the wide range of diversity, that is humanity. Walton raises an issue that will emerge throughout this book: the existence of human diversity and the relationship between diversity and the use of techno-science to alter humans.

Religion and sport scholar Joseph L. Price also recognizes both the limitations and benefits of binaries in sport (and religion). On the benefit side, binaries are part of order and the reassurance that there are some stable, clear-cut rules. For example, in baseball, a hit is either fair or foul; players are safe or out.[41] In hockey, it is either a goal or it is not. Teams win or they lose, and so on. These binary evaluations do not mean there is complete agreement on these calls but that in the end (and during the game) these calls will be made based upon the evaluation of certain criteria and the umpire's or referee's perception of the meeting of these criteria.

Categorical thinking is limited in its contribution to human flourishing. While we need ways to make sense of life, there comes a point at which these tools can be used to stifle growth and the capacity to see and accept the diversity among us. Binaries underscore the existence of difference but can limit the range of diversity by locating it *exclusively* in two poles. However, when binary concepts are held in tension with the recognition that neither

---

[40]Heather Walton, "The Gender of the Cyborg," *Theology & Sexuality* 10, no. 2 (2004): 42.

[41]Price, *Rounding the Bases*, 92. Similarly, Scott Kretchmar argues that some degree of organizing the world in dichotomies is helpful but dichotomies have "limitations" [Scott Kretchmar, "Why Dichotomies Make it Difficult to See Games as Gifts of God," in *Theology, Ethics and Transcendence in Sports*. Jim Parry, Mark Nesti, and Nick Watson, eds. (London: Routledge, 2011): 186.

everything nor every person fit into simple categories, then these poles can become more of an organizing "general" guide rather than a prescriptive "universal" rule.

Binary thinking is in both religion and sport. As historian Steven J Overman puts it, "Sport's symbolic rituals and ceremonies attempt to place events in a traditional and orderly view. Like religion, sport offers its followers a grouping of myths and symbols that facilitate the total experience. Sport serves the function of religious dramatization in that they feed a deep human hunger, placing humans in touch with features of human life within the cosmos."[42] Categorical and binary thinking have helped many to feed this human hunger. But a conflict is emerging between the preference of some for binary ordering in sport and religion and the discomfort experienced by others in response to clear-cut ordering. Postmodern critiques and intentional recognition of the messiness and injustices of life make sense. While the ordering of sport around rules can continue to be attractive, sport is not perfect and not immune to change (and neither are formal religions).[43]

Categorical and binary thinking have restricted the human ability to see the scope of diversity in the world and many of the possibilities that go along

---

[42]Steven J. Overman, *The Influence of the Protestant Ethic on Sport and Recreation* (Aldershot, UK: Avebury Ashgate Publishing, 1997) 7. Or, as Santana and Erickson put it "Because American baseball and religion come out of a white/black, fair/foul, safe/out, and heaven/hell paradigm, they find themselves in tension with an increasingly relativistic and postmodern world that is questioning our knowledge of such concepts as binary truths." [Richard W. Santana and Gregory Erickson, *Religion and Popular Culture: Rescripting the Sacred* (Jefferson, NC: McFarland & Company, 2008) 47.]

[43] Muscular versions of Christianity, Judaism, and Islamism tend to be conservative and evangelical in their approach to sacred text, usually assuming binary relationships between good and evil, heaven and hell, the transcendent and the immanent, and sacred and profane, for example. As historian William Baker observes, "religious devotion and competitive sport share essential attitudes and modes of behavior. They hold similarly polarized visions of good and evil, heaven and hell, winning and losing" [William J. Baker, "Religion," in *Routledge Companion to Sports History*, eds. S.W. Pope and John Nauright (London and New York: Routledge, 2010) 216]. However, not all theologians (nor all sports enthusiasts) understand theological concepts in neither binary terms.

with this diversity. For example, because sport is seen as occupying one realm or category, and religion another, it has been easy to miss or not understand the spiritual qualities in sport. Or because we are comfortable with all people being clearly male or clearly female, those who are more visibly somewhere in the middle disrupt the order. So long as we think universally in binaries, likely we will be tempted to use techno-science developments to support this thinking. But if we move more deliberately to thinking generally in binaries and categories, with an eye to exceptions and overlaps, we can imagine ways to grow and thrive. As pastoral theologian Pamela R. McCarroll argues, hope entails an opening of perspective or a shifting of horizons. Some order in the world helps us to make sense of life, including sport. Too much rigid ordering, or ordering that imposes a lesser value on particular groups, squeezes our ability to see a more complex world and to imagine more life-giving possibilities.

Feminism

Feminist, *mujerista*, womanist, and other liberating theologians have pointed out the damage connected to dualistic theologies. Dualisms reflect and retrench understandings of the world and God that marginalize some groups and over-valorize others. This relational structuring hurts all, since life is interconnected. In some theological quarters, men continue to be valued over women—and are seen as very distinct from women; humans are valued over other creatures; and creation occupies the lowest rung. God, in this paradigm, is seen as above and apart from all life, although closest to men.

Several theologians who resist these hierarchical divisions, including Ivone Gebara and Mayra Rivera, have challenged binary conceptions of God and human experiences of God. Beginning with the contention that all life is interdependent, they reject the assumption that evil is separate from good, or the sacred from the profane, or the transcendent from the immanent. This intertwining in everyday life, they argue, is the point of redemptive possibility as well as the messiness of humanity. This intertwined-ness does not obviate the need to discern good and evil but requires that we understand that this differentiation is more complex than it might appear at first blush.

Feminist critique is important to the illumination of the implications of the intersection of religion, sport, and techno-science. I write from a feminist Reformed Protestant perspective. The theological disposition that I bring is best understood as left of mainstream, informed by my United Church of Canada commitments and my related commitments to social justice and pluralism. Some of the themes common to feminist theologies are relationality, diversity, embodiment, justice, power, and flourishing. These themes will arise throughout this book.

Outline of the Book

In this book I build towards two very connected questions: One, how sport's spiritual dimension might be affected by techno-science and, two, how the valuing of sport's spiritual quality of hope might affect the sport enhancement debate.

Chapter two considers the intersection of sport and techno-science. I describe some of the ways in which techno-science has been and is being used in sport. The meaning of the term "techno-science" is unpacked. The concept of normal and the epistemological question of how we know are explored further. I look at existing advantages (genetic anomalies) possessed by elite athletes, and "added" technological enhancements. Questions regarding the assessment of the acceptability of these advantages and enhancements are posed. Most approaches to the issue of techno-science in sport focus on added technologies. I show why it is important to widen the focus to include science and the assessment of existing advantages.

In chapter three I use Christian theological reflection to help identify and give depth to some of the spiritual and theological issues related to techno-science. This reflection is neither an exhaustive nor systematic theological analysis. The defining Christian moments of creation, fall, and redemption form the structure for this reflection. Issues that surface include embodiment and what it means to be created in God's image; atonement theories and the glorification of pain and suffering; forms of sin including the lack of self-love and ownership of power; and just relationship and the redemptive importance of doing good and moving towards right relationship with God. The relevance of theological interpretation and faith perspectives also are addressed. I suggest how these issues are related to sport.

Chapters four and five explore scholarly literature on the relationship between sport, religion, and spirituality. Chapter four focuses on the range of approaches to, and assessments of, the relationship between sport and religion. After reviewing a substantial selection of this material, I distill three themes that are important to the techno-science conversation: the establishment of a relationship between sport and religion; the relevance of culture, including religion, to values in sport; and the relationship between sport and play.

The themes of immanence and transcendence are explored in chapter five as part of a larger discussion on flow states. Flow experiences have been surmised to have a spiritual quality. However, not all scholars agree that flow is spiritual. This chapter addresses flow experiences for both athletes and fans. I argue that hope, as a spiritual quality, is characteristic of many flow experiences for both athletes and fans. I also suggest that, unlike formal religions, there is no clear normative ethic informing the expression of flow energy.

At this point in the book, hope has been identified as a compelling feature of sport and a significant part of what makes sport meaningful. In chapter six, I discuss four locations of hope in elite sports: winning, losing, and anticipation; star athletes; perfect moments; and relational embodiment. Each of these places in which hope is experienced is promising and problematic. Each is influenced by mixed values. I explore the complicated relationship of some of these values to the spiritual quality of hope, bearing in mind Pargament's understanding of spirituality as a search for the sacred, including an appreciation of the interconnectedness of all life. Of course, there are additional facets of hope in sport that are not presented here in this discussion of elite sports. Of particular note are the locations of hope in everyday sport or exercise. Theological reflection on the meaning of hope in these locations will raise issues that also need to be part of the sport techno-science conversation.

In chapter seven I identify and critically analyze four main approaches to the ethical question of enhancement use in sport. All four approaches are informed by a decisionist focus, meaning that these approaches all are focused on how to decide whether or not an enhancement is acceptable in elite sports. The approaches do not usually address the values that underlie decision-making processes. The first approach understands individual rights

18

and potential physical harms as the most important criteria for assessing the acceptability of an enhancement. The second is most concerned with fairness: Is the enhancement fair to the other competitors? The question of what it means to be fair is explored in this subsection. How an enhancement affects the internal goods and the nature of sport is the focus of the third approach. In this subsection questions about the internal goods of sport are raised. The spiritual dimension of sport is posited as an internal good and part of the nature of sport. Finally, the therapy-enhancement approach is discussed. This approach relies on a distinction between therapeutic interventions and enhancing interventions with the latter usually evaluated as unacceptable. Of course, some approaches to the sport enhancement debate are hybrids of these four. Theological reflection assists in problematizing these approaches. Throughout this chapter questions are raised regarding the relevance of sport's spiritual dimension and particularly hope.

The final chapter proposes a reconstruction of the sport enhancement debate. The proposed approach is most concerned with the implications of techno-science for hope, as part of sport's spiritual dimension. How might hope in sport potentially be affected by techno-science? And how might a valuing of sport's spiritual dimension, and particularly hope, reshape the sport enhancement debate? Aspects of each of the four approaches discussed in chapter seven are adapted and incorporated. Using the creation, fall, redemption model for theological reflection, introduced in chapter three, I offer some last thoughts and cautions on the theological meanings of techno-science in sport.

This book is written for students at both undergraduate and graduate levels, scholars, and enthusiasts of religion and sport. While there are some complex concepts discussed within these pages, they are explained either in the text or in footnotes. Because the interfacing of techno-science with humans challenges conceptions about what it means to be human, we need to engage much more deliberately in this ethical conversation. And because sport functions as a secular religion, it behooves us to ask religious questions regarding sport and enhancements.

Chapter 2

Sport and Techno-science: Setting the Stage

The concept of "normal" is complicated. What is seen as a normal state of health has changed significantly over the centuries and continues to change. It used to be that the expected human lifespan was much shorter than it is today, and diseases such as polio, measles, and tuberculosis were life-threatening or incurable. Even HIV is no longer considered a terminal diagnosis—it has become a chronic, treatable condition. Healing knowledge and therapies have long influenced and improved the human condition. What is different now is the rapidity of scientific and technological developments.[1] With these developments, our understandings of normal health care and natural health have shifted and continue to shift.

For example, in 1944 doctors at Johns Hopkins Hospital were the first to perform a shocking new cardiac surgery, and a child with Tetralogy of Fallot was given a chance at life through what became popularly known as the "blue baby" operation. Prior to this time, heart surgery was thought to be an untouchable domain—the stuff of science gone wild. The heart was seen as the sacred core—God's domain not meant for human intervention. Now heart surgery is normal.

Next it was DNA. Our genetic code, it was commonly thought, was never meant to be broken, but upon completion of the internationally funded Human Genome Project in 2003, scientists had mapped the genes of human DNA. This mapping now provides the foundation for diagnostic testing and medical interventions. Although progress in these areas has been

---

[1] I use the term "developments" deliberately. Although the term is somewhat problematic in terms of being value-laden, it is not as much so as "progress" or "advancements." It is important to refrain from assuming that simply because something is new and innovative that it is furthering the "best" in humanity. Human creations, as will be discussed further later in this book, are not necessarily good or bad. Sometimes we develop things that do more harm than good.

limited, many effective gene therapies are anticipated.[2] This science is relevant to everyone as we "are all carrying … forty to fifty faulty genes" that may or may not manifest as a disease.[3] It is expected that the knowledge afforded by the mapping of the human genome will eventually yield answers to many diseases, although there is much debate regarding how long these discoveries will take. Intervening in DNA is still seen by many as inappropriately playing God, opening the door to unforeseen Frankenstein-type monstrosities created by human hubris. Yet this science is contributing significantly to the prediction of, and hopefully the curing of, many diseases.

Although medical therapy interventions are very different from athletic enhancements, the two overlap. At this point, the enhancement debate becomes more complicated. How do we decide where the line should be drawn between healing an injury (medical therapy intervention) and making an athlete better than what he or she would have been "normally"? If an intervention is available to improve oneself, and it is medically safe to do so, then why not use it? These are only some of the quandaries that emerge when considering the use of technology and science in sport.

Whether or not an enhancement causes external or internal physiological change has been seen as a way to distinguish between the more problematic enhancement technologies and those considered acceptable,

---

[2] There remain many concerns regarding unforeseen side effects of gene therapy. [Theodore Friedmann, Olivier Rabin and Mark S. Frankel, "Gene Doping and Sport," in *Science* 327: 647–48.] In 1999, 18-year-old Jesse Gelsinger died unexpectedly following a gene transfer directly into his hepatic artery for a rare genetic disorder that blocks the body's ability to break down ammonia. The cause of death was not his liver disorder but the genetic modification, which led to multiple organ failure likely as a result of his immune system attacking the injected virus or synthetic gene [Peter Schjerling, "The Basics of Gene Doping" in *Genetic Technology and Sport: Ethical Questions,* eds. Claudio Tamburrini and Torbjorn Tannsjo (London and New York: Routledge, 2005) 27–28]. Additionally, in January 2003 a second child developed a "leukemia-like" condition from another gene therapy trial to treat X-linked severe combined immunodeficiency disease ("bubble baby syndrome"). [Christen Brownlee, "Gene Doping: Will Athletes Go for the Ultimate High?" *Science News* 166, no. 18 (30 October 2004) 280–81.]

[3] Francis S. Collins, "Human Genetics" in *Cutting-Edge Bioethics: A Christian Exploration of Technologies and Trends,* eds. John F. Kilner, C. Christopher Hook, and Diann B. Uustal (Grand Rapids, MI: Eerdmans Publishing, 2002) 5.

with those causing internal change usually seen as suspect. For example, lighter and custom-built running shoes are not problematic enhancements, whereas the drawing and re-introduction of an athlete's own blood back into their own body (blood doping) is seen as very problematic because it changes the athlete's physiology, improving endurance. But even this distinction of external and internal changes is problematic. Consider the example of vitamins. It is generally accepted and expected that most people will not only have access to daily multivitamins but will take them. The taking of vitamins has become "normal" practice; however, it is problematic on a number of levels. Although they are legal and considered therapeutic, vitamins are external substances that alter one's physiology. Furthermore, there are distributive justice concerns: not everyone has access to vitamins. And, to add to the complications, there is ongoing debate regarding the efficacy of some vitamins. One might well ask how a substance becomes considered normal, and who decides.

The question of what enhancements are fair and acceptable in sports competition has been debated for years.[4] Humans have long quested after self-improvement; it seems that this questing is part of being human. Perhaps in no other locus is this quest more evident than sport as techno-science corporeal enhancements are tested and marketed at sports events and particularly the Olympics.[5] The goal is to win, and winning requires that athletes produce better performances than their historical and contemporary peers. "Better" is defined as whatever it takes to legitimately win a competition. There is pressure on elite athletes to use whatever will enhance a performance to improve their chances of winning.

Sociologist Rob Beamish identifies runner Roger Bannister and "the miracle mile"[6] as "the gateway to modernity and the pursuit of sport through

---

[4]See, for example, sociologist Rob Beamish's insightful analysis of historic steroid use and policy changes. [Rob Beamish, *Steroids: A New Look at Performance-Enhancing Drugs* (Santa Barbara, CA: Praeger, 2011)].

[5]Although sport is my interest in these pages, there are many other aspects of life in which self-improvement is the focus. Some examples are cosmetic plastic surgery, the promotion and sale of cosmetics and clothing, and even aspects of education.

[6]On 6 May 1954, Bannister ran the first recorded sub-four-minute mile.

applied science, research, and professionalized training regimes."[7] A medical student, Bannister drew on his knowledge of physiology to develop an effective training regimen. This breakthrough occurred in tandem with other shifts in competitive sport: increased professionalization (rigorous and effective training came to mean that there was not time to work at a separate full-time job if one wanted to win[8]), increased media options and exposure, and increased advertising revenue. The expanding media, including the advent and spread of television, and associated advertising investments furthered the connection between winning elite performances and cutting-edge technology that included sports equipment.

In a significant departure from IOC founder Pierre de Coubertin's Olympic ideals, athletes, as of 1974, became permitted, under certain conditions, to receive money connected to competing in their sport.[9] This decision meant not only the professionalization of athletes but the legitimate availability of advertising and promotion money to fund these endeavors. Increased financial resources combined with emerging insights into how science could make athletes faster, stronger and higher, meant that scientifically informed training regimens and equipment became the norm. It became clear that if science progressed, athletic records would be broken.

Yet, the ideal of the purity of sport as a natural and meritocratic institute—maybe one of the last such societal bastions—has persisted at some level,[10] in spite of the calculated use of enhancements, the invasion of advertising dollars, and the professionalization of sport in general. Regardless of advanced equipment, training techniques, and other aids, many people still insist that sport and athletes are pure and natural and that the astounding performances we witness are proof that humans continue to improve physically and mentally.

In this chapter I will provide an overview of some of the science and technologies used to enhance athletes and sport's competitions. Some of the

---

[7] Beamish, *Steroids*, 60.

[8] Ibid., 68. Research referenced in the 1969 and 1970 reports from the IOC/NOC joint commission "showed that from 1950 to 1970, the time track athletes spent training had doubled and in some cases tripled."

[9] Beamish, *Steroids*, 69–72.

[10] Tara Magdalinski, *Sport, Technology and the Body: the Nature of Performance* (New York: Routledge, 2009).

ethical issues raised by the intersection of sport with technology and science will be identified. I introduce Christian theological reflection to help illuminate spiritual and social convictions associated with these issues. Scholars have shown that sport and Christianity reflect and influence North American cultural norms, particularly since Christianity has attracted more followers than any other religious tradition in contemporary North America.[11] Feminist Christian theologies are drawn on to sketch the contours of an approach informed by marginalized values. A qualifier must be added: My goal is to show how science and technology are intersecting with sport, not to explain details of the actual science informing these innovations.

Techno-science: Technology, Science, and Values

Before I proceed, it is important to discuss my choice of terminology and my understanding of the scope of the sport enhancement issue. I use the term techno-science deliberately because I think that both science and technology need to be considered in the enhancement debate. In brief, the goal of science is knowledge and technology is the practical application of science. There has been much debate concerning the conflation of science and technology; proponents of one side do not wish to be subsumed by the other. Science and technology are connected, but they are not the same.

One distinction that is often—but not always—made between science and technology concerns values: science is purported by some to be objective or value-free, while technology is generally accepted as value-laden.[12] Several European philosophers, including Herbert Marcuse, Jürgen Habermas, and Michel Foucault, have shown that technology promotes values of efficiency and utility.[13] In sport, the uncritical absorption of the technological values of

---

[11]Steven J. Overman, *The Influence of the Protestant Ethic on Sport and Recreation* (Aldershot, UK: Avebury Ashgate Publishing, 1997).

[12]For an excellent discussion of the differences and similarities between science and technology, and for a description of the conversation regarding values and science and technology, see Rodney E. Frey, "Another Look at Technology and Science," *Journal of Technology Education* 3, no. 1 (2011): 1–12. www.scholar.lib.vt.edu/ejournals/JTE/v3n1/pdf/frey.pdf

[13]Herbert Marcuse, *One Dimensional Man: Studies in the Ideology of Advanced Industrial Society* (Boston: Beacon Press, 164); Jürgen Habermas, *Knowledge and*

efficiency and utility has an amplifying effect on the importance of winning, which is a very utility-driven value.[14]

While it is clear that technology is informed by particular values, I am in agreement with American philosopher, historian, and physicist Thomas Kuhn[15] and do not find science's purported objectivity convincing. Scientific knowledge, it has been said, is simply knowledge;[16] the choices around how to apply it have not been made in the science itself. However, factors influencing the framing of science are value-laden and so have an effect on the science: How we choose which scientific inquiries to investigate and who should be involved in these pursuits are value-laden decisions.

These values actualize in ways that are typically self-amplifying. If I value winning most highly, I would likely choose scientific pursuits that may yield insights that could be used to develop performance-enhancing technologies. The use of these technologies by elite athletes would likely result in better performances, which would drive up the expectations in that sport. To use a particular example, for runners, knowledge about oxygen capacity is highly desirable scientific information that is then likely to be well funded by pharmaceutical companies and other interests.[17] Science that is seen to have potential to increase winning performances gets funding. As breakthroughs that contribute to winning athletic performances are made, more funding for more research is predictable, and the perceived importance of science that assists winning increases. The new knowledge is then used to develop enhancement technologies such as hypobaric training chambers, leading to more athletes experiencing faster race times and increased

---

Human Interest (Boston: Beacon Press, 1971); Michel Foucault, *Technologies of the Self* (Boston: University of Massachusetts Press, 1988).

[14] As some recreational sport evidences, it is possible to cultivate more marginalized values such as diversity and the pleasure of playing the game, or competing intensely, regardless of outcome. These values are expressed by some elite athletes, but they are not normative.

[15] Thomas S. Kuhn, *The Structure of Scientific Revolutions* 2nd ed. (Chicago: University of Chicago Press, 1970), 24.

[16] See, for example, Frey, "Another Look at Technology and Science," 2011.

[17] The values of interest groups such as advertisers, pharmaceutical companies, and sports equipment companies who contribute funding dollars to the research areas that are expected to increase their profit margins, influence science.

endurance. Ultimately the expectations for a winning running performance increase.

It is important to bear in mind the relationship of science to values as we consider the relevance of existing advantages to the sport enhancement debate. Questions include why some so-called natural advantages possessed by elite athletes to warrant scientific screening and testing, whereas others are simply accepted, are related to values and need to be asked.

Existing Advantages and Science

Brain activity, not surprisingly, has an effect on athletic performance. In 2007, the *New York Times* reported that USA Track and Field[18] "banned the use of headphones and portable audio players like iPods at its official races … to ensure safety and to prevent runners from having a competitive edge."[19] Professor emerita of social studies of science at the Swiss Federal Institute of Technology Helga Nowotny and molecular biologist Giuseppa Testa explain that iPods were banned in the 2007 New York marathon because they were assessed as a form of "emotional doping" and created an unfair advantage: "the ban on music players was supported by results from studies of metabolism and images of brain activity" that "linked the act of listening to music with a large number of molecular reactions."[20] Brain scans also show that prayer or meditation is a similar form of emotional doping in that brain activity is affected[21] in ways that could enhance athletic performance. Not surprisingly, the ban on music proved impractical to enforce during the marathon. Of course, given the range of "emotional doping" methods, it would be impossible to prevent the use of these methods to enhance one's emotional state. Since the psychology of sport has become accepted as a normal component of athletic training, there is a high interest in promoting at least some forms of what could be called "emotional

---

[18]USA Track and Field is the USA national governing body for running.

[19]Juliet Macur, "Rule Jostles Runners Who Race to Their Own Tune" *New York Times*, 1 November 2007, http://www.nytimes.com/2007/11/01/sports/other-sports/01marathon.html?_r=2&.

[20]H. Nowotny and G. Testa, *Naked Genes: Reinventing the Human in the Molecular Age*, trans. Mitch Cohen (Cambridge, MA: MIT Press, 2010) 29.

[21]See, for example, Graham Ward, "A Question of Sport and Incarnational Theology," *Studies in Christian Ethics* 25, no. 1 (2012): 49–64.

doping," such as visualizing techniques. And now science has provided us with the know how to see brain activity through scanning and imaging, which is helping us to understand the implications of these emotional interventions.

It may be that some athletes respond more intensely or constructively to emotional interventions. The assessment of iPods as an unfair advantage is questionable if all marathoners had the option of using these devices. If some athletes benefit more than others from musical stimulation, then fairness may be an issue; however, the question of why this advantage would be less acceptable than other advantages such as height for basketball players, begs asking.

Another area of science that has implications for making optimal use of inborn advantages is predictive genomics. Predictive genomics DNA profiling may be one of the most talked about scientific developments in regard to sport performance. This science is used not only to enhance individual athletic performance but also to select suitable sports, thus potentially optimizing the sport itself. Predictive genomics allows for individuals to be matched to sports that draw on their genetic strengths. Genes can suggest particular suitability to sports involving strength or speed or flexibility.[22] In addition to aligning prospective athletes with particular genetic characteristics to specific sports, genetic testing can also identify potential vulnerability to certain types of injury or other health risks.[23] Exercise programs can be tailored to an athlete's needs based on this information. More importantly, an athlete's trainability and response to exercise as measured by oxygen uptake and usage is on the verge of being able to be determined.[24]

---

[22] M. Kambouris, F. Ntalouka, G. Ziogas, and N. Maffuli, "Predictive Genomics DNA Profiling for Athletic Performance," *Recent Patents on DNA & Gene Sequences* 6, no. 3 (2012): 229–239.

[23] For example, see House of Commons, Science and Technology Committee, "Memorandum from Professor Julian Savulescu" in *Human Enhancement Technologies in Sport: Second Report of Session 2006 07*, 7 February 2007, London, 82.

[24] Claude Bouchard, "Genetics and Sports Performance," paper presented at the International Convention on Science, Education and Medicine in Sport (Glasgow, UK, 20 July 2012); Sigmund Loland and Hans Hoppeler, "Justifying Anti-Doping:

It is possible that children could be genetically mapped and assessed to maximize their potential in particular sports. Genetic profiling might end dreams of being a top-caliber athlete if one takes a genetic determinist view.[25] But this science is not yet well understood, and it may be that there are more factors that affect athletic suitability and performance than a reductionist approach to DNA interpretation allows.

Another aspect of predictive genomics DNA profiling that could become an important component of athletic training is nutrigenomics or the study of how nutrition affects an individual's entire genome. As ethicist Ruth Chadwick suggests, this knowledge would intensify the already "increasing medicalization of nutrition."[26] This functional approach to food in the world of athletic training raises questions about what we value and what makes us happy. While a particular nutritional regimen informed by a scientific analysis of an individual athlete's physiology may provide him or her with optimal energy, acuity, and muscle development, that athlete may feel happier by eating a dinner of homemade macaroni and cheese, their happiness may also affect their athletic performance as well as life disposition. Being the best possible athlete and the best possible human is not reducible to any one thing. Questions need to be asked: What is enhanced (the person, the sport, the performance) by following particular scientific knowledge? What is possibly lost in choosing an enhancement or enhancing approach? Who decides what makes an athlete better?

One of the most anticipated innovations in sport is the biological "passport" that will not only aid in catching those athletes who cheat by using banned substances, but will also reveal genetic anomalies. The primary

---

The Fair Opportunity Principle and the Biology of Performance Enhancement," *European Journal of Sport Science* 12, no. 4 (2012): 349.

[25]Further, relying on a combination of genetic information and a commitment to providing the "right" environmental factors such as training and appropriate encouragement assumes a genetic and environmental determinism that, as theologian Ted Peters well argues, fails to take into account a necessary third factor—human spirit. [Ted Peters, *Playing God? Genetic Determinism and Human Freedom*, 2nd ed. (New York: Routledge, 2003).]

[26]Ruth Chadwick, "Nutrigenomics, Individualism and Sports," in *Genetic Technology and Sport: Ethical Questions*, eds. Claudio Marcello Tamburrini and Torbjörn Tännsjö (London, UK.: Routledge, 2005) 126.

intention of the Athletic Biological Passport is to catch athletes who use banned enhancements such as blood doping, designer EPO (recombinant erythropoietin), and designer testosterone—all of which appear as naturally occurring substances produced by the body.[27] The passport works by identifying the athlete's phenotype or molecular signatures and comparing these markers to future signatures to determine if any "broad metabolic, genetic, and [or] proteomic" changes have occurred. Changes would flag the possible use of "chemical, biological, or genetic doping agents."[28]

Importantly, the passport is based on the recognition that each person is unique and does not necessarily conform to all "normal" parameters. A problem in testing for banned substances that is addressed by the passport is the effect that the athlete's genotype can have on test results.[29] The genotype is an individual's full hereditary information in their genes. An athlete with a particular genotype may produce what appear to be suspicious results in response to some of the tests for banned substances, even though they have not used a banned substance. Further complicating things, environmental factors influence how the genetically coded traits evolve in an individual in interaction with the individual's environment. The degree to which environment or context affects each individual's genotype is known as phenotypic plasticity. The passport would be able to identify and measure each athlete's phenotype and phenotypic plasticity. Any deviations from an athlete's internal functioning that would be caused by a foreign substance would show up by comparing future tests to their baseline.

Ethicists Sigmund Loland and Hans Hoppeler have been strong proponents of using each athlete's phenotypic plasticity for assessing the acceptability of enhancements. With the passport, the athlete's phenotype becomes his or her individual baseline. After establishing the individual athlete's expected physiological range, future tests are compared to check for any internal deviations instead of relying on a comparison with a standard

---

[27] Pierre-Edouard Sottas, Neil Robinson, Oliver Rabin, and Martial Saugy, "The Athlete Biological Passport," *Clinical Chemistry*, 57, no. 7 (2011): 969–76.

[28] Friedman et al., "Gene Doping and Sport," 647.

[29] Angela J. Schneider, Matthew N. Fedoruk, and Jim L. Rupert, "Human Genetic Variation: New Challenges and Opportunities for Doping Control," *Journal of Sports Sciences*, 30, no. 11 (2012): 1117–29.

average. In so doing, it accounts for natural anomalies that may appear similar to effects caused by banned substances. Any substance that bypasses this baseline range (e.g. takes "short cuts" to get the desired effect such as EPO) would be prohibited.[30] Loland and Hoppeler propose that anything that bypasses particular bodily physiological reaction patterns should be on the banned list; conversely anything that does not should be removed. This approach has the advantage of anticipating more accurate tests for the use of banned substances such as EPO, anabolic steroids, and ephedrine, since it takes into account individual phenotypic variations and plasticity.

As proponents acknowledge, this approach also has limitations. There are numerous ethical issues associated with the proposed biological passport system: the athlete's privacy, knowledge of potential or assured genetically caused diseases, the retention of personal data and its potential uses, and consent to the possible use of this information, to name a few. Furthermore, the passport may not uncover the possible use of genetic modification technologies by an athlete prior to the taking of their baseline test, and will not be useful in assessing the enhancement provided by technological additions such as prosthetic devices or cyber aids such as implanted training chips.

The passport also does not address the issue of how we judge what these tests discover about athletes and their embodied advantages. Values and worldviews inform judgments that we make regarding what are acceptable advantages and what are not. For example, how do we decide what human features are "anomalies," and what anomalies are considered acceptable or unacceptable advantages. These assessments are informed by normative values and categories that we apply to people and the world. One of the most well known cases is that of Finnish athlete Eero Mäntyranta who, in the 1960s, won seven Olympic medals, including four golds, in cross-country skiing. A rare mutation in the gene coding for his EPO receptor resulted in a 25 to 50 percent increase in the oxygen-carrying

---

[30] Loland and Hoppeler, "Justifying Anti-Doping: The Fair Opportunity Principle and the Biology of Performance Enhancement" (2012): 347–53.

capacity of his red blood cells, giving him superior endurance.[31] In 1997, the Fédération Internationate de Ski (FIS) implemented a rule that would have excluded Mäntyranta from competition: a maximum hemoglobin concentration for males was set on the grounds that higher levels are unsafe. (In 2009 a new ruling was introduced allowing for the possibility of exceptions.) However, Mäntyranta's health has not been negatively affected by higher than normal hematocrits.[32]

More recently, winning swimmer Michael Phelps was discovered to have several genetic advantages including: disproportionately long "wingspan" to height ratio; disproportionately large shoe size and hand size; a "greater-than-average lung capacity"; and "muscles [that] produce 50% less lactic acid than other athletes."[33] Such discrepancies have always existed among people. What has changed is that we are now acquiring the ability to know more about who possesses what advantages.

We either admire these anomalous individuals as genetically gifted or see them as monsters and freaks that require fixing. Olympic-level athletes are highly unusual, possessing genetically exceptional or anomalous traits. Otherwise, they would not possess what is needed to be among the best in their sport. And that is how we regard these successful athletes—as the best. However, there are those few exceptions whose difference generates a fascination that is more akin to revulsion than admiration. Caster Semenya appeared too masculine for many people, while Oscar Pistorius's prosthetic legs drew a fascination that included popular support as well as disturbance and concern that he had a unfair advantage or was not really running. Both Semenya and Pistorius visibly violated normative embodiment categories. By identifying these judgments and assumptions as part of the enhancement issue, we can understand better what informs approaches to the debate in sport.

---

[31]Christie Aschwanden, "Gene Cheats," *New Scientist*, no. 2221 (15 January 2000): 24–29; Paul McCrory, "Super Athletes or Gene Cheats?" *British Journal of Sports Medicine London* 37, no. 3 (2003): 192.

[32]Schneider et al., "Human Genetic Variation," 1121.

[33]George Dvorsky, "Michael Phelps: 'Naturally' Transhuman," The Institute for Ethics and Emerging Technologies (2008), http://ieet.org/index.php/IEET/print/2575/.

Added Enhancements

The assumption that the enhancement issue is restricted to *add-ons* to the athlete or sport means that invisible genetic advantages (inborn enhancements) are ignored as is the relevance of how we judge these advantages. Added enhancements are all of those things—accepted or banned—that can be added to an athlete or sport to improve athletic performance, including innovative equipment, training techniques, drugs, vitamins, prosthetics, clothing, and genetic modification technologies. This restricted focus reflects the technological value of utility: In a technological society we are more focused on substances or things that *do something* than we are on self-consciously understanding how we see, judge, and order the world. But if we want to understand more self-critically and thoroughly what informs our approaches to enhancements, we must broaden the scope of the issue to include inborn advantages. How we assess these advantages can tell us more about the values that inform our decisions about added enhancements.

As long as we focus only on the assessment of added enhancements, we also likely will not move beyond action-oriented, decisionist approaches to the use of techno-science in sport. Decisionist ethics are concerned with what to *do* in a situation, and the weighing of the possible outcomes of these choices. Principles, duties, and consequences are accorded varying degrees of importance in decisionist models. Regarding the sport enhancement issue, ethical analyses have focused on how to decide what should be banned and what should be permitted to enhance athletic performances. While these questions are pressing on a public policy level,[34] it is important not to lose sight of virtue ethics questions that are not as immediately concerned with decisions regarding the acceptability of enhancements but with character, including questions of motivation and values.

---

[34]For example, using a decisionist framework, WADA delineates three criteria, two of which must be met if a substance or technology is to be added to the prohibited doping list: 1) It must be performance enhancing; 2) It must be harmful to health; and 3) It must run counter to the spirit of sport. As several ethicists have argued, these criteria are problematic in that they are vague and difficult to define. Yet it is necessary to have some rules in place if there is to be any attempt at consistency and order.

A purely decisionist approach neglects the underlying assumptions about how the world is conceptualized and ordered, and what is desired. The relevance of the spiritual dimension of sport is not likely to be considered. Such an approach risks uncritically reinforcing and amplifying the status quo. For example, although the passport is built on the recognition that each person's biological "normal" is distinct and that each individual has a *particular* baseline phenotypic plasticity, other epistemological issues are not addressed. How we know and categorize the world and people shapes how such information is interpreted and used. For Semenya and others like her who may not fit "normal" gender categories, the question of how we "know" that people are either male or female (in spite of science that shows that are more than two sex categories) is not considered. The assumption that there are only two acceptable sex and gender categories could be reinforced by using the information in an athlete's passport, not as an individual baseline test (as it seems it would be meant to be used), but to see if athletes "fit" in normative epistemological categories. The acceptability of athletes' bodies and perceived advantages rests, in part, on the way that we order the world.

Science is making invisible physiological and genetic characteristics, visible. How we interpret, assess, and use these revelations are important questions that must be considered in tandem with the science. We have looked at some of the ways in which science can reveal genetic anomalies, impart knowledge that can be used to design optimal nutrition or training programs, and make visible brain activity that occurs in response to different stimuli such as music. This discussion, so far, has been about the advantages and characteristics with which athletes are born—including a brain and body that are responsive to certain stimuli, optimal hormonal levels, and oxygen uptake capacities, and ways that we make the most of these characteristics and the knowledge science affords us, in sport.

Enhancements that are not pre-existing but added are the ones most frequently addressed in ethical analyses of sports enhancements. And of these, substance doping is the most prominent enhancement. But there is much more to enhancement issue than the doping by athletes such as Lance Armstrong and Barry Bonds.

Cybernetics, nanotechnology, cognitive sciences, exercise science, and genetic modification technologies are providing options for athletes and sports that go well beyond anabolic steroids, exogenous EPO, and blood doping. There are also added enhancements that are usually not even recognized as enhancements because of their easy availability and their social acceptability: vitamins, energy drinks, and numerous equipment enhancements such as carbon fiber-composite tennis racquets, fiberglass and carbon fiber pole vaults, the klap skate, and super polyurethane swimsuits. Let's first discuss these popularly acceptable added enhancements.

Vitamins, vaccinations, and numerous types of specialty drinks that contain caffeine or sugars and other stimulants are commonplace. They are designed to enhance the body but have become so normal that we do not think of them as enhancing (except when studies suggest that the effects on our bodies are not as simple and consistently good as we have come to believe).

Sports equipment is improved regularly to optimize athletic performances. In tennis, carbon fiber-composite tennis rackets are much lighter and more efficient than the old wooden ones. Steel rackets were introduced in the late 1960s, followed by aluminum in 1975 and carbon fiber-composites began to be created in the 1980s. The more flexible fiberglass and carbon fiber-based pole vaults were introduced in the 1980s, and since then pole vaulters wouldn't dream of using one of the old wooden or metal ones. The fiber-based poles have become normal.

Somewhat similarly, the klap skate (e.g. skates with a hinged blade) was first introduced in 1997 and generated much controversy in speed skating. However, after some issues were addressed, mainly regarding the process by which the skates were introduced, and after some time passed, the klap skate became accepted as the speed-skating skate.[35] In most cases, equipment and training innovations become accepted enhancements unless they significantly improve athletic performance and disrupt continuity with past records, or change the sport. With the passage of time, most changes become regarded as normal and not as enhancements.

There are other added enhancements that are controversial in sports, some of which are allowed and others not. These include Cheetah legs, polyurethane swimsuits, and to some extent hypobaric chambers, to name a

---

[35]See Ivo van Hilvoorde, Rein Vos, and Guido de Wert, "Flopping, Klapping and Gene Doping: Dichotomies Between 'Natural' and 'Artificial' in Elite Sport," *Social Studies of Science* 37, no. 2 (2007): 173–200.

few. These added enhancements are neither ingestible nor injectable, which, I suspect, has contributed to the difficulty in assessing them negatively; they do not generate the immediate revulsion that is associated with substance injection, nor do they alter the body permanently. Pistorius's cheetah legs are more disruptive in some ways, perhaps partly because prostheses are normal and not temporary for him. On the other hand, the fact that the super polyurethane swimsuits are temporary added enhancements did not save them from being banned from competitions since they enhanced swimmers' times to an unacceptable degree.

Hypobaric chambers, which are used by athletes to enhance their endurance capacities, fall on the border between temporary added enhancements and those that change or affect one's physiology. Hypobaric chambers, or altitude chambers, are chambers used to simulate the effects of high altitude on the body. The hypoxia (low oxygen levels) and hypobaria (low ambient air pressure) in high altitudes make it more difficult for athletes to perform well. Time spent in hypobaric chambers, however, can help one's body adapt more easily to high-altitude conditions if one comes from a lower altitude country. When athletes have to compete in altitudes higher than those to which they are accustomed, hypobaric chambers can improve their ability to compete at these higher altitudes. Since athletes who live in high altitudes get this advantage without using the chamber, it is reasoned that hypobaric chambers help even the playing field. It is, after all, a non-invasive intervention that only involves breathing air with different oxygen concentrations. However, some athletes use hypobaric chambers even when they are not preparing to compete in higher altitudes. This is because the number of red cells in the blood is increased by mild hypoxia, and a greater number of red cells improves endurance (similar to the effects of blood doping). Thus, athletes can have different motives for using hypobaric chambers. For some, it is to address an uneven and unnecessary advantage and for others it is to gain an advantage.[36] Because the effect of hypobaric chambers on the number of red cells is temporary (about two weeks) and because the mode of delivery is close to a natural process—breathing a

---

[36]For example, see Andy Miah's discussion of hypobaric chambers and ethics in Miah, "From Anti-Doping to a 'Performance Policy': Sport Technology, Being Human, and Doing Ethics," *European Journal of Sport Science* 5, no. 1 (2005): 54.

different concentration of air—it is possible to perceive hypobaric training chambers as a temporary added therapy instead of an enhancement that changes an athlete's physiology. In truth, it is both.[37] Hypobaric training chambers are not banned by WADA; however, there continues to be debate among ethicists regarding the acceptability of these tents.[38]

Potential cyber technologies are growing and include the possible use of a microchip that can be implanted in the arm that will record physiological changes, work-out data, and other information that could be used in developing an optimal training program for an individual athlete. There is no reason to think that the range of controversial options will do anything but increase.[39]

Although there tends to be a widespread aversion to ingestible, and particularly injectable, substances, with them being viewed as impure and drug-like, there are some ingestible and even injectable enhancements that are not popularly condemned even though they might be on some lists of banned enhancements. These tend to be substances available to the general public such as prescription and over-the-counter drugs. Many of these pharmaceuticals are seen as normal and innocuous. For example, beta-blockers, which are banned in most sports competitions, are now used not only to treat cardiac conditions but also to reduce performance anxiety. University students turn to beta-blockers for exam anxiety, as do many musicians, public speakers, and athletes. Similarly, stimulants such as high

---

[37]Further complicating the ethics of hypobaric training chambers is the cost involved. Many athletes cannot afford this intervention, thus creating unequal access to the chambers.

[38]See, for example, Verner Møller, *The Ethics of Doping and Anti-Doping: Redeeming the Soul of Sport?* (New York. Routledge, 2010) 114.

[39]For example, in 2009 scientists announced they had discovered how to reprogram "somatic cells to pluripotency, thereby creating induced pluripotent stem (iPS) cells." This breakthrough paves the way to regenerative medicine; a goal is to "grow" replacement organs and tissue from existing cells in one's body, thus avoiding autoimmune problems as well as the shortage of organ donors. This has obvious potential application for athletes; torn soft tissue could be regenerated rather than requiring less than certain surgery that requires lengthy rehabilitation [Keisuke Kaji et al, "Virus-free induction of pluripotency and subsequent excision of reprogramming factors," *Nature* 458 (1 March 2009): 771–75, http://www.nature.com/nature/journal/vaop/ncurrent/full/nature07864.html.]

doses of caffeine and sugar in energy drinks are not only available but also are widely promoted through advertising campaigns that are often associated with sports and healthy, strong, winning bodies.

Perhaps most controversial are substances from the ephedra family, particularly ephedrine and pseudoephedrine, stimulants found in some asthma and cold medications. Bans on these substances vary from sport to sport and are often at the center of controversy, as in the case of American swimmer Rick Demont who, following the 1972 Munich Games, was stripped of his gold medal after he was found to have ephedrine in his system from an asthma medication. He had no idea his medication contained a banned substance. Galine Kulakova of the Soviet Union was disqualified after winning bronze in the five-kilometer Nordic skiing event (1976) for testing positive for ephedrine. In perhaps the most recent highly controversial incident, Romanian gymnast Andrea Raducan won the women's Olympic all-around gold medal in the 2000 Sydney Olympics only to have it taken away when pseudoephedrine was discovered in her system. Her coach unwittingly had given her a cold medication containing the banned substance before the event.

Lastly, some banned enhancing substances are used covertly by some athletes. These substances include anabolic steroids, blood doping, EPO, human growth hormone (HGH), and gene doping. They are unacceptable as judged both by popular audiences and by sports regulating bodies. Anabolic steroids are harmful to health (health risks include organ damage, reduced fertility, elevated blood pressure, blood clotting, tendon damage, and psychiatric disorders)[40] but improve athletic performance, and are often used to gain an unfair advantage. EPO and HGH fall into a similar category. Banned in 1985 by the IOC, blood doping provides a different nuance to the challenge of ingested or injected enhancements since the athlete's own blood is used as the doping substance. However, it is an artificial means to improve endurance by increasing blood volume and hemoglobin concentrations. Blood doping also poses health risks (including

---

[40] See, for example, C. Maravelias, A. Dona, M. Stefanidou, and C. Spiliopoulou, "Adverse Effects of Anabolic Steroids in Athletes: A Constant Threat," *ScienceDirect* 158, no. 3 (2005): 167.

an increased risk of stroke, cardiac arrest, or embolism)[41] and is a covert way of gaining a competitive edge, or cheating.

Gene Doping[42]

The International Olympic Committee (IOC) first added "gene doping," or genetic modification technologies, to their list of banned substances in 2003. The IOC's World Anti-Doping Agency (WADA) defines gene doping as "the non-therapeutic use of genes, genetic elements and/or cells that have the capacity to enhance athletic performance."[43] In anticipation of the 2012 London Olympic Games, authorities warned that "gene doping, or the modulation of an athlete's genetic material or its expression to improve performance, is ... thought of as a potential threat to the London 2012 Olympics.... [T]here have already been reports of use of gene therapy in this fashion."[44] Predictive genomics DNA profiling, somatic cell modification, and germline cell technologies are all categories of gene transfer technologies that either will or already do affect sports. Predictive genomics DNA

---

[41]WADA, "Blood Doping," (2014), https://www.wada-ama.org/en/questions-answers/blood-doping.

[42]Material from pages 48–52 inclusive is adapted with permission from an article I published previously: Tracy J. Trothen, "Sport, Religion, and Genetic Modification: An Ethical Analysis of Gene Doping," *The International Journal of Religion and Sport* 1, no. 1 (2009): 1–20.

[43] This definition was included in the WADA 2003 list of prohibited substances. (See E. M. Swift and Don Yaeger, "Unnatural Selection," *Sports Illustrated* 94, no. 20 [14 May 2001]: 88; and www.wada-ama.org or www.olympic.org.) WADA held their first interdisciplinary conference on "Genetic Enhancement of Athletic Performance" in 2002 in which ethical issues were considered in addition to legal, policy, and scientific issues. (WADA, "WADA Gene Doping Symposium Calls for Greater Awareness, Strengthened Action against Potential Gene Transfer Misuse in Sport" [June 2008] on the World Anti-Doping Agency web site; http://www.wada-ama.org/en/newsarticle.ch2?article-Id=3115626).

[44] House of Commons, Science and Technology Committee, *Human Enhancement Technologies in Sport: Second Report of Session 2006–07* (London, 7 February 2007): 40. Neurologist and Sports Physician Paul McCrory states, "Currently there are over 100 chromosomal loci, including nuclear and mitochondrial DNA, involved in human performance with more genes discovered each year." [McCrory, "Super Athletes or Gene Cheats?" (2003): 193.]

profiling has been outlined earlier in this chapter.[45] Potential somatic cell modification technologies raise fewer ethical objections than do potential germline interventions, since germline modifications will affect future generations that cannot consent to these changes. What is popular and desirable today may not be in the future.[46] Somatic cell technologies, on the other hand, target a particular set of cells and only the individual treated.[47]

Somatic cell genetic modification technologies are at a preliminary stage of development but assuredly will, at some point, become available to human subjects. The science typically involves using an ordinary adenovirus, such as the virus for the common cold. The cold-causing genes within the virus are removed and replaced with synthetic genes that direct the body to produce the desired proteins. The newly configured vector is then injected into the animal or human body.[48]

An example of an emerging somatic cell genetic modification technology is Repoxygen, which is "the tradename for a type of gene therapy which induces controlled release of [erythropoietin] EPO in response to low oxygen concentration in mice."[49] The genetic modification of the EPO receptor could be very beneficial to those suffering from anemia associated with diseases such as chronic renal failure. Exogenous EPO has been

---

[45] See pages 28-29.

[46] W. French Anderson, "Human Gene Therapy" in *Contemporary Issues in Bioethics*, 5th ed., eds. Tom L. Beauchamp and Leroy Walters (Belmont, CA: Wadsworth Publishing, 1999) 584; Audrey Chapman, "Religious Perspectives on Human Germ Line Modifications," in *Beyond Cloning*, eds. Ronald Cole-Turner (Harrisburg, PA: Trinity Press International, 2001) 74–76; David R. Cole, "The Genome and the Human Genome Project," in *Genetics: Issues of Social Justice*, ed. Ted Peters (Cleveland, OH: Pilgrim Press, 1998) 63.

[47] However, it is possible that somatic cell interventions inadvertently will affect germline cells. [See, for example, McCrory, "Super Athletes or Gene Cheats?" 192; Mehmet Unal and Durisehvar Ozer Unal, "Gene Doping in Sports," *Sports Medicine* 34, no. 6 (2004): 358; H. Lee Sweeney, "Gene Doping," *Scientific American*, 21 June 2004, http://www.sciam.com/article.cfm?id=gene-doping.]

[48] Simon Eassom, Head of Sports Studies at de Montfort University, United Kingdom, Interview by Amanda Smith, *Sports Factor*, ABC, 12 July 2001, www.abc.net.au/rn/talks/8.30/sportsf/stories/s435073.htm.

[49] House of Commons, Science and Technology Committee, "Human Enhancement Technologies in Sport," 40.

available legally since 1989 for this purpose, and has been procured by some athletes to increase their endurance, notably in the notorious 1998 Tour de France.[50] It is suspected that Repoxygen was used in the 2012 Olympic Games in spite of its experimental status. Lending credence to this suspicion is the indictment of Thomas Springstein, a German track coach who in 2006 was found guilty of trying to procure Repoxygen for his athletes.[51] Another example of a potential somatic cell genetic technology that would enhance endurance is vascular endothelial growth factor (VEGF), which could increase the development of blood vessels and blood flow to muscles and organs, thereby delaying exhaustion.[52]

One more example of a somatic cell genetic modification technology that could be attractive to athletes is the development of insulin-like growth factor 1 (IGF-1) and other anti-myostatin drugs for the treatment of degenerative muscle diseases such as muscular dystrophy. The inhibition of myostatin, which is a negative muscle growth factor, would increase muscle bulk and decrease recovery time for muscle damage.[53] In 1998, scientist H. Lee Sweeney found that IGF-1 gene therapy increased muscle bulk in sedentary mice by 15 to 30 percent.[54] In a later study, Sweeney found that

---

[50] The EPO receptor provides feedback control of red blood cells' oxygen carrying capacity. [See, for example, McCrory, "Super Athletes or Gene Cheats?" 192; A. Gaudard, M. E. Varlet, F. Bressolle et al., "Drugs for Increasing Oxygen and Their Potential Use in Doping: A Review," *Sports Medicine* 33, no. 3 (2003): 187–212; and S. Zhou, J. E. Murphy, J. A. Escobedo et al., "Adeno-Associated Virus-Mediated Delivery of Erythropoietin," *Gene Therapy* 5, no. 5 (1998): 665–70.]

[51] Christie Aschwandan, "The Future of Cheating in Sports," *Smithsonian Magazine* (July 2012), http://www.smithsonianmag.com/science-nature/The-Future-of-Cheating-in-Sports-160285295.html; Friedmann et al., "Gene Doping and Sport," (2013) 647.

[52] Unal and Unal, "Gene Doping in Sports," 357, 359; and House of Commons, Science and Technology Committee, "Memorandum from Professor Julian Savulescu" in *Human Enhancement Technologies in Sport: Second Report of Session 200–07* (London, 7 February 2007) 81.

[53] Schneider et al., "Human Genetic Variation," 1120; Friedmann et al., "Gene Doping and Sport," 647; Unal and Unal, "Gene Doping in Sports," 358–59; E. M. Swift and Don Yaeger, "Unnatural Selection," 86.

[54] Sweeney, "Gene Doping" (21 June 2004).

rats could increase their strength further through weight training.[55] Sweeney also reports that molecular geneticist Nadia Rosenthal's follow-up study, using the same gene therapy, found that the mice had an increased muscle bulk of 20 to 50 percent. Additionally, the mice "retained a regenerative capacity typical of younger animals," indicating the possibility of not losing muscle mass due to aging.[56] Sweeney has received several requests from athletes interested in IGF-1.[57]

It is not unreasonable to surmise that future genetic modification technologies will allow for the possibility of programming an offspring's height particularly if the fetal genetic profile indicates that he or she will be shorter than what is expected for his or her age group. Of course, what is considered a "normal" height today likely will change in the future. It is not a big leap to suppose that a little would be added to that "normal" height, to give a prospective athlete an edge or, particularly for men, increased social standing.

In assessing genetic modification technologies, it is tempting to see them as akin to other "doping" substances including EPO, steroids, blood doping, and human growth hormone. But it is important to be aware of the particular revulsion factor associated with "tampering" with genetics at this point in time. Also, the question of why particular enhancements are singled out as unacceptable when many other unnatural enhancements are accepted needs to be addressed.[58]

Advantages and Enhancements: Questions to Consider

The meanings of the words normal, natural, therapeutic, enhancing, and artificial are complicated. These concepts change with historical and cultural contexts and are value laden. For example, in the sporting world, natural and therapeutic are good whereas artificial and enhancing are bad.

---

[55] Brownlee, "Gene Doping," 281.

[56] Sweeney, "Gene Doping" (21 June 2004).

[57] Brownlee, "Gene Doping," 280.

[58] Andy Miah makes a good case for assessing genetic modification technologies differently from other athletic enhancements [Miah, *Genetically Modified Athletes: Biomedical Ethics, Gene Doping, and Sport* (New York: Routledge, 2004)].

Athletes are expected to perform without aids and are expected to represent ideal body images. They are to be proof that the ways in which we order the world make sense and that new athletic records are possible without enhancements.

Nowotny and Testa ask how society will regard the increasingly visible new forms of humans that will emerge and how they will be "integrated into the existing social order."[59] There is a different question that could be posed, however, and that is, how will the existing social order that is built around particular notions of normality be reconfigured in response to the greater number of visibly diverse bodies? It's hard to say how tenacious our understandings of normal and sameness will be in the face of more "enhanced" humans.

What does it mean to make oneself enhanced or better? In short, what makes a human better and what makes a human in sport better? If we agree that athletes enhance their physical selves through sport, then we are saying something about what makes the physical self "better." In other words, physical strength, speed, agility, flexibility, and other such qualities make humans better on a physical level. Youth and a low percentage of body fat are highly valued. For power sports such as hockey, football, rugby, and wrestling, maleness is valued since men tend to have greater physical strength than women. In contrast, femaleness is valued when greater flexibility is required, such as in some gymnastic and figure-skating competitions.

As humans, for what do we long? What are our desires and our hopes? What do we value? These questions must be raised as part of the sport enhancement debate if we are to critically and prudently consider what the future holds.

---

[59]Nowotny and Testa, *Naked Genes*, 49.

Chapter 3

Theological Reflection on Sport and Techno-science: Creation, Fall, and Redemption

Various voices have weighed in on the issue of possible advantages posed by enhancements and inborn physical attributes of athletes. The power of these respective voices has waxed and waned with changing historical contexts. At one time, the voices of theologians were much more central to this issue, but now, scientists and engineers who specialize in technology have assumed a more powerful voice.[1] The issue, from this perspective, is informed mostly by technological values (e.g., efficiency and utility) with the result that the main concern has been how to improve an athlete's chances of winning. Immediately, several questions emerge: What would make sport better? What do we mean by better? In response to these questions, philosophers and theological ethicists have contributed their analyses. As the connection between sport and religion becomes increasingly explored and debated, it is timely to ask what might be added to the enhancement discussion in light of the "religious" dimension of sport.

Christian theological reflection can help us see that there are different ways to understand the sport enhancement debate. A theological perspective can suggest alternate values to the technological emphasis on utility and efficiency. Not only is the enhancement issue placed in dialogue with an alternate value set and worldview, but issues about the spiritual dimension of sport and what it means to be human are raised more deliberately. Christian theology does not offer a *completely different* set of values and concerns but it does suggest some different perspectives. In short, religion is part of culture, and culture is part of religion. Neither subsumes the other, but the mutual influence of each is apparent. The point here is that the application of a more marginalized perspective can raise additional questions about what is important in sport.

---

[1]Brent Waters, *From Human to Posthuman: Christian Theology and Technology in a Postmodern World* (Surrey, UK: Ashgate Publishing, 2006).

Bringing a Christian lens to the enhancement debate is not new; Christian theologians and ethicists have contributed substantially to the enhancement debate. What is new is theological reflection on human enhancement in sport, when sport is understood to have a religious or spiritual dimension.

Within Christianity, as within all religions, there is a diversity of perspectives. I take a feminist reformed protestant perspective with the hope that this perspective will contribute to the enhancement dialogue through adding a particular Christian interpretation. This is not meant to be a systematic theological approach to techno-science in sport but an attempt to broaden and deepen the sport enhancement conversation, and to illustrate the importance of one's worldview to how we see (and don't see) an issue.

Biblically and theologically, Christianity has three main moments to its story: creation, fall, and redemption. Within these three are several layers, only a few of which will be touched on here as they relate to techno-science and sport. These three moments are intertwined and overlap.

Creation

Revelations of God are both transcendent and enfolded in the world. From a theological perspective, revelation is understood to occur in two forms: in a particular way through scripture and in a general way through the ongoing actions and presence of the Holy Spirit. General revelations are particularly relevant to sport. Experiences of transcendence or flow[2] are sometimes understood as experiences of the sacred. Is it possible for an awe-inspiring experience in sport to be a general revelation of God's spirit?[3] Theologically, the answer is "yes" since God's spirit is not and cannot be restricted. The question concerns discernment. Not every emotion filled moment is a divine revelation.

---

[2] See chapter five for a sustained discussion of flow.

[3] Hopsicker presents an interesting theological argument for the working of God's Spirit when the athlete or fan perceives a "miracle" of God to have occurred in sport. He proposes that even if theologically it makes no sense to see a sports event as a miracle, the fact that some think they have seen God at work serves an evangelical function that in itself may well be of God. (Peter M Hopsicker, "Miracles in Sport: Finding the 'Ears to Hear' and the 'Eyes to See'," *Sport, Ethics and Philosophy* 3, no. 1 [2009]: 75–93).

The theological conversation around how one recognizes a genuine, spiritually filled moment has been ongoing for centuries. German theologians Friedrich Schleiermacher, Rudolph Otto, and Jürgen Moltmann have a much less restrictive view of these moments than do other equally prominent theologians such as Karl Barth. How one approaches this theological topic has to do with how one sees the relationship between the sacred and profane, and the transcendent and immanent. As suggested in the introduction to this book, some theologians see these relationships as clear binaries—not overlapping but distinct: God alone is sacred and transcendent, and God's creatures occupy the profane realm. Feminist theologians largely reject this stark binary, seeing an overlap or even a complete interweaving of these paired elements with the spiritual permeating the mundane world.

If there are moments when athletes and fans "touch" transcendence in sport[4]—believing that they have had a spiritual experience—then it behooves us to ask how various enhancement technologies or science may affect the human capacity for these moments. As ethics professor and theologian Ronald Cole-Turner asks, will enhancing an activity that is in itself enhancing have a doubling effect?[5] Or will we risk compromising, or even ending, spiritual experiences in sport? Theological reflection requires asking difficult questions about what it means to improve or enhance, and what values inform this meaning.

In Christianity, it is believed commonly that God is revealed partially in creation, including the embodied human. Embodiment is an irreducible aspect of humanity created in God's image. By using the term irreducible, I am underscoring the inextricable relationship between body, mind, and soul; any one of these aspects cannot be comprehended apart from the others. For example, how we know the world is mediated by our bodies; if I am in a wheelchair I experience the world as someone who understands physical access issues in a particular way. If I identify as a woman, then I experience the world differently than I would as a recognizably embodied male, especially because of gender stereotyping and other forms of sexism. If I am

---

[4]Mayra Rivera, *The Touch of Transcendence* (London: Westminster John Knox Press, 2007).

[5]I am indebted to Ron Cole-Turner for this observation.

an artist, likely I understand that my mind is not confined to my brain but that my hands can move and create in a way that includes and goes beyond my brain.

Still, there is something helpful about binary categories such as body and soul, or mind and matter. Thinking in these terms *can* help us to be cognizant of the complexity of being human and to avoid reducing people to only one of these aspects. Binaries become more problematic when their elements are assigned values in comparison to each other or when their aspects are regarded as exclusive and not interconnected. Another problem emerges when it is thought that people can be reduced to parts; the Gestalt insight that the whole is greater than the sum of the parts is missed.

Sport is not immune to this type of extreme binary thinking about the athlete. On the one hand, elite sports are a celebration of embodiment and competitive sports are built on the understanding that the human person is multi-dimensional. On the other hand, the body, mind, or spirit can be seen as separate parts that need to be overcome, instead of tapping them as integrated resources in healthy and optimal athletic performance.[6] For example, if an athlete suffers muscle strain, the body needs to heal. A temptation can be to use the mind to overcome the body's pain message instead of listening to that message and seeking treatment for the strained muscle. Even though the athlete may feel inspired and *want* to continue their long run, the pain in their knee tells them that they need to stop. The athlete, as an embodied whole, can be encouraged to know what he or she needs to be healthy, on all levels, to perform optimally.

The overall health of elite athletes can be affected adversely by the perception of mind, body, or spirit as limits that are to be overcome. This is different from athletes pushing themselves to a greater integration in which all human aspects are working together to allow the athlete to be the best that he or she can, "incarnate spirits achieving wonders."[7] Each person has a different "best." Working toward that best involves the recognition of limits,

---

[6] Sigmund Loland, "A Well Balanced Life Based on 'The Joy of Effort': Olympic Hype or a Meaningful Ideal?," *Sport, Ethics and Philosophy* 6, no. 2 (2012): 158–59.

[7] Denise Larner Carmody, "Big-time Spectator Sports: A Feminist Christian Perspective," *New Catholic World* (July/August 1986): 173–77.

the belief that one can become even better at a sport, and the ability to see all human aspects as interconnected resources. This is very different from ignoring creaturely limits and needs. A perception of these limits as unnecessary barriers (and not as human aspects that, while challenging, contribute to excellent athletic performances) promotes unnecessary suffering and excessive self-sacrifice.

In a well documented study, associate professor of physical education and kinesiology at Redeemer University College, Jane Lee Sinden outlines some of the common health problems experienced by elite athletes: "substance abuse, eating disorders, osteoporosis, amenorrhea, overtraining, chronic sport-related injuries, burnout and depression." Sinden concludes that "athletes have learned to disassociate themselves from their bodies."[8] Without changes to these distorted beliefs, there is every reason to anticipate an amplification of this disconnect between body, mind, and spirit with more corporeal enhancement options. This disconnection manifests itself in multiple embodied dimensions. For example, Sinden found that an inability to express stressful emotions makes athletes more vulnerable to physical injury and depression.[9]

The body has not always been celebrated within either elite sports or the Christian tradition. Christianity has often regarded the body and bodily pleasure as suspect. Women have born the brunt of this suspicion, often being portrayed as sexual temptresses. Traditionally, sex has been seen as equivalent to sin; thus, in many classical theologies women have been seen as more ontologically sinful than men. Since the rise of feminist theologians in the 1970s, the created goodness of the body has become more recognized. Traditionally, there are three Christian doctrines that imply the goodness of human embodiment: creation, the Incarnation, and bodily resurrection. Regarding creation, the *imago Dei* or the belief that we are created in the image of God, suggests that embodiment is part of the divine image in some way, and, therefore, that embodiment is good. At their best, elite sports are a celebration of embodiment aimed at excellence.

---

[8] Jane Lee Sinden, "The Elite Sport and Christianity Debate: Shifting Focus from Normative Values to the Conscious Disregard for Health," *Journal for Religious Health* 52 (2012): 338.

[9] Ibid., 335–49.

An approach to the enhancement debate that is consistent with this vision of elite sports will ask how enhancements might affect the whole person. For example, if I choose to use an available genetic modification technology because it will increase my endurance levels and improve my distance running, I must also ask what else might be affected. Will other aspects of my health be affected? How will future generations be affected, particularly if it is a germline genetic modification technology? Will other athletes have equal access to this enhancement? Might I be taking, indirectly, needed resources from someone else? Will this change affect my sensitivity to others? What is my motivation? Is my choice to use this technology about me becoming more authentic and truer to what I believe in, or am I being driven by something else? Will I be healthier spiritually?

In Christianity, it is believed that humanity is made in God's image, but the meaning of this *imago Dei* doctrine has been much debated. To be created in the image of God is not to be the same as God but to be created in a way that reflects glimmers of God. Reflected images are not perfect representations. To appreciate these glimmers in each person, it is necessary to have some idea about the nature of God.

The majority of Christians understand God as trinitarian: three persons and one essence. This concept of three in one is very difficult to understand, owing partly to changes in language and conceptualizations since the formulation of this doctrine. [10] Nonetheless, it is still helpful in communicating human experiences of God. The trinitarian doctrine of God underscores that God *is* community within God's self. It is believed that God has revealed this three-in-one nature through the work of creating (God as source of life), redeeming (Jesus Christ), and sustaining the world (the Holy Spirit). This mystery of God's interior relationality highlights the created nature of humanity also as relational. In Christian terms, relationality means love of neighbor and justice.

God's trinitarian nature also suggests that humans are made to need each other; humans are interdependent, as is God. Yet, dependency—even

---

[10]Elizabeth A. Johnson, *She Who Is: The Mystery of God in Feminist Theological Discourse* (New York: Crossroad, 1992). Johnson notes that neither numbers (one, two, three) nor the term "person" mean the same thing today as when the doctrine of the trinity was formulated.

mutual dependency—is not a favored value in much of today's North American society. Interestingly, those instances in which athletes show vulnerability and fragility are some of the most remembered, discussed, and awe-inspiring moments in elite sports competitions. For example, during the 2010 Vancouver Winter Olympics, Canadians were full of pride at Joannie Rochette's resilient bronze medal performance, a performance that she dedicated to her mother who had died at the beginning of the games. Fans were moved by Rochette's determination to compete even though she was visibly crushed by her mother's death. With the heartfelt support of thousands of fans, she did her best and achieved the bronze medal in spite of being in deep grief. Another moving example, in a different vein, is speed skater Gilmore Junio's decision to give up his spot in the 1,000 meter race to Denny Morrison at the 2014 Winter Olympics. Morrison had twice won the silver medal in the event at the world championship but had failed to qualify for the Sochi race, finishing behind Junio.[11]

Diversity and dignity are connected to relationality and inter-dependence. The diversity of humans reflects the complexity of God. As theologian Mayra Rivera posits, God is "that multiple singularity that joins together all creatures—creatures that are themselves irreducible in the infinite multiplicity of their own singularity."[12] In other words, each person is unique and worthy of dignity simply by virtue of being created in God's image. God is the thread that joins together all unique humans. Only through human diversity can God be "touched" (but never fully "grasped," as Rivera puts it) since each person reflects a particular glimmer of God.

Some of this diversity is represented in elite sports. The embodied beauty of athletes who are of a variety of skin colors, abilities and disabilities, physical proportions, and facial features, is evidenced. This diversity can help stoke awe and appreciation for the diverse Other, if we are open to seeing this beauty. On the other hand, there is always the potential for judgment instead of appreciation. The use and development of technology and science is influenced by our perceptions of diversity, dependence, and vulnerability.

---

[11] Dave Feschuk, "Canadian Speed Skater Gilmore Junio Gives Up His Spot to Denny Morrison," *The Toronto Star* (11 February 2014) wwwthestar.com.

[12] Ibid., 137.

As "created co-creators," to use theologian Philip Hefner's metaphor, humans are meant to create. [13] Although Hefner's proposal has been critiqued as failing to sufficiently acknowledge humanity's hubris and the distinction between God as creator and humanity as creators, [14] it is a useful, albeit limited, metaphor. Theologian Ted Peters has used this metaphor effectively in his theological explorations of biotechnology and genetic science. Understanding the *imago Dei* doctrine as a divine mandate to create with the goal of furthering God's work, Peters cautions against hubris, emphasizing the human propensity to sin. Peters never loses sight that the full realization of what it means to be human will not come until the end times and then in God's terms. [15]

At the core of these theological issues are questions of theological anthropology, or what it means to be human. At what point, if any, does a technologically enhanced human become non-human? Will we gain the capacity and inclination to re-create ourselves so far from God's image that theologically we would become non-human? Much of this line of questioning depends on the meaning of being human and God's grace. Philip Heffner locates the essence of being human in *"the sense that we are*

---

[13]Theological ethicist Grace D. Cumming Long proposes a binding principle of "transcending creativity" based on the *imago Dei* doctrine. This is the duty to create out of a commitment to re-create a more just world. Simply, it is not sufficient to know that aspects of society, church, and world are harmful; because we are made in God's image and sustained by God's Spirit, it is incumbent upon us to use our creative and creating abilities for good. Conditions that are harmful to flourishing must be transcended. This is a proposition built on the contention that none are free until all are free; oppression is a web—all injustices are connected, as is all life. [Grace D. Cumming Long, *Passion & Reason: Women Views of Christian Life* (Louisville, KY: Westminster/John Knox Press, 1993).]

[14]For an excellent discussion of this critique and an in-depth exploration of the *imago Dei* doctrine as it relates to enhancement technology, see Stephen Garner, "Christian Theology and Transhumanism: The 'Created Co-Creator' and Bioethical Principles," in *Religion and Transhumanism: The Unknown Future of Human Enhancement*, eds. Calvin Mercer and Tracy J. Trothen (Westport, CT: Praeger, 2015) 229–44.

[15]Ted Peters, *God: The World's Future: Systematic Theology for a New Era*, 2nd ed. (Minneapolis: Fortress Press, 2000) 157–59.

accountable to something larger than ourselves and larger than our own times."[16] And, psychotherapist Kenneth Pargament offers, "It is perhaps the human yearning for the sacred that makes us most distinctively human."[17] Neither one of these understandings of what it means to be human is confined to a Christian perspective; both point to a sense of spirituality including a sense of sacredness and meaning beyond oneself.

The Fall

Since the fall from the Garden of Eden, humans have been prone to sin. Even so, God has entrusted humanity with the responsibility to create and work towards justice and flourishing. Theological discussions of techno-science and enhancements have attended well to the dangers of hubris, or playing God. Thinking too much of ourselves blinds us to our fallibility and constructive limitations. As history shows, not all that humans create is good.

Upholding the importance of self-critique and humility, Peters nonetheless has debunked hubris as a valid reason to eschew scientific innovations. Since we are created in God's image, part of "playing human" is to create.[18] This creativity has led to much that is good: global communication, life-saving medical interventions, education, travel, and so on. Some of these life-giving creations have also been used in not so good ways. For example, some modes of travel cause excessive harm to the environment. Similarly, the pursuit of techno-science innovations that could be used in sport and physical therapy has potential for both good and bad. And hubris is not the only cause of harm.

The lack of sense of self and voice, too, is a form of sin. When marginalization cultivates *feelings* of powerlessness, one can be tempted to

---

[16]Philip Hefner, "The Animal that Aspires to be an Angel: The Challenge of Transhumanism," *Dialog: A Journal of Theology* 48, no. 2 (June 2009): 165.

[17]K. I. Pargament, "The Pursuit of False Gods: Addressing the Spiritual Dimension of Addictions in Counseling" in *Psychotherapy as Cure of the Soul*, eds. Thomas St. James O'Connor, Kristine Lund, and Patricia Berendsen (Waterloo, ON: Waterloo Lutheran Seminary Press, 2014) 245–54. More will be said about spirituality in sport, in chapter five.

[18]Ted Peters, *Playing God? Genetic Determinism and Human Freedom*, 2nd ed. (New York: Routledge, 2003).

accept that one *is* powerless. Oppressive powers and structures compromise one's moral agency,[19] but women and other marginalized groups have found creative and strategic ways to claim voice and resist. When oppressed people are courageous enough to exercise power—in any small way—it does at least two things: it opens the door to more transformative work, and it demonstrates that people are rarely without *any* power. On the one hand, it may seem harsh to call acquiescence "sin." On the other, if we do not name the giving up of power and self as sin, we buy into the lie that marginalization removes personhood. Excessive pride or hubris is not usually the main sin of the marginalized. Rather, more pride is needed.[20]

In an age when techno-science is rapidly developing and when winning is so important in elite sport, athletes need courage and confidence to speak out when feeling pushed to use enhancements. Sports participation has been a double-edged sword in terms of cultivating this courage and confidence. On the one hand, sports participation at all levels has been shown often to build confidence, particularly in those who struggle with claiming their own power, including many women and girls. This added confidence can make a big difference. Sport can help one to feel stronger and to recognize the strength that one possesses, both physically and as a moral person.

On the other hand, sport does not always contribute to athletes' courage and confidence. The power differential between coach, owners, and athletes has attracted predators who abuse athletes.[21] It also has meant increased pressure on athletes to do whatever they can to achieve the goals of their sport.[22] Christian theology has not always been helpful to this dynamic. Traditional theologies often have glorified physical suffering and self-sacrifice as moral goods in and of themselves. Feminist, womanist, mujerista, and other theologians who write from the "underside" have critiqued these

---

[19]Moral agency is the capacity to make decisions and act on them.

[20]Hubris and a lack of self are not mutually exclusive.

[21]See, for example, Laura Robinson, *Crossing the Line: Violence and Sexual Assault in Canada's National Sport* (Toronto, ON: McClelland & Stewart, 1998); and Sandra Kirby, Lorraine Greaves, and Olena Hankivsky, *The Dome of Silence: Sexual Harassment and Abuse in Sport* (Halifax, NS: Fernwood, 2002).

[22]The ethical question of individual choice is explored more thoroughly in chapter seven.

theologies as especially unhelpful and dangerous to women.[23] Instead of fostering a constructive, healthy sense of one's own power and value, these theological messages have contributed to self-abnegation and sometimes self-destruction. And these theological messages have not been restricted to Christian followers; at some level they have permeated popular culture.

In particular, some atonement theories have been used to support the dangerous interpretation that because Jesus suffered on the cross, all suffering is part of emulating God and is, therefore, good. Because oppressed people experience much of the suffering in the world, these interpretations are most harmful to them. The acceptance of all suffering as God's will maintains unjust power systems and abuse. Countering this, theological ethicists including Barbara Andolsen, have argued that Jesus' suffering on the cross was not an end in itself. Rather Jesus was killed because he upset the unjust balance of power through his ministry of solidarity with the oppressed. In this view, God's promise of new life is not contingent upon physical suffering but upon working towards an eschatological vision of mutual well-being, justice, and love.

The Gospel stories of Jesus' physical healing miracles are another indication of God's desire for embodied humanity to be well and not suffer unnecessary pain. For example, Jesus healed the blind man (Mark 8:22–25) and the hemorrhaging woman (Mark 5:25–34). Self-sacrifice that is not for a greater good, and unnecessary suffering, are not consistent with a Christian message of wholeness and life.

Yet it is the theological glorification of violence, not so much the celebration of bodily well-being, that has seeped into culture, including sport. Most sports intrinsically involve some degree of physical violence to the athlete; hard training, for example, pushes the body to its physical limits and often causes injury. Not all violence is bad; hard training and some degree of risk can be exhilarating, and foster persistence and discipline. But complicating this intrinsic violence is a range of banned and accepted "enhancements" that are widely available to athletes. Elite athletes will often be among the first to try new ways to improve their performances even if it

---

[23]See Tracy J. Trothen, "Holy Acceptable Violence?: Violence in Hockey and Christian Atonement Theories," *Journal of Religion and Popular Culture*, special edition: Religion and Popular Culture in Canada (2009): 1–42.

might cost them a little (or a lot of) pain or risk to health. Athletes' willingness to risk their well-being can be seen in many aspects of competitive sport ranging from pride in physical injuries taken "for the team" to starvation to accomplish a certain body weight or image.[24] Pain is not seen as a bad thing in sport. What is seen as bad is if the athlete cannot tolerate the pain or if the cause of the pain is understood as incongruent with the values of naturalness and purity (values that also correspond to traditional Christian values).

An example of how this view of pain may eventually interact with enhancement use is an emergent genetic transfer technology—the modification of the DREAM gene. Scientific research has made inroads in the genetics of pain sensation. A protein called the Downstream Regulatory Element Antagonistic Modulator (DREAM) is associated with how we experience pain sensations. It is possible in future that genetic transfer technologies could provide athletes with what ethicist Andy Miah calls "the DREAM gene for the posthuman athlete"[25] by blocking the production of prodynorphin, a chemical produced by the body in response to pain or stress. Prodynorphin seems to lessen pain sensations. Early tests on mice in which the DREAM gene is inhibited or removed show promise for the reduction of pain, but any application of this science to humans remains prospective. While such a genetic transfer technology might be used in sport, it is possible that some athletes will not find this modification attractive because it would make pain tolerance and self-sacrifice relatively meaningless. However, if modification of the DREAM gene allowed athletes to still experience pain, but only after more intense training, it might be very attractive even though it would increase the chance of serious injury.

---

[24]Michelle M. Lelwica, "Losing Their Way to Salvation: Women, Weight Loss, and the Salvation Myth of Culture Lite," in *Religion and Popular Culture in America*, eds. Bruce David Forbes and Jeffrey H. Mahan (Berkeley: University of California Press, 2000) 180–200. The traditional Christian distrust of the body, especially women's bodies, as possessing uncontrollable appetites, passion and propensity to sin, has not assuaged these messages.

[25]Andy Miah, "The DREAM Gene for the Posthuman Athlete: Reducing Exercise-Induced Pain Sensations Using Gene Transfer," in *The Anthropology of Sport and Human Movement: A Biocultural Perspective*, eds. Robert R. Sands and Linda R. Sands (Plymouth, UK: Lexington Books, 2010) 327–41.

Unfortunately, some Christian theologies continue to propagate the belief that unnecessary suffering and self-sacrifice are noble and strong qualities. Additionally, the body remains suspect and is sometimes regarded as a tool to be shaped and controlled. This perception is related to the high value placed on individualism and utility in North American culture. And the pressure to win at any cost grows. These are persuasive messages that can lure the elite athlete to consider using a wide spectrum of techno-science options, whether banned or not. But a bind is created by the contradictory message that athletes are natural, pure, and paragons of virtue.[26] It is this bind that fosters shame in using banned enhancements[27] or, possibly, some level of guilt if one isn't willing to try anything to optimize performance regardless of cost to health. And at least as importantly, these messages also make it difficult for the athlete (or fan) to question the use of techno-science in elite performance if it is not on the banned list.

The reduction of the embodied athlete to Descartes's body-as-machine status is manifest in extreme training regimens that treat the person as a mechanized and dehumanized body. Christian theologies that glorify unnecessary bodily suffering and pain contribute to the message that the athlete's body is only a tool to be honed for winning. On the other hand, the theological messages that the body is good, that embodied humanity is created in God's image, and that self-love and empowerment contribute to overall human flourishing counter this reductionist message. The theological celebration of the body and of the power to claim voice can foster critical dialogue regarding the use of techno-science in sport.

The development of enhancement technologies demands more sustained critical conversation. This conversation needs the voices of those who do not often speak. Theologically, a failure to trust in something larger than ourselves is at the root of the sins of pride and a lack of self-love. When the commitment to wider flourishing and the confession that humans are

---

[26]Tara Magdalinski, *Sport, Technology and the Body: The Nature of Performance* (New York: Routledge, 2009).

[27]Kate Kirby, Aidan Moran, and Suzanne Guerin, "A Qualitative Analysis of the Experiences of Elite Athlete Who Have Admitted to Doping for Performance Enhancement," *International Journal of Sport Policy and Politics* 3, no. 2 (2011): 205–24.

created in the image of God are forgotten,[28] then, as Hefner reminds us, from a Christian perspective our very humanity is subverted: "*Essential human nature is violated when we obliterate or no longer acknowledge the sense that we are accountable to something larger than ourselves and larger than our own times ... Our humanity is compromised when we forget that our personhood is defined in the engagement with this something larger.*"[29]

From a Christian perspective, the acknowledgment that humans are prone to sin must be part of ethical analyses. Sin must be taken seriously as must the recognition that humans are created in the image of God and accountable to God. Since we have the capacity to sin, we must exercise caution in the matter of enhancements. This sense of caution does not mean that humans should avoid enhancements, but it does mean that we should always question what values, motives, and desires underlie our choices.[30]

Redemption

Christianity is built on the belief that Christ was incarnate among humanity as Jesus. Jesus stood in solidarity with all people, particularly with the marginalized. The Christian tradition holds that he performed miracles,

---

[28]There is increasing debate regarding the assumption that humans only are created in the image of God. [See, for example, Joshua M. Moritz, "Evolution, the End of Human Uniqueness, and the Election of the *Imago Dei*," *Theology and Science* 9, no. 3 (2011): 307–39.]

[29]Hefner, "The Animal that Aspires to be an Angel," 165. (Italics are in the original text.) These larger purposes to which we are accountable are explained summarily by ethicist Karen Lebacqz: "as stewards of the life we have been given by God, it is our task to preserve God's values and intentions to the best of our ability" [Karen Lebacqz, "Dignity and Enhancement in the Holy City," in *Transhumanism and Transcendence: Christian Hope in an Age of Technological Enhancement*, ed. Ronald Cole-Turner (Washington, DC: Georgetown University Press, 2011) 57. Also see Trothen, "Redefining Human, Redefining Sport: The Imago *Dei* and Genetic Modification Technologies," in *The Image of God in the Human Body: Essays on Christianity and Sports*, eds. Donald R. Deardorff and John White (New York: Edwin Mellen Press, 2008) 217–34.

[30]Ted Peters, "Progress and Provolution: Will Transhumanism Leave Sin Behind?" in *Transhumanism and Transcendence: Christian Hope in an Age of Technological Enhancement*, ed. Ronald Cole-Turner (Washington, DC: Georgetown University Press, 2011) 63–86.

heard confessions, promised redemption, and through parables communicated wisdom and his messianic identity. He was crucified and raised three days later from the dead in the promise that salvation, including eternal life, was available to humanity. In short, redemption is the means by which one moves into right relationship with God. This right relationship is salvation.

Much debate has occurred within Christianity over the ages about how one moves into right relationship with God. Generally it is agreed that Jesus as God Incarnate saved humanity. But it does seem that what "saved" means is neither clear nor agreed upon. Jesus' nature as fully divine and fully human was necessary to accomplish redemption. As fully human, Jesus continues to be a powerful exemplar of what it means to be human. The doctrine of the incarnation resists the separation of body, mind, and soul. Jesus was integrated wholeness: the soul is body is mind; embodiment is of God.

Feminist theology has challenged the interpretation that it was Jesus' crucifixion and subsequent resurrection that was *the* saving act. Many feminists have proposed that it is not the violence of the crucifixion that saved humanity but rather Jesus' lived ministry of justice and love that continues on through the work and inspiration of the Holy Spirit.

Redemption is needed to offset humanity's inclination to sin and to effect God's promise of healing from sin in the shape of renewed right relationship. The means by which one moves toward this right relationship with God is through God's grace, which was actualized partly in Jesus' salvific acts. What is debated among Christians is the role of good works in this movement toward right relation. Feminist and liberationist theologians tend to agree that, if one opens oneself to receiving God's redemptive grace, then good works will necessarily accompany this opening. Following Jesus does not mean that these works will be perfect but rather that they will be messy since humans cannot live *fully yet* in the relational ways that God desires.

A question to consider is what good works look like in the context of techno-science and sport. Since redemption is concerned with right relationship with God, and since all life is interdependent, redemption is concerned also with right relationship with self, others, and creation. This right relationship involves an appreciation that everyone is created in God's image.

It also involves an appreciation of human capacity for both sin and redemptive acts.

A Christian theological view demands that the principle of beneficence, or doing good, be a priority, not an afterthought in deference to a culture that favors individual rights over other principles. If doing good is the top priority, an improved chance of winning is not a sufficient reason to use an enhancing technology, nor is it enough that an enhancing technology meets health safety criteria. Beneficence reaches beyond both these reasons to bigger questions concerning doing good. In this view technologies need to contribute to healthy and just relationships, and promote the best spirit of sport.

For example, if science can help us better understand human diversity, as it may with the Athletic Biological Passport, then it has potential to be used in relationally enhancing ways. The passport could be used to help us better appreciate that one size does not fit all and that humans are much more physically diverse than the limited categories that we use, such as male and female. Awareness of embodiment diversity can enhance relationship through assisting us to see past our epistemological categories and assumptions. There are many, including Pistorius and Semenya, who do not fit well into these categories. If an increased awareness of human diversity can help illuminate the limitations of categories, then it may become more possible to maintain some of these ways of ordering the world but with more nuance. Or we may be inspired to create more inclusive categories. Order is helpful if we understand it to be a limited human mechanism that confines neither God nor God's creations but helps us, in our limited way, to begin to understand diversity.

The knowledge provided by the passport could also help in the tailoring of training programs that bring out the best the athlete has to offer, while avoiding over-training and injury. In turn, more marginalized athletes may increase their confidence. It may also be that enhancing interventions could be developed to heal injuries more effectively and be used to help everyday people get the physical exercise they need to feel better physically, emotionally, and spiritually.

The capacity of techno-science for increasing healing, well-being, and appreciation of diversity holds transformative and liberatory potential but not promise. As techno-science pushes awareness of human diversity, values will either become more entrenched and categories of thinking narrowed *or* new ways of thinking built on the appreciation of diversity will emerge.

In my view, when one moves closer to right relationship with God, one discovers delight in difference and a growing hunger for justice and compassion. This relational opening of the self to the Other enhances human capacity for hope and meaning.[31] As Pamela McCarroll proposes, hope is *"the experience of the opening of horizons of meaning and participation in relationship to time, other human and nonhuman beings, and/or the transcendent."*[32] Another possibility is that instead of opening horizons, the revelations of techno-science might squeeze the mystery out of elite sports as we find it harder to ignore the role of the genetic lottery in winning performances. The question is how we perceive the meanings of human diversity and well-being, as well as what values we hold. If winning is all that is hoped for, then the meaning of human diversity is reduced to utility: what body is best suited for winning. But if beauty, persistence, courage, teamwork, and other goods are valued as also important, then there is more room for hope beyond utility driven visions.

Salvation through God's redemption of the world is part of Christian hope. And, from a feminist perspective, salvation is not restricted to life after death. Theological ethicist, Ronald Cole-Turner in his analysis of enhancement technology explains that for the Christian, salvation "is expressly not the fulfillment of our desires for ourselves. It is the replacement of our desire for the self with a desire for God."[33] Salvation is right relationship with God—the possibility of which has been given to humanity through God's grace-filled redemption of the world.

---

[31] Rivera rests her theology of transcendence on authentic encounters of the other person and the holy Other as partially revealed in each person as created in God's image. In constructing her theology she draws heavily on the philosopher Emmanuel Levinas who describes the encounter with the Other as the constitutive element of ethics [Emmanuel Levinas, *Humanism of the Other* (Champaign: University of Illinois Press, 2006)].

[32] Pamela R McCarroll, *The End of Hope—The Beginning: Narratives of Hope in the Face of Death and Trauma* (Minneapolis, Fortress Press, 2014) 48.

[33] Ronald Cole-Turner, "Transhumanism and Christianity," in *Transhumanism and Transcendence: Christian Hope in an Age of Technological Enhancement*, ed. Ronald Cole-Turner (Washington, DC: Georgetown University Press, 2011) 197.

The reception of God's redemption means, as Cole-Turner wisely suggests, an opening of self to others and to God. This action involves both the releasing of egoistic wants and an opening to God's radical love. From a Christian perspective, both excessive self-interest and a lack of self-love crumble with the valuing and recognition of human diversity and interdependence. The prioritizing of beneficence, or doing good, changes not only how enhancing technologies might be assessed but also how the elite athlete is perceived and for what they are valued—by others and by themselves.

Chapter 4

Sport and Religion:
Why the Relationship Matters

What does religion have to do with the use of techno-science in sport? In addition to the application of theological reflection to the intersection of sport and techno-science, sport itself functions for some people as a form of religion. To understand more fully the implications of the intersection of ' sport and techno-science, it is necessary to understand also the intersection of sport and religion. This chapter reviews approaches to the relationship between sport and religion, and identifies some issues emerging from this body of work that are particularly relevant to sport and techno-science questions.[1]

In assessing the religious function of sport, several scholars note the decline of institutional religious attendance particularly in Canada, parts of the United States, and the United Kingdom.[2] Yet there seems to have been a concurrent increase of interest in spirituality.[3] The decline in religiosity

---

[1] The chapter following this one looks more specifically at spirituality and flow.

[2] For example, see Nick J. Watson and Andrew Parker, "Sports and Christianity: Mapping the Field," in *Sports and Christianity: Historical and Contemporary Perspectives*, eds. Nick J. Watson and Andrew Parker (New York: Routledge, 2013) 22; Joseph L. Price, "An American Apotheosis: Sport as Popular Religion," in *Religion and Popular Culture in America*, eds. Bruce David Forbes and Jeffrey H. Mahan (Berkeley: University of California Press, 2000) 202; Timothy R. Steffensmeier, "Sacred Saturdays: College Football and Local Identity," in *Sporting Rhetoric: Performance, Games, and Politics*, ed. Barry Brummett (New York: Peter Lang, 2009) 219; Sean P. Sullivan, "God in My Sporting: a Justification for Christian Experience in Sport," *Journal of the Christian Society for Kinesiology and Leisure Studies* 1, no. 1 (2010): 10; and Dean Garratt, "'Sporting Citizenship': the Rebirth of Religion?" *Pedagogy, Culture & Society* 18, no. 2 (2010): 123.

[3] See, for example, Simon Robinson, "The Spiritual Journey," in *Sport and Spirituality: An Introduction*, eds. J. Parry, S. Robinson, N. Watson, and M. Nesti, 38–58 (London: Routledge, 2007); and Kevin O'Gorman, *Saving Sport: Sport, Society and Spirituality* (Dublin, UK: Columba Press, 2010) 61–63.

does not mean that religious notions have left people's imaginations or have ceased to influence how they make sense of life. However, the decline in institutional participation has meant changes in terms of where one finds community and communal identity. It has also left a vacuum for some people in terms of structured and intentional places to experience aspects of religious expression. Some argue that this vacuum is being filled, at least partially, by sport for many athletes and fans. As religious studies scholar Joseph L. Price suggests, "Although we might be living in a post-ecclesiastical age, ours is one in which persons still cling to religious affections and actions, often transferring them in unconscious ways to secular ceremonies and events that have begun to render their lives entertaining and thus residually religious if not fully meaningful."[4]

A relationship between sport and religion has been established by several well-regarded scholars. While the claim that sport is a religion has been debated passionately, most who have participated in this debate agree that features of sport are religious-like or that sport can function similarly to a religion for some followers. Whether or not sport is actually a religion is a debate that has at times distracted deeper attention to other questions. The more important questions, for the sake of this book, concern how sport intersects with religion—regardless of whether or not we think it should—and what this intersection says about what it means to be human at this point in time. Judging by the appearance of scholarly publications, there is a growing interest in the relationship between sport and religion-—a relationship that may well suggest the ongoing importance of the search for meaning and hope.[5]

The Sport Is/Is Not A Religion Argument

Scholarship on sport and religion has been focused on two main areas: historical analyses (particularly the Olympic roots of sport and the

---

[4]Joseph L. Price, *Rounding the Bases: Baseball and Religion in America* (Macon, GA: Mercer University Press, 2006) 210–11.

[5] After exploring the relationship between sport and both religion and spirituality, later in this book I will consider why this search is relevant to the use of techno-science in sport.

development of muscular Christianity and Judaism)[6] and the contemporary relationship between sport and religion, including religious experience.[7] The relationship between sport and religion is a strongly interdisciplinary field with important contributions from scholars in history, anthropology, psychology, sociology, theology, religious studies, philosophy, leisure studies, sports studies, and kinesiology, among others. Most of the scholarship thus far has been by scholars writing out of the United States context, with some notable works from elsewhere, particularly the United Kingdom.

Research on the contemporary relationship between sport and religion (including religious experience) has focused on two areas: first, the possible parallels and connections between religion and sport, and second, sport experiences that have been variously called "flow," "shining moments," "Zen," or transcendence. These two areas overlap but have a degree of distinction.[8]

Nick Watson and Andrew Parker, in their very helpful survey of research on sport and Christianity, begin by noting that "[h]istorians and anthropologists have mapped a relationship between religion and sport that spans approximately three thousand years."[9] American sociologist Robert Bellah, in 1967, was the first to propose sport as a civil religion.[10] He understood civil religion to mean "a collection of beliefs, symbols, and rituals

---

[6]See, for example, William J. Baker, "Religion," in *Routledge Companion to Sports History*, eds. S. W. Pope and John Nauright (London and New York: Routledge, 2010) 216–28; Steven J. Overman, *The Influence of the Protestant Ethic on Sport and Recreation* (Aldershot, UK: Avebury Ashgate Publishing, 1997); and Tony Ladd and James A. Mathisen, *Muscular Christianity: Evangelical Protestants and the Development of American Sport* (Grand Rapids, MI: Baker Publishing House, 1999).

[7]Theologian Annie Blazer posits a third kind of research that she calls "cultural analyses of the role of sport in religious life after muscular Christianity," which is the least developed area of scholarship in sport and religion [Blazer, "Religion and Sports in America," *Religion Compass* 6, no. 5 (2012): 287].

[8]I will consider scholarly approaches to possible parallels and connections between religion and sport in this chapter, and flow experiences in the next chapter.

[9]Watson and Parker, "Sports and Christianity: Mapping the Field," 9.

[10]Shirl J. Hoffman, *Sport and Religion* (Champaign, IL: Human Kinetics Books, 1992) 9.

with respect to sacred things and institutionalized in a collectivity" that functions as a representation or "vehicle" of American national religion.[11]

Theologian Michael Novak, author of the first comprehensive examination of the contemporary relationship between sport and religion,[12] argued that sport is a form of civil religion in the sense that it is a natural religion (or as he writes elsewhere, "a form of a lower religion"[13]). According to Novak, sport is a religion centered in nature and primal being: "sports flow outward into action from a deep natural impulse that is radically religious; an impulse of freedom, respect for ritual limits, a zest for symbolic meaning, and a longing for perfection. The athlete may of course be pagan, but sports are, as it were, natural religions."[14]

Novak also pays attention to another theme in many of the writings on sport and religion—the relationship between sport and play. Sport, he offers, belongs in the realm of play and not work. However, organized sport, like religion, has become very structured. This structure is reassuring but has its limitations; to much structure can make sport more like work than play. Novak presents play as serious, authentic, meaningful, and often inspiring. While work is to Novak an "escape," "play is reality"[15] because of its embodiment of "the almost nameless dreads of daily human life: aging, dying, failure under pressure, cowardice, betrayal, guilt."[16] Contrary to Novak's claim that sports are metaphors or symbols for life's greatest questions, philosopher Randolph Feezell argues that it is actually its very

---

[11]Robert N. Bellah, "Civil Religion in America," in *Religion in America*, eds. W.G. McLoughlin and R.N. Bellah (Boston: Houghton Mifflin, 1967) 8, 12.

[12]Michael Novak, *The Joy of Sports: End Zones, Bases, Baskets, Balls and Consecration of the American Spirit* (New York: Basic Books, 1967/1994).

[13]Michael Novak, "The Joy of Sports," in *Religion and Sport: The Meeting of Sacred and Profane*, ed. Charles S. Prebish (Westport, CT: Greenwood Press, 1993) 162.

[14]Ibid., 152. The quest for, and meaning of, perfection is multi-layered and contextual. Christian theological perfection is directed toward right relationship with the triune God and living in such a way to deepen this connection. As religiosity declines, the meaning of perfection is becoming more secular and shaped by socially normative values including efficiency and utility as embedded in technology.

[15]Ibid., 165–67.

[16]Ibid., 161.

lightness—its "splendid triviality" [17] —that makes sport a meaningful activity.[18] A hierarchical distinction between sport and play, usually favoring play as the purer and more religious-like activity, characterizes much of the literature on sport and religion. Unlike many writing on the sport-religion relationship, neither Novak nor Feezell[19] see sport and play as fully separate.

Theologian Tom Sinclair-Faulkner, one of the few Canadian religious scholars to address the relationship between sport and religion, laments the seriousness of hockey: "hockey is more than a game in Canada: it functions as a religion for many, and does so at the expense of is own playfulness."[20] Similarly to Novak, Sinclair-Faulkner expresses concern that sport is becoming more like work: "in modern Canadian society the formerly clear line differentiating work from play is being destroyed. Work is increasingly dissociated from its product, play is increasingly organized and disciplined."[21] Sinclair-Faulkner recognizes the attraction of certainty and clear-cut categories in hockey, but cautions against too much structure. He proposes that hockey played as a game is superior to hockey as a professional form of work. Writing in the 1970s, he critiques the masculinity of Canadian hockey as perpetuating "gender distinctions," and equating masculinity with violence.[22]

Another perspective on the relationship between sport and religion that has generated controversy and resonance is the proposal by sociologist James Mathisen that sport is a folk religion. Contesting Bellah's claim that sport is a civil religion in America with a national collective function, Mathisen proposes that sport is a "form" of civil religion without Bellah's nationalist or implicit prophetic claims. Mathisen's conception of sport as a folk religion corresponds to his understanding that sport reflects social norms: "sport encapsulates, magnifies, and reflects back to us the primary beliefs and

---

[17]Randolph Feezell, *Sport, Philosophy, and Good Lives* (Lincoln: University of Nebraska Press, 2013) 66.

[18]Ibid., 214.

[19]Ibid., 28.

[20]Tom Sinclair-Faulkner, "A Puckish Reflection on Religion in Canada," in *Religion and Culture in Canada/Religion et Culture au Canada*, ed. Peter Slater (Ottawa, ON: Wilfrid Laurier University Press, 1977) 401.

[21]Ibid., 400.

[22]Ibid., 400, 393.

norms of the surrounding American culture with a normative certitude. It is this authority that emphatically characterizes sport as a folk religion."[23] Although, as Mathisen points out, sport promotes some of its own distinct "values and myths," it does not dispute the "primary beliefs and norms of ... American culture." Further, while civil religion is "institutionalized," folk religion is "more diffuse but less obvious to its practitioners."[24] Sport, Mathisen proposes, is best understood as a folk religion that embodies recognizable popular myths, ritual, and values.

More recently, education scholar Dean Garratt applied Mathisen's analysis to the United Kingdom in anticipation of the 2012 London Olympic Games. He concluded that sport at this international championship level does indeed function as a folk religion but only for the working class. However, he also laments that, unlike traditional religions, this folk religion does little to foster social integration since it is, as Mathisen agrees, diffuse.[25] On the other hand, there are scholars who see sport's primary religious-like characteristic as fostering social group identity, but these scholars tend to mount more particular cases such as "local identity" for college football team followers in the United States.[26]

Theologian and religious studies professor Robert Ellis recently conducted one of the few empirical studies of athletes and sports spectators to see if sport was, in some way, replacing religion in people's lives. Based on his survey of 468 respondents, he concluded: "The responses to this survey give some grounds for believing that sport is performing a quasi-religious function in the lives of many of our contemporaries."[27] He found that in addition to having a formative influence on identity and creating a sense of belonging, sport also provided participants and followers with moral

---

[23] James Mathisen, "From Civil Religion to Folk Religion: The Case of American Sport," in *Sport and Religion*, ed. Shirl J. Hoffman (Champaign, IL: Human Kinetics Books, 1992) 20, 22.

[24] Ibid., 22; Ladd and Mathisen, *Muscular Christianity*.

[25] Garratt, "'Sporting Citizenship': The Rebirth of Religion?" 123–43.

[26] Steffensmeier, "Sacred Saturdays: College Football and Local Identity" 218–234.

[27] Robert Ellis, "The Meaning of Sport: An Empirical Study into the Significance Attached to Sporting Participation and Spectating in the UK and US," *Practical Theology* 5, no. 2 (2012): 186–87.

messages that shaped character, a source of aesthetic pleasure, and opportunities to engage with existential questions.[28]

Joseph Price highlights the parallels between American baseball and organized religion, concluding that sport is a form of popular religion: "For tens of millions of devoted fans throughout the country, sports constitute a popular form of religion by shaping their world and sustaining their ways of engaging it. Indeed, for many, sports are elevated to a kind of divine status, in what I would call an American apotheosis."[29] Price illustrates similarities between established religion and baseball including the rituals and myths in baseball, impressive attendance statistics, its communal function, its structured symbols and calendar, and its "transformative potential."[30] He concludes that sport is a religion since sport satisfies the criteria for a religion as identified by religious studies scholar Ninian Smart.[31] More recently, Italian social scientist Roberto Cipriani has argued similarly for understanding "sport as spirituality" particularly on the basis of ritual parallels and the celebration of embodiment in both sport and Christianity.[32]

Others agree that sport is a type of religion but choose varying terms to describe this type. For example, religious studies scholar Catherine Albanese

---

[28]Ibid., 169–88.

[29]Price, "An American Apotheosis: Sport as Popular Religion," 202.

[30]Ibid., 209. As I have noted elsewhere [Trothen, "Hockey: A Divine Sport?: Canada's National Sport in Relation to Embodiment, Community, and Hope" *Studies in Religion/Sciences Religieuses* 35, no. 2 (2006): 292], hockey in Canada similarly "exhibits many characteristics of a religion: star players are like gods or heroes and heroines, sport's historical icons such as hockey's Wayne Gretzky are saints; coaches, owners, and scouts are akin to high councils, elders, and other institutional religious figures; reporters and colour commentators are similar to scribes; uniforms and pre-game ritual parallel religious regalia and ceremony; arenas function similarly to places of worship; there are hockey shrines including the current shrine honoring Maurice Rocket Richard at Canada's Museum of Civilization in our nation's capital; fans have at least near ecstatic experiences; the Stanley Cup and other lesser awards are similar in some ways to religious icons; and the list goes on."

[31]Price, *Rounding the Bases*, 111–75.

[32]Roberto Cipriani, "Sport as (Spi)rituality," *Implicit Religion* 15, no. 2 (2012): 139–51.

called sport a form of cultural religion.[33] Historian of religion Charles S. Prebish insists simply that sport *is* a new American religion.[34]

These claims have prompted some, such as Robert J. Higgs, to declare that "heresy ... is afoot in the land."[35] Higgs, professor emeritus of English literature and former football player at Navy, sees much that is suspect in sport's relationship to religion; he is concerned that sport is being elevated to God-like status and cautions against the dangers of idolatry and pride.[36] He sees play as more redemptive than sport (for example, play is oriented to intrinsic not extrinsic gifts) but still not to be confused with religion.[37] Further, in Higgs's mind, play is associated with the supposedly more virtuous feminine and sport with the masculine. He does not claim that all play is virtuous and all sport sinful (nor all women virtuous and all men sinful), but sees sport as less virtuous and more stereotypically masculine

---

[33] Catherine Albanese, *America: Religions and Religion* (Belmont, CA: Wadsworth, 1982).

[34] Charles S. Prebish, *Religion and Sport: The Meeting of Sacred and Profane* (Westport, CT: Greenwood Press, 1993) 16.

[35] Robert J. Higgs, *God in the Stadium: Sports and Religion in America* (Lexington: University Press of Kentucky, 1995) 21.

[36] Writings on sport and religion have often suffered from a neglect of theologies from the "underside" that have been prominent theologies since the 1980s. These theologies include liberation, feminist, womanist, and queer among others. One of the earliest and seminal critiques was by Valerie Saiving, "The Human Situation: A Feminine View," *Journal of Religion* 40 (April 1960): 100–12. Her paper addressed the normative white Euro-American male conflation of sin with pride; women, she contended, did not share this as their central temptation. Rather, women were more inclined to self-negation with an attendant denial of responsibility and power. From such a perspective, sport *can* be a vehicle for empowerment of marginalized people [Some phenomenological studies have demonstrated this liberatory potential of sport. See, for example, William Bridel and Genevieve Rail, "Sport, Sexuality, and the Production of (Resistant) Bodies: De-/Re-Constructing the Meanings of Gay Male Marathon Corporeality" *Sociology of Sport Journal* 24 (2007): 127–44.]

[37] Higgs, *God in the Stadium*, 3; and Higgs, "Muscular Christianity, Holy Play, and Spiritual Exercises: Confusion About Christ in Sports and Religion," in *Sport and Religion*, ed. Shirl J Hoffman (Champaign, IL: Human Kinetics Books, 1992) 89–103.

when athletic success is reduced to winning.[38] Sinclair-Faulkner likely would have agreed judging by his laconic observation that "we may consider a typification which is implicitly tied to masculinity in hockey: violence and aggressivity, qualities which are virtually equated. I note in particular the only NHL trophy which bears a woman's name is the Lady Byng—for gentlemanly conduct."[39] Higgs, together with Michael Braswell in their important 2006 volume *An Unholy Alliance*, continues to caution against the tendency to mistake the profane (sport) for the sacred (God).[40]

Shirl Hoffman also understands there to be a disjuncture between sport and religion. Similar to Higgs, he elevates play as closer to the sacred realm (but not quite in the sacred realm, which is God's alone) than sport, which he sees as instrumental and oriented to extrinsic goods. Hoffman paints a grim picture of professional sport, seeing only the ideal of winning at work. This value he contrasts sharply with a Christian sports ethics.[41] Hoffman finds arguments that claim some sport is a religion, a type of religion, or like a religion, troubling. Although there are parallels to aspects of religion, such as rituals and a structured environment in which emotions, including elation, are expressed, sport is in no way a religion. In sum, Hoffman's main concern is that an understanding of sport as a form of religion "humaniz[es] the sacred" and so reduces God to the profane, human level.[42]

Joan Chandler also objects to claims of sport's religiosity, but her core argument differs somewhat from Hoffman's. Sport is not a religion since, she contests, sport fails to address the meaning of life and death: "Sport, like

---

[38] Higgs, *God in the Stadium*, 4–5. A binary approach to sex and gender—male/female—is in danger of buying into stereotypes of men and women. Even when the intent is respect or regard for women, when women are put on a pedestal of virtue, the result often is continued exclusion from the supposed male realm of public life, including competitive sport.

[39] Sinclair-Faulkner, "A Puckish Reflection on Religion in Canada," 393.

[40] Robert J. Higgs and M. C. Braswell, *An Unholy Alliance: The Sacred and Modern Sports* (Macon, GA: Mercer University Press, 2004).

[41] Shirl J. Hoffman, "The Sanctification of Sport: Can the Mind of Christ Coexist with the Killer Instinct?" *Christianity Today* (April 1984): 17–21; Hoffman, *Good Game: Christianity and the Culture of Sports* (Waco, TX: Baylor University Press, 2010).

[42] Shirl J. Hoffman, "Recovering a Sense of the Sacred in Sport" in *Sport and Religion*, ed. Shirl J Hoffman (Champaign, IL: Human Kinetics Books, 1992) 158.

so many other human activities, may give us some hints, some paradigms of the unique events of birth and death; it cannot attempt to explain them. That is the function of religion." [43] Agreeing with Chandler, Tara Magdalinski and Timothy Chandler, in their notable edited volume *With God on Their Side*, are clear that "sport cannot offer, nor does it even profess to offer, answers to some of life's most enduring questions: Who are we? Where are we going? Why are we here?"[44]

Sifting Through Approaches to the Sport-Religion Relationship

In one of the first articles to describe the different types of approaches to this debate, religious studies scholar Annie Blazer argues that contemporary sport and religion scholars tend to frame the relationship between sport and religion on understandings of religion that are based primarily on form, function, or content. Blazer mounts a good case that form-based (e.g., arguments posed by Albanese or Novak) or function-based (e.g., Price's approach) arguments tend to be successful in arguing that sport is like or is a religion, whereas content-based arguments are most successful in demonstrating a disjuncture between sport and religion.

Form-based arguments appeal to the similar construction of religious and sports communities: For example, "Novak's claim that sport is a religion relies on understanding religion as an organized community bound together by rules, rituals, and a shared understanding of human perfection. Due to these formal similarities between religion and sport, both Albanese and Novak treat sport as a religion."[45]

Blazer appeals to Émile Durkheim's and Mircea Eliade's understandings of religion to explain function-based approaches as those approaches that explore "what religion accomplishes in the lives of its adherents."[46] For example, comparative religion scholar David Chidester builds on American anthropologist Clifford Geertz's definition of religion as a "system of

---

[43]Joan M. Chandler, "Sport is Not a Religion," in *Sport and Religion*, ed. Shirl J. Hoffman (Champaign, IL: Human Kinetics Books, 1992) 57.

[44]Tara Magdalinski and Timothy J. L. Chandler, eds., *With God on their Side* (London: Routledge, 2002) 7.

[45]Blazer, "Religion and Sports in America," 288.

[46]Ibid.

symbols"[47] and concludes that baseball is a religion because it has a communal function nurtured by recognizable structure, rules, rituals, and the provision of sacred space and time.[48] Similarly, in their argument that baseball is a popular religion, professors Richard W. Santana and Gregory Erickson use a functional approach, defining popular religion as "the ways that ordinary people use religion to make sense and give meaning to their lives, a religion more about bumper stickers than about philosophy and theology and less about the Bible than about religious tracts."[49] As such, they claim that baseball provides "a window into part of our [United States] national religious psyche."[50]

Blazer describes the approach of Joan Chandler, professor emerita of historical studies at the University of Texas, as content-based. Content-based definitions "are theological and involve claims about the existence of the supernatural."[51] Explicit claims about the existence of the supernatural are not a formal part of sport. However, implicit claims about the supernatural can be argued to be part of sport. Content regarding the supernatural includes, but is not limited to, explicit doctrine. Metaphorical content, such as that in sport, is also important. As Price puts it, "sports are not religions in the same way that Christianity and Islam, Buddhism and Taoism are religions."[52] While sport does not claim to offer concrete theological claims pertaining to life after death, for example, as Robert Ellis' study suggests, it does offer opportunities to struggle with questions of meaning. Novak, for example, controversially contends that in sport losing is a symbolic kind of death.[53] While clearly losing is not a literal death,[54] the

---

[47]As quoted in David Chidester, "The Church of Baseball, the Fetish of Coca-Cola, and the Potlatch of Rock 'n' Roll," in *Religion and Popular Culture in America*, eds. Bruce David Forbes and Jeffrey H. Mahan (Berkeley: University of California Press, 2000), 219.

[48]Ibid., 219–38.

[49]Santana and Erickson, *Religion and Popular Culture: Rescripting the Sacred*, 18.

[50]Ibid., 35.

[51]Blazer, "Religion and Sports in America," 288.

[52]Price, "An American Apotheosis," 209.

[53]Novak, "The Joy of Sports," 153.

[54]See Feezell, *Sport, Philosophy, and Good Lives*, 70. Philosopher Feezell rejects Novak's conclusion that in sports "losing is like death" not so much because it seems

metaphor implies the despair and sadness that losses in sport can generate. Sport's losses are temporary, but can still put one in touch with some of the risks of investment in a person or team. Theological questions that have long been debated—such as the meaning of salvation—can take on a greatly felt but less explicit meaning in sport.

As with any categorizing system, every scholar's argument does not fit neatly into one category. In talking about form, for example, it is not uncommon to consider how these forms affect follower's lives (function). Consider Price's arguments. While they may be described as mostly functional, they are not exhaustively so. Price also makes form-based and content-based arguments. Regarding the latter, for example, he considers theological approaches to hope and transcendence and how these are important aspects of baseball. The categories of form, function, and content often overlap. Nonetheless, they help us to understand that approaches to the question of whether sport is or is not like a religion are informed by the writer's explicit or, more often, implicit understanding of religion.

Not all who write about sport and religion do so with the intent of making a case for sport being like or not like a religion. Others are more concerned with how sport can be useful to religion, or a means by which religious convictions can be lived out. For example, many American conservative evangelical Christians promote a type of contemporary muscular Christianity that, it is hoped, serves "as a means for Christian outreach to change evil to good" and not simply to "make the 'good of society better'" as intended by the original muscular Christianity that arose in England.[55] These promoters of sport understand the mission of pro-athletes as the conversion of souls. Among the best known of these current Christian sports stars are Jeremy Lin and Tim Tebow, both of whom have

---

to trivialize death—although this is part of it—but because this claim undermines the potential of sport as a locus for meaning and happiness: "It assumes that winning is the only good or primary good in sports, and it based on an optimizing approach to happiness that ignore what the adapter emphasizes—that avoidance of unhappiness, or at least its reduction, is possible by moderating our passions, refocusing our attention, and reshaping out attitudes."

[55]Ladd and Mathisen, *Muscular Christianity*, 13.

promoted their faith convictions on the field.[56] These public displays of evangelical testimony in elite sports are called "total release performance" or "praise performance," meaning that these athletes are releasing themselves to a higher power that can then work through them in their athletic performances.[57] In "total release," athletic performance is a public testimony and act of love toward God, requiring the athlete's dedication and other resources.

Problematically, when these athletes lose it can be thought that they did not put 100 percent into their efforts or open themselves sufficiently to God.[58] Also, Peter Hopsicker points out that "popular and thin definitions"[59] of miracles are used often to claim God's favoritism in sport's competitions. Ultimately, Hopsicker—similar to Price[60]—reasons that even though these interpretations of miracles are at best theologically thin and based in "self-interest,"[61] they can serve a divine purpose by providing a seedbed for "spiritual conversion."[62] In short, by "catalyzing the conversion of individuals to more holy and sacred lives, [perceived] miracles in sport demonstrate the saving grace of God."[63]

There are still other ways in which faith influences or is engaged to benefit athletes' performances both on and off the field.[64] Sean Sullivan writes that "sport can become an opportunity for worship," although—like

---

[56]For example, see Feezell, "Sport, Religious Belief and Religious Diversity," *Journal of the Philosophy of Sport* 40, no. 1 (May 2013): 135–63.

[57]For example, see Wes Neal, *Total Release Performance: A New Concept in Winning* (Grand Island, NE: Cross Training Publishing, 2000).

[58]Jane Lee Sinden, "The Elite Sport and Christianity Debate: Shifting Focus from Normative Values to the Conscious Disregard for Health," *Journal for Religious Health* 52 (2012): 337. This theological reasoning is similar to the dysfunctional theodicy theological claim that attributes suffering and calamity to a lack of true prayer or faith.

[59]Peter M. Hopsicker, "Miracles in Sport: Finding the 'Ears to Hear' and the 'Eyes to See'" *Sport, Ethics and Philosophy* 3, no. 1 (2009): 81.

[60]Price, *Rounding the Bases*, 219–37.

[61]Hopsicker "Miracles in Sport," 70.

[62]Ibid., 75.

[63]Ibid., 90.

[64]See, for example, Christopher Stevenson, "Christian Athletes and the Culture of Elite Sport: Dilemmas and Solutions" *Sociology of Sport Journal* 14 (1997): 241–62.

most scholars who have argued that sport is a type of religion—he qualifies this statement:"[s]port as religion in the traditional sense would amount to a contrived substitution of the secular in place of the sacred."[65] Drawing on the example of Eric Liddell as portrayed in the film *Chariots of Fire*, philosophy professor Mike Austin posits: "sport can provide a context for and be exercises in Christian spiritual formation" such as "solitude, prayer, and meditation."[66] Similarly, author and professor emeritus Ignancio Gotz suggests that sport provides opportunities to engage in spiritual disciplines.[67] And others such as Cipriani discuss the superstitious use of religious acts to increase one's chances of winning.[68] Additionally, scholars including Austin, Rolf Kretschmann and Caroline Benz, and Nick Watson and Mark Nesti show that religious practices can serve as coping mechanisms and performance-enhancing techniques for athletes.[69]

This overview of some of the scholarly explorations of the relationship between sport and religion demonstrates the range of approaches used as this scholarly field continues to take shape. This overview suggests themes that are relevant to the intersection of sport, religion, and the use of techno-science. The themes that will be considered in the rest of this chapter are: 1) that there is general agreement that sport and religion are related; 2) that culture, religion, and sport are connected and this connection is partly about shared values and virtues; and 3) that the way in which the relationship between sport and play is understood is related to the intersection of sport with religion and, I will suggest, enhancement use in sport.

---

[65] Sullivan, "God in My Sporting: A Justification for Christian Experience in Sport" (2010): 14, 15. Interestingly, one of the features differentiating sport from religion, according to Sullivan, is the "private" nature of religion (13). Hoffman echoes this claim. Feminist theorists have established strong arguments against a binary approach to public/private. In brief, religious beliefs are not strictly private as they are meant to influence one's behavior in all contexts.

[66] Mike W. Austin, "Sports as Exercises in Spiritual Formation," *Journal of Spiritual Formation & Soul Care*, 3, no. 1 (2010): 66, 68.

[67] Igancio L. Gotz, "Spirituality and the Body" in *Religious Education* 96, no. 1 (Winter 2001): 2–19.

[68] Cipriani, "Sport as (Spi)rituality," 144.

[69] Watson, Nick J. and Mark Nesti, "The Role of Spirituality in Sport Psychology Consulting: An Analysis and Integrative Review of Literature," *Journal of Applied Sport Psychology* 17, no. 3 (2005): 228–39.

Themes

1. There Is a Relationship Between Sport and Religion

The body of work overviewed in the preceding pages suggests that these interdisciplinary scholars generally agree that sport possesses many features and functions that are similar to religion or, at least, that sport and religion can affect each other. The meaning of these similar features and functions is not agreed upon but the existence of a relationship is not much contested.

It is difficult to organize the arguments made by these scholars and to put them all into conversation with each other due to their diverse foci and perspectives. Since the intersection of sport and religion is a multi-disciplinary field (attracting scholars from such diverse disciplines as sports studies, kinesiology, theology, religious studies, literature, history, philosophy, and sociology) different bodies of knowledge inform each approach. To this diversity we must add the lack of agreement over definitions of both sport and religion, which is partially due to disciplinary perspective and partially due to individual faith convictions and worldviews.

Interpretations of the relationship between sport and religion are influenced by perspectives and convictions. For example, those writing from a conservative theological perspective tend to be skeptical about claims that there is anything religious in what they might understand to be profane activities, such as sport. A serious concern is idolatry: that players or a sport become regarded as God-like. Those with more left-leaning theological perspectives, for example, are more likely to focus on the possible revelation of God's immanence and transcendence in sport. Writers with no specific institutional religious identity also have commitments to values and views that influence their perspectives on the possible relationship between sport and religion. There is not a problem having commitments or values—everyone does. The challenge is to recognize these commitments and values and understand how they affect and limit understandings of the world, including the relationship between sport and religion. The perspectival nature of arguments is part of being human. Simply put, we need to be aware of authorial perspectives in order to engage in effective critical conversation.

Defining Religion and Sport. Definitions of concepts such as religion and sport are complicated. And postmodern thought has further problematized these. Are definitions even needed? Philosophical ethicist Jim Parry cautions that "… there are dangers in assuming that … [definitions] must be provided; and provided in advance of an investigation."[70] The dangers, he posits, include "scientism" which cloaks arguments as "objective facts." As the history of science demonstrates, no definition or argument is "crisp once-and-for-all" and one must be open to the possibility of being proven wrong. Magdalinski and Chandler similarly note:

> Whilst it may be useful to determine precisely what we mean when we speak of "religion" securing a suitable definition has proven a complex task. Religious studies experts disagree on a singular definition of "religion" with some contending that one definition of religion may be neither necessary nor appropriate. Indeed, the desire to define, categorize and delimit culturally variant concepts seems reminiscent of rationalist paradigms that suggest all aspects of culture can be scientifically labeled and constrained.[71]

Furthermore, as Price points out, no one religious tradition (or sport) has "all characteristics of a religion … because such comprehensive definitions of 'religion' are simply ideal norms against which actual religions are measured."[72] Definitions of both religion and sport, and of their relationship, must be regarded as contextual and dynamic.

Postmodern thought emphasizes the importance of a critical approach to context and the partiality of any argument. But this does not mean that attempts at defining and understanding concepts are not needed. Sports ethics scholars Lisa Edwards and Carwyn Jones have argued that extreme postmodern critiques have undermined effective ethical critique through the rejection of *universal* norms because this rejection has generated suspicion of

---

[70] Jim Parry, "Must Scientists think Philosophically about Science?" in *Philosophy and the Sciences of Exercise, Health and Sport: Critical Perspectives on Research Methods*, ed. Mike McNamee (New York: Routledge, 2005) 22.

[71] Magdalinski and Chandler, *With God on Their Side*, 2.

[72] Price, "An American Apotheosis: Sport as Popular Religion," 204.

general, binding norms.[73] As Santana and Erickson ask, "if the experience of God or of baseball is now one of blurred edges, no beginnings or endings, and no definitions, how do we proceed?"[74]

Given the fluid and perspectival nature of definitions, determining whether or not sport satisfies a definition of religion may be less important than phenomenological claims of subjective experiences of sport as spiritual.[75] Yet it is helpful, as Blazer points out, to attempt to describe what I mean by religion, if I am assuming a connection between sport and religion. Moreover, if one takes the position that anything is a religion (or spiritual) so long as one person experiences it that way, then religion (or spirituality) becomes a meaningless concept. I stop short of suggesting a "definition" of religion; preferring, instead, the more open-ended and modest concept of an "understanding" of religion.

Not surprisingly, as someone who sees sport as "like a religion," I favor a more functionalist understanding of religion mixed with implicit supernatural content. Some such as Kevin Schilbrack, professor of philosophy and religion, argue that an adequate definition of religion must be both functional and ontological (content-based with reference to a "superempirical reality"[76] or, as Blazer would say, a "supernatural" realm). There are well-established definitions of religion that are often appealed to in discussions of

---

[73]Edwards and Jones, "Postmodernism, Queer Theory and Moral Judgment in Sport" (2009): 331–44. See chapter one for more discussion of the difference between general claims and universalism claims.

[74]Santana and Erickson, *Religion and Popular Culture*, 49.

[75]There is good reason for the varied understandings of religion. As Sheila Greeve Davaney [Sheila Greeve Davaney, "Theology and the Turn to Cultural Analysis," in *Converging on Culture: Theologians in Dialogue with Cultural Analysis and Criticism*, eds. Delwin Brown, Sheila Greeve Davaney, and Kathryn Tanner (Oxford, UK: Oxford University Press, 2001) 190] observes, "… religions are increasingly viewed as cultural processes and artifacts that are not disconnected from other dimensions of human cultural and social institutions, discourses, and networks of power. They are now taken to be both products of and contributors to the negotiations around cultural resources. As such, religions, like cultures in general, are viewed as always concrete and particular, lacking essences that provide a common character across traditions and a singular identity within traditions."

[76]Kevin Schilbrack, "What Isn't A Religion," *The Journal of Religion* (Chicago Journals) 93, no. 3 (July 2013): 316.

religion, including definitions by William James, Clifford Geertz, and Émile Durkheim. I have found Durkheim's definition particularly meaningful. He defined religion as "a unified system of beliefs and practices relative to sacred things, that is to say, things set apart and forbidden—beliefs and practices which unite into one single moral community called a Church, all those who adhere to them."[77] Apart from his reference to Church, his definition fits with my understanding of religion and extends, in most ways, to my understanding of sport. Moreover, Durkheim, building on his definition of religion, proposed the sociological concept of "collective effervescence"—a phenomenon that can be experienced by a community or society coming together and participating in the same action creating a "frenzied" excitement by entering into the sacred. The notion of collective effervescence provokes reflection on the experiences of sports fans and athletes.

I propose that sport functions as a type of secular religion for many but not all participants and fans. Briefly and intentionally vaguely, *for these people, sport is a secular religion because sport functions as a communal belief system and it is characterized by the spiritual quality of hope.*[78] My understanding of religion draws on themes that appear in many definitions of religion. A religion is characterized by: a sense of and desire for the sacred; the propagation and development of important myths; the enactment of these myths in ritual practices; a sense of community and a cohesion in that community that comes from the sharing of common beliefs; some form of regular worship; doctrinal beliefs that are reflected in normative moral convictions or values; and attention to the meaning of the human condition in relation to the supernatural or sacred things. I take these themes as guideposts and want to be clear that I see sport as a secular religion but not as a formally organized or established religion or way of being religious such as Daoisim, Jainism, Buddhism, Hinduism, Aboriginal Spirituality, Islam, Judaism, or Christianity among others. Not all sports followers—fans and athletes—would agree that they understand an ontological supernaturalism as the source of what moves them in sport. Some would connect sports

---

[77]Émile Durkheim, *The Elementary Forms of the Religious Life* (New York: Free Press, 1965 [1912]) 62.

[78]I will explore the meaning of spirituality in chapter four, and hope in chapter five.

experiences explicitly to a theistic or nontheistic set of beliefs while others would not. For this reason, I do not see sport as being the same as organized religions, but I do see sport as a secular religion for many of its participants and followers.

Not only are definitions of religion difficult and perhaps undesirable, definitions of sport also are difficult with no one definition being fully adequate. There are debates regarding the appropriate place of character in sport; which activities are seen as sports and which not; the importance or not of winning; professional versus amateur sport, and so on. Sports scientist Verner Møller proposes a working definition of sport that applies well to elite level sport:

1) The activity is played out as a competition, which is taken seriously even though it serves no external purpose and in that sense can be regarded as not serious.

2) The aim is to win and to move upwards within the activity's hierarchical structure.

3) The activity is organized and functions in an institutionalized framework, in which results are recorded and are ascribed significance.

4) The activity is governed by a written set of rules, which are administered by a judge who ideally is impartial.[79]

Because it is possible for a sport to have multiple aims, including, but not fully limited to, winning (as suggested in Møller's second criterion), this definition enjoys some elasticity.

As techno-science usage in sport advances there is an increasing need for ethical analyses and evaluation. While these normative judgments must be partial and not absolute, particularly since the use of technology and science and sport will continue to development and likely in some unanticipated ways, engagement in the debate is critically important. Multiple voices need to weigh in if the debate is to take account of the range of possible consequences. These consequences include effects on sports'

---

[79]Verner Møller, *The Ethics of Doping and Anti-Doping: Redeeming the Soul of Sport?* (New York: Routledge, 2010) 15.

religious form, function, and content. A robust ethical discussion of techno-science usage in sport must consider the religious dimension.

2. Culture, Religion, and Sport: Values and Virtues

Sport reflects and shapes cultural contexts, and culture includes religion. It is helpful to repeat Mathisen's description of this dynamic: "sport encapsulates, magnifies, and reflects back to us the primary beliefs and norms of the surrounding American culture.... At the same time, sport raises up particular values and myths of its own and projects them onto the culture with a normative certitude."[80] And historian of sport and religion, Steven J. Overman sees the influence of religious, and particularly Christian values, on contemporary sport as the link between sport and religion: "it isn't so much the forms of religion but the values of religion which have carried over into modern sport ... [which then] modern sport disseminates, reaffirms, and reinforces...."[81]

Hoffman takes particular note of problematic values in competitive sport, which he understands as arising from secularism, not Christianity: sport is "narcissistic, materialistic, violent, sensationalist, coarse, racist, sexist, brazen, raunchy, hedonistic, body-destroying, and militaristic."[82] Also observing that sport often exemplifies values incongruous with Christian faith such as those associated with gambling, drugs, excessive money, violence, and narcissism, Austin proposes that faith can modify and improve

---

[80]Mathisen, "From Civil Religion to Folk Religion: The Case of American Sport" (1992): 22. Overman [*The Influence of the Protestant Ethic on Sport and Recreation*, 193], agrees regarding this relationship between sport and culture, and cautions that while sport "supplements" religion, it cannot "replace" religion: "Sport, like religion, can serve as a model for and model of reality. Both are cultural systems with symbols, established moods and motivations, and formulated conceptions of the general order. Both perform the functional requisites of society. They socialize novices into the values of the society, reinforce behaviors, and reaffirm cultural values. If an overlap occurs in the functions of sport and religion, this doesn't imply that sport is a religion but that sport can act as a functional equivalent of religion...."

[81]Overman, *The Influence of the Protestant Ethic on Sport and Recreation*, 8.

[82] Shirl J. Hoffman, "Whatever Happened To Play?" *Christianity Today* (February 2010): 23.

sport through the cultivation of virtues such as trust, courage, and fairness.[83] Scholar Wolfgang Vondey also contrasts elite sports' focus on winning and overcoming "one's boundaries" with his understanding of Christianity's focus on "God's gift of justification" although he does not express the optimistic view that religion can uplift sport.[84]

Professor of kinesiology Rolf Kretschmann and sport and exercise science specialist Caroline Benz agree that religion is usually morally superior to sport, and that sport and religion are, in many ways, polar opposites:

> First of all sports are competitive and individualistic while religion is non-competitive and communal.... [S]ports are instrumental and goal oriented, whereas religion is expressive and process oriented. Sports are part of the secular, material, profane world, whereas religion is part of the sacred and the supernatural. Beliefs of sports are diversified and related to every day life whereas beliefs of religion are commonly held and related to the sacred. Sports are clear-cut and crude whereas religion is mystical and pure.[85]

Dualistic depictions of religion and sport such as this are not uncommon. Unfortunately, such depictions obscure realities concerning both religion and sport. For example, while some sporting experiences, such as distance running, may be very individualistic, other sporting experiences are very communal, drawing people together with common hopes (e.g. many baseball teams). Even in the case of distance running, the runner may feel very connected to the world. Similarly, not all religious groups are non-competitive. I've certainly witnessed some very competitive dynamics on church committees, for example.

---

[83] Austin, "Sports as Exercises in Spiritual Formation," 67, 71.

[84] Wolfgang Vondey, "Christian Enthusiasm: Can the Olympic Flame Kindle the Fire of Christianity?" *Word & World* 23, no. 3 (2003): 318.

[85] Kretschmann and Benz use comparisons of sport and religion put forward by Higgs and sports studies scholar Jay Coakley in arriving at this description. [Rolf Kretschmann and Caroline Benz, "Morality of Christian Athletes in Competitive Sports—A Review," *Sports Science Review* 21, nos. 1–2 (2012): 20 and 10, respectively.]

Whether or not sport has been positively or negatively influenced by Christian values is an ongoing debate. This debate about values in religion and sport has at least two problems. First, some scholars fall into the trap of binary thinking and claim that either sport or religion is the source of good values and the other the source of bad values[86] when it is more accurate to suggest that both sport and religion offer much that is life-enhancing and also much that can be life-denying.[87] Related to this trap are the assumptions that institutional religion and sport are essentially good or bad. Second, there is an implicit assessment that some values are morally good and other values are morally bad. For example, pride is often seen as bad; it goes hand-in-hand with egocentrism and narcissism. But pride can be a virtue if pride is understood as connected to healthy confidence and belief in oneself.

More even-handedly, Price identifies the ethical issue of "the inculcation and transmission of values" as part of sport and religion.[88] Both organized sport and organized religion have promoted divisive and oppressive messages that run counter to their respective potentials to enhance diverse lives and relationships; yet, both can also cultivate human love and flourishing. Although values espoused by organized religions sometimes conflict with elite sport values, often values are shared, for better or for worse. One example that we explored is the value placed on pain and suffering in sport and in interpretations of Christian theology. The values we hold have much to do with our approach to the use of techno-science in sport. Some of the values that are most often discussed in the religion-sport conversation are bodily goodness, purity, pride, self-love, and relationship.

---

[86]For example, Raphaël Massarelli and Thierry Terret argue that sport has been negatively affected by the decline of religious influence ("The Paradise Lost? Mythological Aspects of Modern Sport," *Sport, Ethics and Philosophy* 5, no. 4 [2011]: 400.)

[87]As Feezell puts it [Feezell, *Sport, Philosophy, and Good Lives*, 37]: "defenders of religion insist that religion can be corrupted, a religion can be misunderstood or debased, but that need not affect our love or respect for the thing itself. Likewise, sport may be corrupted, but that need not affect our attachment to the elements of sport that are the basis for our love of these activities or our sense that involvement in sports may enhance our lives."

[88]Price, "An American Apotheosis: Sport as Popular Religion," 214.

How Christianity has influenced sport regarding the valuing of embodiment has been debated. Some say that Christianity has imparted a valuing of bodily goodness. Others see the influence of a distorted Christianity that has distrusted the body, seeing the body, and particularly the female body, as a source of temptation that needs to be controlled. Overman points to the historical influence of Puritan fears of human bodily pleasures and "appetite."[89] Compounding this distrust of the body is the historic influence of the Protestant work ethic on sport. The Protestant work ethic holds that activities should be oriented to a practical end such as paid work, the management of a household, or the construction of useful and needed items such as furniture or tools. Play and sport are frivolous and therefore suspicious. The body, in this view, is not supposed to be indulged in as a source of pleasure or delight.

Despite impassioned protests by some apologists who argue that the Christian tradition celebrates "the goodness of the human body,"[90] many Christian thinkers have denigrated the body, most notably the female body. This negative influence continues to be felt. For example, some empirical studies show an association between religiosity and a lower incidence of binge drinking, nicotine addiction, and drug abuse among young athletes,[91] but this finding does not seem to be associated with experiences of positive body image.[92] The explanation behind these finding is likely proscriptive religious messages against drinking, smoking, and drug use, but few body-affirming religious messages. If body-affirming messages predominated in

---

[89]Overman, *The Influence of the Protestant Ethic on Sport and Recreation*, 347.

[90] See, for example, Stefano Scarpa and Attilio Nicola Carraro, "Does Christianity Demean the Body and Deny the Value of Sport?—A Provocative Thesis," *Sport, Ethics and Philosophy*, 5, no. 2 (2011): 110–23; and Gregg Twietmeyer, "A Theology of Inferiority: Is Christianity the Source of Kinesiology's Second-Class Status in the Academy?" *Quest* 60 (2008): 453.

[91]See, for example, See, for example, Mike Cavar, Damir Sekulic, and Zoran Culjak, "Complex Interaction of Religiousness with other Factors in Relation to Substance Use and Misuse Among Female Athletes," *Journal of Religious Health* 51 (2012): 381–89.

[92]See, for example, Val Michaelson, T. Trothen, F. Edgar, and W. Pickett, "Eucharistic Eating, Family Meals and the Health of Adolescent Girls: A Canadian Study," *Practical Theology* 7, no. 2 (2014): 125–43.

religious communities, one would expect that these findings would also include a more-positive-than-average body image. There continue to be less-than-celebratory interpretations of the body within many Christian and other religious communities.

The question of the "true" meaning of Christian doctrines and sacred texts is at the root of this debate about Christianity's influence on attitudes toward embodiment. Certainly Christianity has been interpreted in ways that have undermined embodiment, sometimes seeing the body as a barrier between humans and God, and a source of sexual temptation (tempting one to "impure" thoughts and behaviors), with the female body being most problematic. However, feminist theologians usually agree that, understood properly, the Christian message is body and life-affirming; Christian doctrines of creation, the Incarnation, and resurrection all support positive understandings of the body. Others disagree, convinced that Christianity is, at root, body-denying and damaging.[93]

Møller sees a Christian influence on values in sport. In Møller's view, Christianity tells athletes that they ought to prioritize supporting the weak over winning. However, the bottom line in elite sports is the pressure to win. Thus, Møller argues, Christianity has contributed to the pressure on athletes to be the impossible: not only pure, which includes siding with the weak, but also the best. According to Møller, this message has generated a "fault-line between the will to purity and the will to win,"[94] and it is this fault-line that is at the root of some athletes' covert use of banned performance enhancing drugs (PEDs); athletes want to win but they have a sense that this is not a good desire and so some pursue winning through hidden means.

Winning *can* be contradictory to protecting the weak, as Møller argues, but not necessarily so. One can strive to win and prioritize becoming the best athlete possible without trying to damage those who are not as good.

---

[93] See, for example, Mary Daly, "Theology After the Demise of God the Father: A Call for the Castration of Sexist Religion," in *Sexist Religion: Women in the Church*, ed. Alice L. Hageman (New York: Association Press, 1974) 125–42; Ronald B. Woods, *Social Issues in Sport* (Champaign, IL: Human Kinetics, 2007) 257; and R. A. Mechikoff and S. G. Estes, *A History and Philosophy of Sport and Physical Education*, 4th ed. (New York: McGraw-Hill, 2005).

[94] Møller, *The Ethics of Doping and Anti-Doping: Redeeming the Soul of Sport?*, 1–2.

Winning performances can even be inspirational to those who are "weaker" or in need of encouragement. And losing is part of sports competitions and life.[95]

Some athletes such as Jeremy Lin and Tim Tebow believe that winning is not in conflict with their Christian faith, sometimes citing Paul's exhortation to win the race (1 Corinthians 9:24) as evidence that winning is good as long as it is done for Christ. Exegetically it does not seem that this passage is meant literally but metaphorically; however, such popular interpretations of biblical passages and theological doctrines are still influential.

Just as Lin and Tebow subscribe to particular understandings of the meaning of faith in sport, athletes may see winning as good for reasons other than self-aggrandizement, including reasons such as self-satisfaction, contribution to a larger effort (such as adding to the overall national performance at the Olympics), and the opportunity to be an empowering role model. For example, after the Canadian women hockey team's gold medal victory in the 2010 Olympics and the relative success of the 2012 women's soccer team, many interviews with girls and young women affirmed the inspiration that winning had provided. In this way, the goals of winning and supporting others are not in conflict.

The devaluing of women in sport is often noted,[96] as is the hypervaluing of traditional masculine characteristics such as aggression,[97] and a win-at-any-cost mentality. Of course, sexism is not the only systemic

---

[95]A greater problem, as I discuss, regarding the influence of Christianity on sport is the glorification of suffering and pain.

[96]See, for example, Ladd and Mathisen, *Muscular Christianity*, 243; Eleanor J. Stebner and Tracy J. Trothen, "A Diamond Is Forever? Women, Baseball and a Pitch for a Radically Inclusive Community," in *The Faith of 50 Million: Baseball, Religion, and American Culture*, eds. Christopher H. Evans and William R. Herzog, II (Louisville, KY: Westminster John Knox Press, 2002) 167–86; Anita DeFrantz "An Open Letter: Sport Belongs to Us All," *Journal of Women and Religion* 18 (2000): 13–14; Susan Birrel and Diana M. Richter, "Is a Diamond Forever? Feminist Transformations of Sport," in *Women, Sport and Culture*, eds. Susan Birrell and Cheryl L. Cole (Windsor, ON: Human Kinetics, 1994) 221–44; and Laura Robinson, *Crossing the Line: Violence and Sexual Assault in Canada's National Sport* (Toronto, ON: McClelland & Stewart, 1998).

[97]Sinclair-Faulkner, "A Puckish Reflection on Religion in Canada" (1977) 393.

oppression absorbed and perpetuated in organized sport. So, too, are racism, classism, ableism, and commercialization. As theological ethicist Gregory Baum observes, "structured games mirror a structured society,"[98] which suggests that the systemic oppression perpetuated by sport is more deeply rooted in culture.

It has become the norm to assume that "pride, arrogance, self-centeredness, and narcissism" are connected and undesirable, particularly from a faith perspective.[99] For example, Hoffman states that one reason for Christianity's incompatibility with sport is that Christianity "says all are unworthy and undeserving," whereas sport is a "microcosm of meritocracy."[100] He cautions against the narcissism of competitive sport. Theologian Lincoln Harvey echoes this concern, stating that "[f]allen play has become self-worship."[101] Austin, too, shares this concern but modifies it, drawing a helpful distinction between self-interest and self-centeredness: a "morally and spiritually dangerous aspect of sport is their potential to elicit egocentric reasoning.... Sometimes, the shift from a morally justifiable self-*interested* perspective to an immoral self-*centered* perspective is quite subtle."[102]

From a feminist theological perspective, self-interest and, particularly, the cultivation of personal confidence, the claiming of one's value, and the fostering of inner strength, are consistent with the theological message of self-love and dignity associated with the *imago Dei* doctrine. Sport can

---

[98] Gregory Baum and John Coleman, "Editorial: Sport, Society and Religion," in *Sport*, eds. Gregory Baum and John Coleman (Edinburgh, UK: T & T Clark, 1989) 5.

[99] Austin, "Sports as Exercises in Spiritual Formation," 74.

[100] Hoffman, "The Sanctification of Sport," 18.

[101] Lincoln Harvey, "Towards a Theology of Sport: a Proposal," *Anvil* 28, no. 1 (2012): 13.

[102] Austin, "Sports as Exercises in Spiritual Formation," 70. Sports theological ethicist John White ["The Enduring Problem of Dualism: Christianity and Sports" *Implicit Religion* 15, no. 2 (2012): 225–41] provides a very insightful critique of Hoffman's dualistic approach to sport and religion. White rejects Hoffman's negation of sporting values of "excellence, dedication, and hard work" and reclaims them as "spiritual" and consistent with Christian faith, but does not challenge Hoffman's contention that self-interest is inconsistent with Christian faith. Likely this is because self-interest has been mistakenly equated with "self-centredness," as Austin suggests.

provide opportunities for marginalized people including females, people from poorer families and countries, and visible/invisible minorities to develop self-love and perhaps also become role models or signifiers of hope to others. Latina theologian Ivone Gebara shows that the same value can serve both good and evil.[103] As she illustrates, sometimes evil comes from the excess of that which is good. It is possible for self-empowerment and self-love to distort into narcissism. This potential for distortion does not mitigate the goodness of the self-love and inner strength that can be cultivated through sport. The possibility of never developing a positive sense of one's created goodness and value perhaps should be a seen as more serious risk than narcissism. Feminist, womanist, and mujerista theologians have been making the case for decades now that more pride and self-interest are needed among marginalized persons if their human flourishing is to be cultivated. Focus on pride as a sin has been the preoccupation of largely white, male Euro-American theologians. Their mistake has been in assuming that this temptation applies equally to all groups regardless of power imbalances.

The issue of values and virtues in sport is complicated. What is virtuous for some athletes may too easily become a trap for others. Pride can be empowering and inspiring, particularly for marginalized persons, but pride can also become egoism for others, particularly the already socially privileged. The assessment of virtues must be contextual. Adding to this complexity is the question of the origin of normative values. Both religion and sport, as aspects of culture, necessarily influence values. How religious claims are interpreted also influences how fans and athletes understand sport, and values and virtues affect how enhancements are used.

3. The Relationship Between Sport and Play

The contrast of sport and play in the literature on religion and sport helps to illuminate the meaning of sport. In this literature, sport and play are often presented as mutually exclusive binaries. Sport is seen as the evidence of secular immorality while play is that pure form of sport, which in moderation is good. Drawing on Dutch cultural historian Johan Huizinga,

---

[103]Ivone Gebara, *Out of the Depths: Women's Experience of Evil and Salvation* (Minneapolis: Fortress Press, 2002).

many scholars see play as having pure intrinsic value unlike most elite sports.[104] Play is an autotelic activity, an activity whose meaning, and end, is the activity itself.

Feezell is one of the few who understands sport as being in "the neighborhood of play."[105] He thinks that sport, like play, can provide "meaningful experiences" that contribute to happiness as long as sport is not perceived as a matter of life and death.[106] Observing that some participants and fans tend to experience happiness in sport while others tend to experience devastation, Feezell concludes that sport experiences are not monolithic. Other scholars such as Hoffman and Higgs, are more critical regarding sport, seeing it as a distortion of play. As such, they point out that sport is directed toward extrinsic ends that are consistent with undesirable socially normative values. Like Hoffman, Higgs understands sport as "athletic competition for an extrinsic cultural prize, in contrast to play, the indulgence in physical or mental activity for an intrinsic natural gift (not to be confused, at least in my mind, with what have been called spiritual gifts)."[107] Play holds more redemptive possibilities than sport in Higgs's view, but as a profane activity play still must not be mistaken for the sacred. This distinction between internal and external ends, with internal ends associated with the moral goodness and external ends with the morally problematic, is not so easily made in reality.

While Higgs and Hoffman see professional sports as unredeemable in their present state, others, including legendary sports attorney Howard Slusher and sports ethicist Robert L. Simon, see the state of competitive sports as more mixed. Lamenting the instrumentalization of sport that has accompanied its professionalization, Howard Slusher calls attention to the damaging effects of a focus on external ends, concluding "sport is more than

---

[104] See, for example, Harvey, "Towards a Theology of Sport: a Proposal," (2012): 5–15; Feezell, *Sport, Philosophy, and Good Lives* (2013); Robert Ellis, "'Faster, Higher, Stronger': Sport and the Point of It All," *Anvil* 28, no. 1 (2012): 5–13; Hoffman, "Whatever Happened To Play?" 21–25.

[105] Feezell, *Sport, Philosophy, and Good Lives*, 28.

[106] Ibid., 19. Harvey, too, defines sport as falling within the wider class of play. [Harvey, Lincoln, "Towards a Theology of Sport," 5–15.]

[107] Higgs, *God in the Stadium*, 3.

an instrument. It is something itself."[108] Simon too sees sport, even at the most competitive levels, as utility driven in part but also driven by both intrinsic and extrinsic ends. Recognizing the complexity of athletes' motives, Simon rejects a binary understanding of extrinsic and intrinsic ends (sport and play) even at the professional level: "some seem to compete as much for the love of the competition as for financial reward."[109]

Along the same lines, researcher and professor Michael Grimshaw makes the case that winning is not the only end in sport; anticipation and hope are also important ends for athletes and fans. Grimshaw explains that the excitement generated before a sports competition is as important to fans and players as the final outcome. Before the last inning (baseball), round (boxing), or period (hockey), there is still hope that the favored team will win. This hope is itself a meaningful end in sport. Theologian and religious studies scholar Robert Ellis draws attention to the questing for the transcendent that characterizes sport. The reaching for self-transcendence or the sense of awe that can be experienced in competitive sport is, Ellis, offers, what distinguishes sport from play. Grimshaw and Ellis make the point well that sport offers hope and experiences of reaching toward transcendence. These internal goods are not available in the same way, in play.[110]

However, theological ethicist Dietmar Mieth observes that the more sport "comes under the rule of goals, success, and achievement, the more one-dimensional is the possible communication of the participants" and so the less able sport is to foster personhood.[111] Highly competitive sport can become predominantly shaped by normative values of winning, prestige, money, and conformity to norms of physical attractiveness.[112]

---

[108] Howard Slusher, "Sport and the Religious," in *Religion and Sport: The Meeting of Sacred and Profane*, ed. Charles S. Prebish (Westport, CT: Greenwood Press, 1993) 190.

[109] Robert L. Simon, *Fair Play: The Ethics of Sport*, 2nd ed. (Boulder, CO: Westview Press, 2004) 70.

[110] Ellis, "The Meaning of Sport: An Empirical Study into the Significance attached to Sporting Participation and Spectating in the UK and US," 170, 174.

[111] Dietmar Mieth, "The Ethics of Sport" in *Sport*, eds. Gregory Baum and John Coleman (Edinburgh, UK: T & T Clark, 1989) 85.

[112] See, for example, Bridel and Rail, "Sport, Sexuality, and the Production of (Resistant) Bodies," 127–144.

I agree with Slusher, Simon, Grimshaw, and Ellis that elite-level sport is characterized by both intrinsic and extrinsic ends, and that premier athletes would tend to be informed by mixed motives. Many sports theorists draw on Alasdair MacIntyre's definition of "practices" as including sport and "hold that in developing skills such as speed, strength, and tactical imagination the cultivation of certain virtues, such as trust, courage, and fairness, is paradoxically both a necessary condition and a consequence of proper engagement."[113] Sport pushes athletes to understand themselves better, including their limitations and their possibilities. Sport provides obstacles and the challenge to overcome these through creativity, being in the moment, celebrating embodiment, physical conditioning, strategic thinking, teamwork, and having fun. As Feezell proposes, sport can be meaningful in its very triviality. And sport can be a source of hope and awe.

On the one hand, many scholars writing about sport and religion tend to elevate play at the expense of sport,[114] even though, as philosopher Scott Kretchmar's analysis shows, sport and games demand more intelligence than play since they need "at least three kinds of logic that are not required by play."[115] On the other hand, play is suspect in a socio-cultural context in which external ends are valued above internal ends.[116] This is not dissimilar to the paradoxical elevation and marginalization of women. The elevation of subjects or activities as morally righteous can go hand-in-hand with their dismissal. There are a number of obvious problems with this dynamic. First, neither play nor women are in themselves virtuous, and neither sport nor

---

[113] Austin, "Sports as Exercises in Spiritual Formation," 71.

[114] R. Scott Kretchmar, "The Normative Heights and Depths of Play," *Journal of the Philosophy of Sport* 34, no. 1 (2007): 1–12; and Kretchmar, "Why Dichotomies Make it Difficult to See Games as Gifts of God," 189–90.

[115] Kretchmar, "The Normative Heights and Depths of Play," 6–7. Kretchmar identifies these three types of logic as: conventional logic [the logic that "stipulates relationships between means and ends in order to know "what counts' in a game" (7)], the logic of formalism (this is required for understanding the requirements for a game and the boundaries between cheating and playing), and the logic of gratuity [in sport we seek artificial challenges and reason that "harder is better" (7)].

[116] Overman, *The Influence of the Protestant Ethic on Sport and Recreation*, 347, 351. Play, Overman tells us, in Puritan times was regarded as dangerous since it was not goal directed and therefore invited temptation. Further, he argues, this "distrust of play" persists.

men are in themselves morally defunct. On a functional level, society tends to value sport and men more highly than play and women if, for example, viewership (in the case of sport) and political representation (men over women) are valid indicators. Further, play and women are linked, just as are sport and men. It is not by accident that male athletes and male athletic leagues garner more media coverage than do their female counterparts.[117]

Part of the tendency to separate play from sport and work is related to an embedded notion of the purity of "the Game." This notion insists that there was a glory time when athletes played without being paid, when the way one played the game mirrored one's personal good values and when nothing mattered but love of the game regardless of outcome.[118] Power, prestige, status, money—none of these mattered, simply love of the Game. Even winning was not the main concern. One played as well as one could.

In some ways, the Garden of Eden is a parallel notion to the purity of the Game. There is a sense in both of a state that preceded the messy mix of good and evil; an isolated innocence imbues the Garden and the Game.[119] The innocence of the Game is understood as a virtue much like the innocence of Adam and Eve before they partook of the apple. This glorification of innocence has a very dangerous dimension; innocence is not always virtuous and/or desirable.[120] And longing for something that we

---

[117]For a fuller discussion of these dynamics, including empirical evidence, see Andrei S. Markovits and Emily K. Albertson, *Sportista: Female Fandom in the United States* (Philadelphia: Temple University Press, 2012).

[118] See, for example, Ralph Andreano, "The Affluent Baseball Player," in *Games, Sport and Power*, ed. Gregory P. Stone (New Brunswick, NJ: Rutgers University, 1972): 117–26; and Jeffrey Scholes, "Professional Baseball and Fan Disillusionment: A Religious Ritual Analysis," *Journal of Religion and Popular Culture*, 7 (Summer 2004): 1–14.

[119]Kretchmar, "Why Dichotomies Make it Difficult to See Games as Gifts of God," 191.

[120]Rita Nakashima Brock, "And a Little Child Will Lead Us: Christianity and Child Abuse," in *Christianity, Patriarchy, and Abuse: A Feminist Critique*, eds. Joanne Carlson Brown and Carole R. Bohn (New York: Pilgrim Press, 1989) 42–61. In most Christian traditions, Jesus is painted as the innocent lamb of God taken to slaughter. The assumption of his innocence can negate his moral agency. As prophetic messiah, Jesus was politically savvy and committed to a set of virtues that included standing up for the marginalized and neighbor love. He would have

never fully had, and yet have always had, can be distracting and blind us to beauty and possibility of the present moment.

Athletes in sport, even at the highest level, share some of the same motivations as those engaged in play. In fact, competitive sport seems to involve a questing for the transcendent, *unlike* play.[121] And both sport and play have the opportunity to cultivate values and virtues that are consistent with a faith that seeks the flourishing of all life. If sport presents possibilities for cultivating goods, as I believe it does, then one must be attentive to choices that will affect these goods or values. As our capacity for engineering enhancements increases, discussions regarding what it means to enhance sport are needed. Are there values and virtues in elite sport that could be enhanced or compromised? How might techno-science use be evaluated in light of these values and virtues? For what do we hope?

---

understood that crucifixion was a possible consequence of his ministry; he was not innocent but was rather fully committed to divine love and justice.

[121] Ellis, "The Meaning of Sport: An Empirical Study into the Significance attached to Sporting Participation and Spectating in the UK and US," 174, 186.

Chapter 5

The Spiritual Dimension of Sport: Flow

"I'm spiritual but not religious" has become a common refrain. Institutional religion, and particularly Christianity, in some quarters has come to be regarded as undesirable if not repugnant. The push back against institutional religion grew in the 1960s with the emergence of the New Age movement. The postmodern rejection of grand narratives fits with New Age spiritualities that focus on the individual's interior and support each person's freedom to experience the spiritual in whatever ways work for them. To reiterate an earlier point, although formal church participation is on the decline in the United Kingdom and North America,[1] studies and anecdotal experience continue to suggest that spirituality and faith claims remain operative and emerge particularly during times of crisis.[2]

In chapter one I introduced Kenneth I. Pargament's definition of spirituality as "a distinctive ... human motivation, a yearning for the sacred" and explored his understanding of the meaning of sacred.[3] Pargament expands on the implications of spirituality—or the search for the sacred—for "how we live our lives": 1) "people invest more of themselves in those things they hold sacred;"[4] 2) "perceptions of the sacred appear to act like an emotional generator," stimulating feelings of awe, elevation, love, hope, and

---

[1] See for example, Robert Ellis, "The Meaning of Sport: An Empirical Study into the Significance Attached to Sporting Participation and Spectating in the UK and US," *Practical Theology* 5, no. 2 (2012): 175.

[2] See, for example, Simon Robinson, "The Spiritual Journey," in *Sport and Spirituality: An Introduction*, eds. J. Parry, S. Robinson, N. Watson, and M. Nesti (London, UK: Routledge, 2007) 38–58. Robinson references UK empirical studies by Grace Davie.

[3] Kenneth I. Pargament, "Searching for the Sacred: Toward a Non-Reductionist Theory of Spirituality," in *APA Handbooks in Psychology, Religion, and Spirituality: Vol. 1 Context, Theory, and Research*, eds. K. I. Pargament, J. J. Exline, and J. Jones (Washington, DC: American Psychological Association, 2013) 258.

[4] Ibid., 261.

gratitude;[5] 3) "people derive more support, strength, and satisfaction from those parts of their lives that they hold sacred;"[6] and 4) "sacred objects are likely to become organizing forces that lend coherence to other lower-level goals and motivations."[7] Furthermore, it seems that "once people discover something they perceive as sacred," they want to hold onto it.[8]

Spirituality is part of, but not restricted to, organized religions. Some see spirituality as the core goal of religion. Pargament emphasizes the distinctive character of institutional religion in the spiritual quest: religion has as its purpose, he contends, the nurturing of a relationship with the sacred.[9] Indeed, this is what differentiates institutional religion from sport— the *deliberateness* of religion regarding the search for the sacred.

Writing on the relationship between spirituality and sport, Simon Robinson defines spirituality in a way similar to Pargament but emphasizes the importance of relationship to spirituality. Robinson states that a key part of spirituality is "[a]wareness and appreciation of the other (including the self, the other person, the group, the environment and, where applicable, deity).... [t]he capacity to respond to the other ... [and the development of] significant life meaning based upon all aspects of awareness and appreciation of and response to the other."[10] The interdependence of all life becomes clearer with a deepened spirituality. Like Mayra Rivera, he understands the sacred to be partially revealed, or immanent, in relationships.[11] Thus, he reasons, unhealthy spiritualities are *overly* self-interested, unconcerned with relationships with others, the divine, or the world.

---

[5]Ibid., 262.

[6]Ibid.

[7]Ibid.

[8]Ibid.

[9]Kenneth I. Pargament, "Spirituality as an Irreducible Human Motivation and Process," *International Journal For The Psychology Of Religion* 23, no. 4 (2013): 271–81.

[10]Robinson, "The Spiritual Journey," 24.

[11]Robinson explains that spiritual awareness includes "... knowledge of ... the interdependence of the different others; the nature of the other as always emerging, as always learning and therefore never totally knowable; the other as involving both immanence, awareness of the self, and transcendence, a movement beyond the self" (Ibid., 28).

Tracy J. Trothen

As will become evident, Pargament's four implications of spirituality (e.g., the search for the sacred), and Robinson's emphasis on the relational nature of spirituality, can all be found in the spiritual dimension of sport for many followers. But first, however, we will consider the theological concepts of immanence and transcendence and their relationship to sport.

Immanence and Transcendence

A sense of the sacred in mundane experiences such as sport evokes consideration of God's immanence and transcendence. There is a strong tradition in the history of Christianity of separating God from the messiness of humanity; God's transcendent and perfect nature has been thought to entail distance from fallible humanity. Proper awe and respect for God underlie some of this tendency to exteriorize God; there is concern that we might minimize and be blind to true sacredness if God is experienced on too familiar a level.

Rivera proposes that "… God is irreducibly Other, always beyond our grasp. But not beyond our touch." [12] Rivera rejects the dichotomous categories of immanent and transcendent, and sacred and profane. For her there is no distinct theological category of immanence since immanence is necessarily part of transcendence. This view of God's nature is a departure from some traditional theological claims that God is transcendent in a way that separates God from and places God above humanity and creation. A corollary of this later claim is that God is sullied by too close a connection with humanity; that such a connection brings God down and unduly elevates humanity. Yet, as Rivera points out, this claim that God is different and, therefore, exterior to and above humanity establishes "difference as antithetical to close relationships." [13] Thus, she proposes a relational transcendence that implicitly challenges assumptions of power, distance, and separation.

Connected to this idea and important to this discussion on sport and techno-science is the theological claim of God's perfection. If God's perfection separates us from God, then can this perfection really be perfect?

---

[12]Mayra Rivera, *The Touch of Transcendence* (London, UK: Westminster John Knox Press, 2007) 2.
[13]Ibid., ix.

While it is important to see that humans are not God, we have at times overstated the danger of hubris, running at least two risks: one, the clouding of other forms of sin[14] and two, the failure to take seriously the relational dimension of the *imago Dei* doctrine.

Rivera's theology is illuminating in this regard. She understands that God is present in a limited measure in each person since all are created in God's image. Rivera does not see this theological claim compromising God's Otherness. In fact, she argues that such a theology underscores God's irreducible Otherness through an insistence on our ability to "touch" God only through a desire to truly meet the irreducibly different other person, who also is created in God's image.

This reasoning is consistent with the theory of the eschatological proviso that says we can have temporary and powerful moments of realized eschatology in this lifetime even though we cannot fully realize God's eschaton; moments of profound hope, fulfillment, perfection, and joy occur that give us glimpses of how the world could be.

The eschatological proviso has ethical implications. We are given opportunities to draw closer to God through authentic encounters with the Other. Transcendence is, according to Rivera, an "ethical opening of the self to the Other."[15] This means that we are obligated to get to know other people and let them know us. Experiences of diverse humanity can broaden our understandings of the world, humanity, and therefore God. The multiplicity and irreducibility of the Other are joined together in God's "infinite singularity."[16] That different parts of God can be touched through each life invites greater inclusion and valuing of diversity.

Rivera is neither the first nor the only theologian who has challenged the notion of God's Otherness as meaning that God is fully exterior and separate from humanity and the world.[17] Perhaps most prominently,

---

[14]See chapter three for a discussion of sin.

[15]Rivera, *The Touch of Transcendence*, 25.

[16]Ibid., 136.

[17]Ivone Gebara proposes a similar theological approach that she applies to the questions of good and evil, understanding that evil is threaded throughout what is good and goodness throughout evil: "the transcendence and immanence of evil calls me to be converted to the reality I observe, this mingled reality where no word can be complete, no God can be all-powerful, no good can be completely victorious, and

theologian Jürgen Moltmann coined the terms "immanent transcendence" and "transcendent immanence" to reflect his conviction that God could be found in, but never confined to, lived experience: "*To experience God in all things* presupposes that there is a transcendence which is immanent in things and which can be inductively discovered. It is the infinite in the finite, the eternal in the temporal, and the enduring in the transitory."[18]

In my view, the separation of the immanent from the transcendent, the sacred from the profane, limits God and limits relationship. It is possible and probable that awareness of God's presence in all experiences, and particularly through relationships with others, will enlarge our capacities to imagine God and experience genuine spiritual awe. Touching God and allowing that grace to transform us is salvific.

Introducing Flow: Athletes

In his study on transcendence in Eastern and Western religions, religious studies scholar Lawrence Fagg posits that the concept of

---

no evil can have the last word over life." Rivera and Gebara construct complicated understandings of God and God's relationship with humanity that fit with the messiness of life. These theologies challenge notions that are too neat and clear-cut. They uphold hope that is grounded in relationship and the persistent indwelling of God's Spirit that draws us continually into life. [Ivone Gebara, *Out of the Depths: Women's Experience of Evil and Salvation* (Minneapolis, MN: Fortress Press, 2002) 58.]

[18]Jürgen Moltmann, *The Spirit of Life: A Universal Affirmation*, trans. Margaret Kohl (Minneapolis: Fortress Press, 1992) 35. See also, *God in Creation: A New Theology of Creation and the Spirit of God*, trans. Margaret Kohl (San Francisco, CA: Harper & Row Publishers, 1985) 15. Others writing about sport and theology also have wrestled with the binary construction of transcendence and immanence, and the sacred and profane. Karen Joisten sees transcendence and immanence intertwined in athletic experiences, referring to what she calls the "the process of immanence of transcendence" in athletes as they strive to fulfill their vision of a perfect performance. [Karen Joisten, "Man, Mortality, and the Athletic Hero: Yesterday and Today," in *Sport and Christianity: A Sign of the Times in the Light of Faith*, eds. Kevin L. C. Lixey, Christoph Hubenthal, Dietmar Mieth, and Norbert Muller (Washington, DC: Catholic University of America Press, 2012) 21.] Others remain committed to a clear demarcation between the sacred and profane, the immanent and the transcendent, and avoid what they see as the overemphasis of God's immanence.

transcendence is included in all these religions and is not clearly differentiated from the concept of immanence. The concepts of immanence and transcendence, rather, are intertwined, forming a continuum. Fagg sees the pervasive "thirst for transcendence" evidenced in these religions as "intimately related to our quest for meaning."[19] A sense of the immanence of a divine, transcendent presence, assures followers that there is meaning in life. The topic of meaning is related to hope and what it means to be human.[20]

For athletes, transcendence has been equated with, or at least related to, what is sometimes called flow,[21] a peak experience,[22] ecstasy, transcendence,[23] a Zen state,[24] or the zone. Similar in some ways are the experiences of fans as they get caught up in a "wave" or a "shining moment."[25] First, we will consider the flow experiences of athletes.

Although the status of canoeing as a sport has been debated,[26] people have claimed to experience a profound sense of spirituality while canoeing. Canoeing, historian Thomas Peace observes, can facilitate "divine experiences and spiritual growth." Peace's definition of spirituality begins with the individual's experience and extends outward. He defines spirituality partially as "searching for the truth behind our known existence ... or as

---

[19]Lawrence W. Fagg, "Are There Intimations of Divine Transcendence in the Physical World?" *Zygon* 38, no. 3 (2003): 571. William James, in his classic *The Varieties of Religious Experience*, put forth that transcendence was the primal form of all religious experience describing it as ineffable, revelatory, passive, and transient.

[20]The topic of hope and sport will be discussed more fully in chapter six.

[21]Mihaly Csikszentmihalyi, *Beyond Boredom and Anxiety* (San Francisco, CA: Jossey-Bass, 1975).

[22]Abraham H. Maslow, *Toward a Psychology of Being* (Princeton, NJ: Van Nostrand, 1962).

[23]Mihaly Csikszentmihalyi, "The Concept of Flow," in *Play and Learning*, ed. Brian Sutton-Smith (New York: Gardner Press, 1979) 261.

[24]Eugen Herrigel, *Zen in the Art of Archery* (New York: Random House, 1999/1971).

[25]Hubert Dreyfuss and Sean Dorrance Kelly, *All Things Shining: Reading the Western Classics to Find Meaning in a Secular Age* (New York: Free Press, 2011).

[26]Some contend canoeing is a leisure activity. Further, all canoeing does not satisfy Møller's definition of sport. However, arguably rowing is related to canoeing, and rowing is an Olympic sport.

developing a deeper knowledge and understanding of self."[27] He outlines the importance of spirituality in generating social action that is grounded in an awareness of the sacredness of life. At root, he suggests that canoeing fosters connection to people and the environment, and that this sense of connection is part of the spiritual.

Similarly, A. Whitney Sanford investigates the perceived spiritual or sacred dimension of whitewater kayaking. She concludes that these subjectively defined "sacred, spiritual, or religious" experiences should be recognized as valid "self-declared religious practices of many North Americans."[28] In conversations with whitewater kayakers, Sanford found that North American whitewater kayakers prefer to use Asian or indigenous religious terms such as "Zen-like" or "mindfulness" to describe their experiences. She understands this preference as resistance to the normative emphasis on the transcendent at the expense of the immanent, and to the "Western assumptions of the sacred/profane dichotomy" found in Judaism and Christianity.[29]

Both Peace and Sanford draw a link to psychologist Mihaly Csikszentmihalyi's concept of flow in the actions of paddling and kayaking, respectively.[30] Interestingly, Peace aligns the sense of calm with flow while Sanford associates it with the sense of chaotic danger. In both contexts, the participant's experience of time changes. Flow in sport has been linked to spirituality and to a sense of meaning.[31] For athletes, past studies indicated

---

[27]Thomas G. M. Peace, "Journeying by Canoe: Reflections on the Canoe and Spirituality," *Leisure/Loisir* 33, no. 1 (2009): 218–19.

[28]A. Whitney Sanford, "Pinned on Karma Rock: Whitewater Kayaking as Religious Experience," *Journal of the American Academy of Religion* 75, no. 4 (2007): 888.

[29]Ibid., 878–79.

[30]Peace, "Journeying by Canoe: Reflections on the Canoe and Spirituality," 223–24; Sanford "Pinned on Karma Rock: Whitewater Kayaking as Religious Experience," 885.

[31]See, for example, Susan Jackson and Mihalyi Csikszentmihalyi, *Flow in Sports: The Keys to Optimal Experiences and Performance* (Champaign, IL: Human Kinetics, 1999); Nick J. Watson and Mark Nesti "The Role of Spirituality in Sport Psychology Consulting: an Analysis and Integrative Review of Literature," *Journal of Applied Sport Psychology* 17, no. 3 (2005): 228–39; and Kathleen M. Dillon and

that flow occurs most often during those times when skill level is commensurate with the challenge,[32] but more recent studies suggest that flow states occur most commonly when the challenge is perceived as slightly higher than one's perceived skill level. This small margin seems to contribute to greater concentration that assists in creating optimal conditions for flow experiences.[33]

Flow can occur in a variety of activities beyond religious activities including sport, musical and theatrical performances, work, writing, and fine art.[34] Flow experiences can bring a sense of moving "almost automatically" with all of one's effort but no effort at all;[35] alertness; a profound sense of connection with the self and the world that "some people describe...as a transcendence...a merging with the environment, as a union with the activity or with the process";[36] inner peace and harmony; a change in one's experience of time; the loss of fear and anxiety; a sense of mystery and awe; and a sense of mastery.[37] As sport psychology researcher Susan Jackson and

---

Jennifer L. Tait, "Spirituality and Being in the Zone in Team Sports: A Relationship?," *Journal of Sport Behavior* 23, no. 2 (2000): 91–100.

[32]Csikszentmihalyi, "The Concept of Flow," 257.

[33] Mihalyi Csikszentmihalyi and Giovanni B. Moneta, "Models of Concentration in Natural Environments: A Comparative Approach Based on Streams of Experiential Data," *Social Behavior and Personality* 27, no. 6 (1999): 630; Csikszentmihalyi, "The Concept of Flow," 257.

[34]Csikszentmihalyi 'The Concept of Flow," 268, 271.

[35]Ibid., 260. See also Dreyfuss and Kelly, *All Things Shining*, 11; and Patrick Kelly, "Flow, Sport and the Spiritual Life," in *Theology, Ethics and Transcendence in Sports*, eds. J. Parry, M. Nesti and N. Watson (London, UK: Routledge, 2011) 167.

[36]Csikszentmihayli, 'The Concept of Flow," 261. Kelly describes this as a sense of being "a part of something larger than oneself" (Kelly, "Flow, Sport and the Spiritual Life," 167). See also Jackson and Csikszentmihalyi, *Flow in Sports: The Keys to Optimal Experiences and Performance* (1999); Watson and Nesti, "The Role of Spirituality in Sport Psychology Consulting: an Analysis and Integrative Review of Literature," 233.

[37]See, for example, Richard Pengelley, "Sport and Spirituality: An Ancient Connection for Our Modern Times," *Dialogue Australasia* 20 (October 2008): 5–6; Csikszentmihalyi, 'The Concept of Flow," 257–67.

Csikszentmihalyi conclude, "Flow provides a glimpse of perfection, which is why we seek it again and again once we attain it."[38]

Often, flow experiences are brief and all are involuntary. One can foster conditions that are more likely to lead to flow experiences but one cannot choose to create flow; flow is beyond control. Flow states can result in surprising athletic performances, sometimes generating personal bests and unexpected championship victories.

Is Flow Spiritual?

There has been much debate regarding the meaning of flow experiences. Some understand these experiences as sacred while others are adamant that while sports experiences can be very pleasurable or even awe-inspiring, they are neither sacred nor spiritual.[39] Are there criteria that can be applied to determine whether these experiences are spiritual?

Through an extensive examination of research on altered states of consciousness experienced by athletes, Michael Murphy and Rhea A. White conclude that "sport has enormous power to sweep us beyond the ordinary sense of self, to evoke capacities that generally have been regarded as mystical, occult or religious."[40] Kathleen M. Dillon and Jennifer L. Tait conducted the first study to test the relationship between spirituality and being in the flow state. Their findings cautiously support the spiritual quality of flow. They created two new tests for this study: the Zone Test (ZT) and the Spirituality in Sports Test (SIST). Both tests were shown to have high reliability, but because they were both new, the nature of this study is exploratory. The sample size was sixty-two students at a "nonsectarian college ... who said they were or had been members of a sports team."[41]

---

[38]Jackson and Csikszentmihalyi, *Flow in Sports: The Keys to Optimal Experiences and Performance* (1999) 31.

[39]See, for example, Nick J. Watson and Andrew Parker, eds., *Sports and Christianity: Historical and Contemporary Perspectives* (New York: Routledge, 2013) 18; and Robert J. Higgs and M. C. Braswell, *An Unholy Alliance: The Sacred and Modern Sports* (Macon, GA: Mercer University Press, 2004) 219–24.

[40]Michael Murphy and Rhea A. White, *In the Zone: Transcendent Experiences in Sports* (New York: Open Road Integrated Media, 1978) 4.

[41]Dillon and Tait, "Spirituality and Being in the Zone in Team Sports: A Relationship?" 94.

Spirituality or religiosity was defined loosely as "experiencing the presence of a power, a force, an energy, or a God close to you."[42] The researchers did not offer any elaboration on this definition; it was left to the participants to interpret. Their hypothesis "that being more spiritual in sports is related to being in the zone more often was supported by the significant correlation between the SIST and ZT."[43]

In a more recent publication, Patrick Kelly sees clear connections between an athlete's flow states and Christianity. He emphasizes the "ego-lessness" of flow, noting that the self does not "disappear" but that any conscious focus on self dissipates and is replaced by an awareness of connection to something larger. During transitory moments of flow, one loses ego involvement but gains a deeper comprehension of one's identity as part of a whole that is far greater than the self. This comprehension, Kelly reflects, is consistent with the "emphasis on community in Christian spirituality."[44]

In his comparative phenomenology of contemplative prayer and athletes' flow states, Graham Ward, unlike Kelly, sees this ego-lessness in flow as "self-forgetfulness" that he contrasts with the "self-realisation" of contemplative prayer. Ward identifies the difference in intention and motivation between the athlete and one who prays; prayer is oriented to intimacy with God whereas the athlete, Ward suggests, is concerned with self-performance; "the athlete's faith is in himself or herself."[45] Ward does not acknowledge the mix of motivations and intentions that can inform an athlete. For example, a runner may choose to use long runs as prayer time since the consistent physical motion can help some people to be more centered and less distracted. While it is possible that the athlete in flow is oriented purely to oneself, studies of the flow state suggest otherwise.[46] Ward also makes the point that the zone, or flow, is "self-generated," whereas science "cannot determine whether these experiences [those

---

[42]Ibid., 93.

[43]Ibid., 96.

[44]Kelly, "Flow, Sport and the Spiritual Life," 167–70.

[45]Graham Ward, "A Question of Sport and Incarnational Theology," *Studies in Christian Ethics* 25, no. 1 (2012): 61, 64.

[46] Jackson and Csikszentmihalyi, "Flow in Sports: The Keys to Optimal Experiences and Performance," (1999): 27.

associated with meditation] are self-induced or coming from outside altogether." However, earlier in the article Ward also admits that science cannot determine the origin of the flow "propulsion."[47]

Price sees the introspective, quiet, and focused dimension of sport, including flow experiences, as necessarily spiritual: "To engage the most profound level of truth requires that one become introspective and meditative, opening oneself to the Other that resides at the innermost dimension of self. In this sense, then, sports constitute an essential, spiritual pursuit–seeking truth and self-awareness." [48] Again, much of this conversation has to do with one's understanding of spirituality and one's faith convictions. Price's observation fits with Rivera's theology of transcendence and with my own convictions. Not all athletes' experiences in sport are characterized by this opening to the Other and self, and no one sports experience encapsulates all that there is to spiritual searching, but it does seem that some sports experiences have a spiritual dimension.

The Wave: Fandom and Spirituality

Pargament's four implications of spirituality for how we live our lives seem to be met by passionate sports fans. For them, the sport experience is an "emotional generator"—creating and magnifying feelings of awe, elevation, hope, gratitude, and maybe even love. One can infer that fans "derive support, strength, and satisfaction" from their sport, and that the symbols of sport are "organizing forces" in their lives, from the time invested in following their team, the "great lengths" they will often go to protect their team, defend them publicly, identify with a like-minded community, and exhibit support through flags, team shirts, and cheering.

Eric Bain-Selbo, professor of philosophy and religion, suggests that "the experience of the religious adherent and the experience of the Southern college football fan are essentially the same flow experiences, they are simply

---

[47]Ward, "A Question of Sport and Incarnational Theology" (2012): 57.

[48]Joseph L. Price, "An American Apotheosis: Sport As Popular Religion," in *Religion and Popular Culture in America*, eds. Bruce David Forbes and Jeffrey H. Mahan (Berkeley: University of California Press, 2000) 210.

labeled differently."[49] He bases this conclusion on survey data from his extensive study of Southern college football fans in the 2005 and 2006 seasons (220 surveys were completed) and the participants' usage of terms he identified as religious descriptors.[50] Bain-Selbo's conclusion that Southern college football fans have "religious experiences as a consequence of their participation in Southern college football rituals"[51] hinges on his assessment of the religious meaning of the participants' selected words.

To some degree, whether or not these words express a religious quality must depend on one's understanding of religious experience. The relevance of the individual fan's interpretation of what counts as a religious experience likely explains why several survey participants who used some of Bain-Selbo's religious terms did not think that their football experiences had a religious dimension. Bain-Selbo's understanding of religious experience is based primarily of the works of philosopher William James, and theologians Friedrich Schleiermacher and Rudolph Otto, all of whom saw the theological relevance of personal inner experience including emotional states.

While it seems that many sports fans have religious-like flow experiences when watching their team play, Bain-Selbo's conclusion that these fan flow experiences are essentially the same as flow experiences of the religious adherent, may need some further nuancing. If sport is like a religion, and if these flow experiences are the same, or mostly the same, it makes sense to surmise that these flow experiences would stimulate similar behavioral responses. In other words, is not one's response to flow, part of the flow experience? Schilbrack develops the argument that an adequate definition of religion must be both functional and ontological (content-based with reference to a "superempirical reality"[52]). The functional component concerns how one expresses one's faith convictions in the world and suggests that a

---

[49] Eric Bain-Selbo, "Ecstasy, Joy, and Sorrow: the Religious Experience of Southern College Football," *Journal of Religion and Popular Culture* 20 (Fall 2008): 9.

[50] There are very few empirical studies dedicated to the study of the relationship between sport and religion. (Csikszentmihalyi's studies on flow did not explicitly link flow with spirituality or religion.)

[51] Bain Selbo, "Ecstasy, Joy, and Sorrow," 5.

[52] Kevin Schilbrack, "What Isn't A Religion," *The Journal of Religion* (Chicago Journals) 93, no. 3: 316. See chapter 4 for more analyses of the relationship between sport and religion.

religion provides guidance regarding these expressions. Yet, at least one preliminary study suggests that the behaviors of religious fans differ from the behaviors of fans who do not subscribe to a traditional religion.

In 2006, Stephen Reyser investigated the relationship between fan behavior and religious beliefs, hypothesizing that religious commitments do not affect fan behaviors and beliefs. His subjects were fans of sports, music, and media, among others. He used a survey to "examine differences between secular and religious fans with respect to fan behaviors and beliefs."[53] His findings, based on a sample size of 158, countered his hypothesis.[54] This study is limited by the small numbers of participants representing each fan group and by the strong representation of one particular Christian faith group among the religious fans. Based on the findings, Reyser theorizes that the religious fans are governed more by an "explicitly stated doctrine of love" than are the secular fans.[55] Although Reyser's sample is limited, he found that, like religious fans, secular fans tended to exhibit similar behaviors and beliefs within their group. Noting that the particular behaviors and beliefs differed between the secular and religious groups, he concludes that religious commitments affect fan behaviors and beliefs. It may be the case that both religious and secular fans can have flow experiences as sports fans but that each group *expresses or interprets* these spiritual experiences differently. Again, the one thing that seems clear is that some fans use what are commonly recognized spiritual or religious terms to describe their fan experiences.

---

[53]Stephen Reyser, "Secular Versus Religious Fans: Are They Different?: An Empirical Examination," *Journal of Religion and Popular Culture* 12, (Spring, 2006): 1. In the survey, religion was defined simply as a "'commitment or devotion to religious faith'" (1).

[54]Ibid., 3. He surveyed a variety of secular fans (music 32.28 percent; media 14.56 percent; sports 7.59 percent; other 5.06 percent) and religious fans (Assembly of God 32.9 percent; other religions 7.59 percent). Reyser found that secular fan group responses were different from religious member responses. The 11 item survey results showed, for example, that 62.4 percent of secular fans deal with disagreement by ignoring it while 56.3 percent of religious fans deal with disagreement with "love" or "prayer." Also, 62.4 percent of secular fans compare themselves with other fans whereas only 46.8 percent of religious fans tended to do so.

[55]Ibid., 10.

Not all flow experiences can or ought to be understood as spiritual. One indicator of a spiritual flow experience is the response to that experience. Flow experiences include the awareness of the interconnection of all life.[56] If they are spiritual experiences, flow experiences should not end with the dispersal of the congregation, or game crowd. Rather, spiritual experiences, at least as Pargament, Robinson, and I understand them, ought to propel one to life-enhancing actions. When fan flow experiences are transient moments, they are better understood as adrenaline induced isolated moments. This critique applies equally to religious flow experiences and sport flow experiences.

Price's analysis of the fan experience as a communal, and "sort of" conversion experience helps to make sense of the intensity of the fan-flow experience. As Price puts is, "A fan's identification with his or her favorite team as family indicates a rebirth that is remarkably similar to a convert's identification with his or her new brothers and sisters in Christ.... More than merely the sense of the sacred that one gets at a fabled stadium or baseball shrine, the Church of Baseball is fundamentally the community of like-minded believers."[57] Robert Ellis's empirical study of 468 sports spectators and athletes supports Price's insight regarding the importance of communal belonging. Ellis found that sport serves as an organizing principle in people's lives.[58] The intensity of communal fan identity and sense of belonging, add to the euphoria that a group of fans can experience at various moments in a game. The sense of connection among "like-minded believers" can amplify fan euphoria and flow experiences.

This euphoric state has been variously called a wave, effervescence,[59] flow, "anonymous enthusiasm,"[60] or "shining moments."[61] As contemporary

---

[56]Robinson, "The Spiritual Journey," 56. Robinson sums up: "Transcendence is not about a separation for [sic] the world but rather is an engagement with it." This engagement, he posits, involves empathy for the other.

[57]Joseph L. Price, "Here I Cheer: Conversion Narratives of Baseball Fans," *Criterion* 42, no. 2 (2003): 12–19.

[58]Robert Ellis, "The Meaning of Sport: An Empirical Study into the Significance Attached to Sporting Participation and Spectating in the UK and US," *Practical Theology* 5, no. 2 (2012): 175.

[59]See Martyn Percy and Rogan Taylor, "Something For the Weekend, Sir? Leisure, Ecstasy and Identity in Football and Contemporary Religion," *Leisure*

philosophers Hubert Dreyfuss and Sean Kelly explain, "[T]here are moments in sport—either in the playing of them or in the witnessing of them—during which something so overpowering happens that it wells up before you as a palpable presence and carries you along as on a powerful wave. At that moment there is no question of ironic distance from the event. That is the moment when the sacred shines."[62] In those moments, any remaining sense of distance between fans and the players disappears; the physical separation between fans and players that never seemed fully real disappears in an overwhelming sense of oneness. Similar to athletes' experiences of flow, these shining moments hold transformative potential. They are extraordinary, and temporary, and they seem to be propelled by an external force.[63] These characteristics align with Pargament's observation that perceptions of the sacred "act like an emotional generator, stimulating feelings of awe, elevation, love, hope, and gratitude."[64]

Several scholars approach this topic of fan effervescence with caution. Since this energy or "whooshing up"[65] usually happens in large fan crowds, and in fact often increases with the size of the crowd, the potential for an intense response is high. Reyser's study supports the notion that flow does not necessarily lead to particular moral behaviors.[66] Theologian Wolfgang Vondey sees these moments of intense fan energy as dangerous in their anonymity and force. Vondey contrasts fan enthusiasm with Christian enthusiasm that he describes as "never anonymous, never automatic, never excessive. It enhances the unity of the body and is an expression of the

---

Studies, 16 (1997): 37–49. Durkheim and Eliade also both recognized the quality of "effervescence" in groups.

[60]Wolfgang Vondey, "Christian Enthusiasm: Can the Olympic Flame Kindle the Fire of Christianity?" Word & World 23, no. 3 (Summer 2003): 319.

[61]Dreyfuss and Kelly, All Things Shining, 81.

[62] Ibid., 194.

[63] Often the spectator-participant relationship to sport is considered dichotomous; spectators or fans are passive, participants or athletes, active. This dichotomy is false.

[64]Pargament, "Searching for the Sacred," 262.

[65]Dreyfuss and Kelly, All Things Shining, 201.

[66]Watson and Parker, eds., Sports and Christianity, 18. Higgs and Braswell, and Hoffman mount similar arguments [Higgs and Braswell, An Unholy Alliance: The Sacred and Modern Sports (2004) 219–24.]

shared hope to participate in the glorious promises of God."[67] Vondey's description of Christian enthusiasm is an ideal that is not always realized in Christian faith communities. Christian enthusiasm, as a human expression, bears a propensity for missing the mark or, in other words, sin. History has witnessed many mass atrocities perpetrated and justified by distortions of Christian enthusiasm. Not all Christian enthusiasm inspires virtuous behavior; humans are imperfect and we often get it wrong.

Robinson considers the destructive potential of ecstatic sports crowds, referring to the ecstatic crowd response at the Nuremberg rallying fields: "At the rallies there was a strong emphasis of spiritual well-being connected to physical activity and sports.... Hitler developed a belief system ... [that] denied the presence or value of the other, of any group that was different from the Aryan race." Dreyfuss and Kelly make a similar point: "There is ... a vanishingly small distance between rising as one with the crowd at a baseball game and rising as one with the crowd at a Hitler rally."[68] Reyser's finding that there is not a clearly defined set of values informing secular fan beliefs and behaviors, in contrast with the religious fans surveyed, is interesting and potentially important. In short, without a clearly defined value base that informs behaviors and desires, the crowd energy that can be generated at large sports events can be expressed in harmful ways. And belonging in a faith community does not ensure virtuous behavior and regard for the Other. There are many examples of this destructive potential of crowd energy ranging from trampling deaths at soccer matches to the riot after the 2012 Stanley Cup final in Vancouver. By contrast, crowd energy can also inspire good actions: supporting one's team, increasing camaraderie amongst strangers, and appreciation for the opposing team. I experienced this energy and behavior following the Blue Jays' 1993 World Series win, as I joined thousands of fans to fill Yonge Street in Toronto.

The causes of fan violence are complex. At times fan violence derives from "personal and political identities involving economic and ethnic issues" and stimulates these "hooli-fans" to victimize others just as they feel

---

[67]Vondey, "Christian Enthusiasm: Can the Olympic Flame Kindle the Fire of Christianity?" (2003): 319.

[68]Dreyfuss and Kelly, *All Things Shining: Reading the Western Classics to Find Meaning in a Secular Age* (2011) 203.

victimized.[69] Flow can seem to be happening outside of oneself, propelled by an external force, but one always has the ability to control the outcomes of flow experiences through the "retrain[ing of] our desires" so that our responses reflect what is meaningful and shining or sacred to us.[70] Research on crowd behavior shows that although crowds can engage in passive, "automatic thinking," they can also function proactively.[71] Desires are associated with values; if we value winning highly then we desire to win. Desire, similar to hope, is subject to choice. If we uncritically accept that it is most important to win, then we desire that above all. But, if we deliberately explore the importance we place on winning and consider this in comparison with other values, we may choose to modify the intensity of our desire to win or to value other goods, such as life, even more intensely than winning. Feezell suggests adaptation strategies that can be used to modify attitudes, particularly attitudes to winning and losing since often the desire to win leads to unhappiness. Refuting Novak's assertion that in sport "losing is like death," Feezell suggests that re-conceptualizing sport as "splendid triviality" will enhance human happiness: "We need not assume that winning is the only good or primary good in sports, avoidance of unhappiness, or at least its reduction, is possible by moderating our passions, refocusing our attention, and reshaping out attitudes."[72] We can add to this Jackson and Csikszentmihalyi's research finding that "the most memorable and happy moments in people's lives usually involve a job well done that required skills and concentration or a struggle to overcome a difficult obstacle."[73] It seems we need reasonable challenges and a level of investment in these challenges that does not paralyze us when we do not succeed.

---

[69]Kevin O'Gorman [*Saving Sport: Sport, Society and Spirituality* (Dublin, UK: Columbia Press, 2010) 133] addresses fan violence and sums up the explanation for this provided by Franklin Foer [*How Football Explains the World* (London: Arrow Books, 2004) 13].

[70]Csikszentmihayli, 'The Concept of Flow," 261; Dreyfuss and Kelly, *All Things Shining*, 81, 119; Feezell, *Sport, Philosophy, and Good Lives?*, 49.

[71]Percy and Taylor, "Something for the Weekend, Sir?" 38.

[72]Feezell, *Sport, Philosophy, and Good Lives*, 70.

[73]Jackson and Csikszentmihalyi, *Flow in Sports: The Keys to Optimal Experiences and Performance* (1999) 35.

Flow and Techno-science

The increasing use of enhancement technologies will affect flow experiences. At this point we do not know what these effects will be but based on what we know about the dynamics of flow, we can pose some questions regarding the potential effects of increased enhancement use on flow.

If equipment modifications, dietary supplements, or genetic modifycations increase an ahlete's abilities, the challenge-skills balance is affected. If the challenge is no longer perceived to be slightly higher than the skills possessed by an athlete, then the possibility of flow decreases. Also, the potential for record breaking and new personal bests increases. The sport may become less interesting to watch if it is not as challenging. On the other hand, fans may enjoy seeing even more records broken and personal bests recorded. However, this will also affect the continuity of a sport; new successes will be less and less comparable to past successes. This lack of continuity combined with the diminishment of flow experiences may make sports competitions less meaningful. Flow, in its unbidden-ness and power to move the spirit, and so the whole person, in unexpected ways, contributes to the inspirational quality of sports competitions. With fewer or no athletes experiencing flow states, likely we would see fewer surprising performances and surprising successes.

However, if the challenges in a sport are increased concomitantly with any increased skill levels that result from enhancement use, the incidence of flow experiences may remain the same. But an increase in a sports challenge level has implications for the sport including the meaning of personal bests and championship records. Also, at what point does an increase in challenge, or an increase in collective skill level, fundamentally change the nature of a sport?

And, if skills are improved continually because of better equipment, training regimens, or other enhancement interventions, will sports competitions devolve into spectacle or entertainment that is so far removed from average human experience that one cannot imagine identifying with elite athletes? If this happens, the dissolving of the "ironic distance"[74] between fans and athletes that is part of fan flow experiences will become

---

[74]Dreyfuss and Kelly, *All Things Shining*, 194.

less likely. Without that sense of closeness, will fan flow experiences be diminished or even extinguished?

Enhanced athletes may have less interest in nurturing the conditions for flow if flow becomes seen as an unimportant or even undesirable factor in achieving excellence. It is possible that personal bests and winning will become more and more predictable based on what is known about the competing athletes' attributes. Tailored enhancements may become the only reliable and accepted way of achieving athletic success. The unpredictable human factor may not be valued and, in fact, may be seen as more of a hindrance than possible advantage. For example, would coaches and athletes choose to use interventions that block emotions if they become more available? Because flow is contingent on a number of human factors including emotional centeredness or deep attention,[75] it seems that flow relies on the (unpredictable) emotional dimension of being human.

On the other hand, it is possible that more will become known about the physiological dimension of flow, and the option of enhancing flow possibilities may present itself. Flow experiences of both athletes and fans may become more accessible and even enhanced, *if* these are seen as valuable. Techno-science may be used to magnify this human capacity and experience.

There are many possible implications of such a magnification. For example, it will become even more important to understand fan behavior that seems to be related to crowd energy. If fans are able to magnify their experiences of flow, will this energy be expressed in positive ways or will hooliganism increase? Also, will athletes' flow experiences become predictable? If so, how will this predictability affect the meaning and attraction of flow and of sport? And if sport is a source of hope for many followers and participants, how might flow be connected to this hope and how might techno-science developments and use affect this hope?

---

[75] Sam Elkington, "Articulating a Systematic Phenomenology of Flow: An Experience-Process Perspective," *Leisure/Loisir* 34, no. 3 (2010): 327–60. Elkington found that there is a "pre-flow" stage that has three discernible moments: initial investment of attention, activation and energization, and the trust-flow imperative. Each of these involves the subject as a whole person.

Chapter 6

Hope in the Secular Religion of Sport

The most significant potential cost of an uncritical embrace of techno-science interventions in sport would be the erosion of hope, which is the single most important issue arising out of the intersection of techno-science, sport, and religion.

The technological age poses challenges to what is meaningful about being human. As our capacities to create and use human enhancements increase, the conversations regarding which enhancements will truly improve humanity must consider all the layers of being human, including spirituality. The search for the sacred continues to be very important for humans.

We need meaningful experiences in our lives. As technology removes many of the challenges that humans have found meaningful to overcome in the past, we find new challenges. So it is in sport. The challenge of the activity must be preserved if sport is to keep its meaning and attraction. If we introduce a skate that propels the hockey player and senses the most appropriate direction, then a significant challenge is taken out of hockey, changing the game in a way that relies less on human abilities. By removing core challenges, the meaning and implicit hope in an excellent play would be diminished.

Sport at its best cultivates happiness through trivial but meaningful activities. Our human incompleteness stokes spiritual yearning. The quest for perfection and transcendence is about fulfillment. The human ability to overcome hurdles and reach new plateaus, makes us happy and hopeful.[1] And these memorable and happy moments need not be particularly significant beyond the actual moment of meaningfulness:

> athletes and even everyday participants in sports find these relatively trivial activities highly meaningful, because they do have a point, a purpose, a context for intelligible goals. They represent the attempt to

---

[1] Susan Jackson and Mihalyi Csikszentmihalyi, *Flow in Sports: The Keys to Optimal Experiences and Performance* (Champaign, IL: Human Kinetics, 1999) 35.

overcome some (artificial) difficulty, yet when successful, such overcoming constitutes real achievement. Sporting activities take place in a context of meaning, a "world," involving clearly delineated goals, standards of excellence, and meaningful ends, internal to the sport.[2]

Sport, at its best, provides many opportunities for these moments.

The rise of technology has changed the way we approach many everyday hurdles such as using a remote to start the car in cold winters or using a machine to wash our dishes. Some writers, including Dreyfuss and Kelly, also see technology as reducing our capacity for wonder, awe, and hope.[3] The fast-paced technology and science industries present a seemingly endless stream of new ways to enhance athletic performance by helping competitors to become faster, stronger, or otherwise more able to win. Yet thus far we have failed to take seriously the question of whether sporting achievements enhanced through these innovations will also enhance human happiness or increase the sense of meaning that imparts hope. In addition to doping and other scandals, the dramatic rise in enhancement availability is reducing the need for human skill and this reduction affects human experiences of meaning, hope, and happiness.[4]

McCarroll's definition of hope is pertinent: *"Hope is the experience of the opening of horizons of meaning and participation in relationship to time, other human and nonhuman being, and/or the transcendent."*[5] In light of this definition, we need to consider how techno-science might affect hope and meaning. The sport enhancement debate is about more than fairness in athletic competition; it is about hope and what it means to be human. The question of what is important—what we value, desire and hope for—is becoming acute in the secular religion of sport. The rise of enhanced or even trans-athletes is generating questions and uncertainty regarding what counts as an authentic sports record or achievement. Who are our heroes? What is

---

[2]Randolph Feezell, *Sport, Philosophy, and Good Lives* (Lincoln: University of Nebraska Press, 2013) 213.

[3]Hubert Dreyfuss and Sean Dorrance Kelly, *All Things Shining: Reading the Western Classics to Find Meaning in a Secular Age* (New York: Free Press, 2011).

[4]Technology "strips away the need for skill" [Dreyfuss and Kelly, *All Things Shining*, 214].

[5]Pamela R. McCarroll, *The End of Hope—The Beginning: Narratives of Hope in the Face of Death and Trauma* (Minneapolis, Fortress Press, 2014) 48.

authentic? For what do we hope? As Dreyfuss and Kelly worry, "The nihilism of our secular age leaves us with the awful sense that nothing matters in the world at all."[6] Sport has become an important source of communal hope for many of its followers in this secular age,[7] and the potential effects of techno-science on hope in sport need to be taken seriously.

Several scholars make reference to meaning and hope in sport.[8] Discussions of the relationship between religion and sport, and of sport's spiritual dimension are almost always about hope and the human quest for meaning that is part of that hope. I propose that hope in sport is generated in four main locations: 1) winning, losing, and anticipation; 2) star athletes; 3) perfect moments; and 4) relational embodiment. Each of these locations is explored below. I use Christian theological reflection to help illuminate the spiritual and social convictions associated with these locations of hope.

Winning, Losing, and Anticipation

Sport can provide a rich ground for faith through the cultivation of values that do not simply mirror normative values but instead inculcate values that are more connected to the goods internal to sport. Some of these goods are community, teamwork, discipline, justice, prudence, joy, pleasure, integrity, humility, courage, self-confidence, acceptance of weakness and strength, commitment, loyalty, persistence, the ability to risk, excellence, and the acceptance of failure as well as success. As Ellis found, there seems to be

---

[6]Dreyfuss and Kelly, *All Things Shining*, 71.

[7]Ibid., 142, 220.

[8]For example, see Simon Robinson, "The Spiritual Journey," in *Sport and Spirituality: An Introduction*, eds. J. Parry, S. Robinson, N. Watson, and M. Nesti (London, UK: Routledge, 2007) 38–58; Jeffrey Scholes, "Professional Baseball and Fan Disillusionment: A Religious Ritual Analysis," *Journal of Religion and Popular Culture* 7 (Summer 2014): 1–14; Joseph L. Price, *Rounding the Bases: Baseball and Religion in America* (Macon, GA: Mercer University Press, 2006) 117, 125; Christopher H. Evans and William R. Herzog, II, eds. *The Faith of 50 Million: Baseball, Religion, and American Culture* (Louisville, KY: Westminster John Knox Press, 2002) 7, 48; and Michael Grimshaw, "I Can't Believe My Eyes: The Religious Ascetics of Sport as Post-Modern Salvific Moments" *Implicit Religion* 3, no. 2 (2002): 87–99.

widespread agreement that goods such as these have a formative influence on the character of sports followers and athletes.[9] As Feezell points out, sport, at its best, is meaningful activity in its "splendid triviality."[10] And the notion of meaningful moments in such trivial occurrences is perhaps as grandiose a notion as is needed.

Part of the meaningfulness of sport is hope. Fans and athletes share in the jubilation of success and the sadness of losing. Sometimes we make the mistake of thinking that hope is only alive in the winning. But the truth is much stranger. Losing does not seem to crush hope, and a shared loss can sometimes bring a community closer together. Furthermore, after the sadness of a loss is experienced, it is usually not long before talk of the next game, match, or event surfaces. For example, in 2014 tennis player Eugenie Bouchard made it to the Wimbledon finals, becoming the first Canadian to do so. She lost, and much lamenting followed among her Canadian fans. But almost immediately the media began to show interviews with people who had refocused on next year with optimism and hope for her success.

It is not losing that diminishes hope and fan support. Certainly the Chicago Cubs and their fans know this phenomenon (and, I should add humbly, the Toronto Maple Leafs and their fans, including me). Rather perhaps the greater threats to hope are those things that run contrary to the goods of sport. But even then, most fans seems to regroup and find some other reasons to keep cheering. For instance, it has been argued that since the mid-1990s fan support for professional baseball has taken a hit as a result of the greed of Major League Baseball players and owners. With no salary cap on what professional players can earn, only the teams with large markets and deep pockets can acquire the most able players. This reality sets up a self-perpetuating dynamic: the richest teams get the best players, win the most games, and so make more money increasing their profit margin over the poorer teams. This dynamic can disillusion fans, dampening hope that their team, if it is a financially poorer one, will ever win. Hope can be ground down by a system that favors the wealthy. Scholar Jeffrey Scholes

---

[9] Robert Ellis, "The Meaning of Sport: An Empirical Study into the Significance Attached to Sporting Participation and Spectating in the UK and US," *Practical Theology* 5, no. 2 (2012): 181.

[10] Feezell, *Sport, Philosophy, and Good Lives*, 66.

contends that such a system erodes hope even *"before the season starts....* [W]hen this hope is altered and diminished by agents operating outside of the means to better a baseball team from within, this religious dimension cannot exert itself fully into the psyche of certain fans, and the game that used to evoke fervor will continue to disappoint fans for all the wrong reasons."[11] Unlike Scholes, I am not convinced that overall fan hope is eroded; I think fan frustration is increased and the hope for an even playing field is diminished. But hope for the success of one's team, even against all odds, seems to persist. There is persistent belief in the David and Goliath tale; youthful David might still defeat the experienced giant; and the higher the odds against him, the greater the win.

Everyone wants "their" team or athlete to win. Sometimes against all odds winning happens, and the jubilation of that success is felt well beyond the participating athletes. These moments, though fleeting, are anticipated eagerly by athletes, coaches, and fans. Many team sports, including baseball, basketball, hockey, and football, are structured around predictable seasons with a beginning and an end. With the end of each season a championship team is crowned. The fans of the winners are jubilant and the losers, especially the team in the dreaded second place position, are left to mourn their loss. But these sorrows too are temporary; soon a new season will begin and with that season new hope.

Anticipation of the next season, game, or even play is an important component of hope. Winning is not the only thing that motivates athletes and fans; anticipation of competing and being in those moments is a powerful force. Dreams preceding an athletic event may know no bounds; athletes and fans almost always hold out hope for a repeated championship or an unexpected dramatic win. Even when victory does not occur, the hope preceding the outcome is powerful.

The hope experienced in watching a team compete is not only escapism. Watching a favorite team can stir more intense and lasting emotion than watching a good movie, reading a good book, or, sometimes,

---

[11]Scholes, "Professional Baseball and Fan Disillusionment: A Religious Ritual Analysis" (2004): 2, 10, 11. It should be noted that others including Price [*Rounding the Bases*, 73] refer to the *overall* doubling in pro-baseball attendance figures between approximately 1980 and 2005.

attending a worship service. Part of the experience is the communal character in a crowd of invested followers; there is a sense of belonging and sharing in a moving experience. These events, while trivial in some sense, are real. Real people, real dreams, real struggle, and the overcoming of obstacles are involved in the journey to each competition. Fans identify with their team and share in the wins and losses, and for some, hope for their team is connected to hope for transcending even greater limitations of everyday life including poverty, racism, and sexism. The determination of teams and individual athletes to never give up is enough, it seems, to ignite similar hope in their fans. While hope is stoked by winning, it also can be stoked by losing, because of the repeating structure of the seasons, and the communal nature of the experience.

Theologically, it is not winning to which Christians are exhorted. Rather it is to be in solidarity with the marginalized. Excessive self-glorification and disregard for one's competitors runs counter to Jesus' modeling of care and empowerment. The athlete who cares only about winning and is prepared to do so at any cost demonstrates no interest in the good that goes beyond being number one. Also, theologically, it is not sufficient to win at any cost even if one attributes one's win to God. Such claims raise questions about the meaning of losses and God's favor. Is God only with us when we win? Does God prefer one team or country over another? Does losing indicate God's rejection or negative judgment? Most theologians do not see God's presence and love as conditional but as free gifts of grace. To suggest that God is pleased only with a win (or a loss) is to refuse this grace and attribute to God human traits of petty punishment and conditional reward.

Christianity neither supports only those who win nor only those who lose. The narratives of Jesus' ministry have been understood as promoting hope for healing and success during this life. Much of the moral evaluation of success depends on the interpretation of success. Success, in the Jesus narratives, is not the accumulation of wealth or status but is faithfulness, solidarity with the marginalized, and the capacity to love.

The refusal to concede permanent defeat is congruent with Christianity, as is the celebration of a well-played game, win or lose. The healthy owning of one's power and successes, both in victory and defeat, is consistent with the conviction that everyone has been made in God's image. Everyone has the potential, therefore, to reveal a glimpse of God. Measured pride, combined with the humility of knowing that everyone is fallible, can help one to rise to one's potential. The refusal to take appropriate pride in an excellent performance is, in some sense, a refusal to accept the doctrine of the *imago Dei*.

The hope associated with anticipation has obvious religious parallels, as does the need to prepare and witness to one's faith through communal gathering, doing one's best, and the valuing of team mates and opponents.

Star Athletes

Identification with a team and their fan group makes one part of a community. Often, particular star athletes are singled out for admiration and emulation, thereby becoming role models. Fans buy shirts with their favorite player's number on them. Posters of individual athletes adorn walls. If one plays the same sport as one's favorite athlete, it can be a big coup to get that player's number as one's own. Followers often seek to play the game or perform in the sport using the same style as their role model.

Star athletes are regarded by some fans as more than role models; they become regarded as moral exemplars. Yet there is no reason to expect exemplary or even good moral behavior from someone known for the athletic skill alone. Although there are opportunities to develop virtuous character traits through sports participation such as loyalty, the ability to work well with others, dedication, persistence, and grace in winning and losing, there are also opportunities, particular at highly competitive levels, to learn less admirable traits. As we have discussed, power can be abused, teammates and coaches can be ruthless in their evaluations of each other, and players can be encouraged to carve out any kind of niche for themselves including that of a goon or intimidator. Sport (or institutional religion) does not necessarily instill good character; athletes are not better people simply because they perform their sport well or even superbly.[12]

Yet when we discover that our sports heroes have used banned substances, their fall from grace can be taken as a personal affront. For

---

[12] See for example, Joseph L. Price, "An American Apotheosis: Sport as Popular Religion" in *Religion and Popular Culture in America*, eds. Bruce David Forbes and Jeffrey H. Mahan (Berkeley: University of California Press, 2000) 214; and Randolph Feezell *Sport, Philosophy, and Good Lives*, chapter six.

example, Ben Johnson—Canada's running hero who won gold and set a new record in the 100-metre race at the Seoul Olympics—was stripped of his medal after being disqualified for doping. The attention paid to Johnson's disqualification twenty-five years later by the media is an indication of the national impression made by this event. Similarly, star athletes such as Olympian Oscar Pistorius who are charged criminally—but may have no sports infractions—also attract a lot of media attention and shock as these athletes have violated the moral expectations that are attached to being a sports star.

Fans invest in their favorite stars, and usually are very disappointed when their star's behavior does not measure up to high standards on or off the sports venue. Fans are proud to be associated with their star when their hero or heroine does something admirable, and can be defensive when their hero or heroine does something scandalous.

Loyal fans persistently defended Lance Armstrong, standing by him when he insisted repeatedly that he had not used banned substances. No matter how many witnesses said otherwise, Armstrong's staunchest defenders did not give up. As evidence mounted that he had used banned substances to win the Tour de France not once but seven times, there were still supporters who did not want to believe this. Others could not deny the evidence but stood by him, nonetheless, attributing responsibility to the nature of the Tour de France and the particular sports culture.[13] Armstrong came to represent not only the hope of repeated wins in what is one of the most grueling athletic competitions, but also the hope that comes from beating cancer *and* being the star athlete. Armstrong was the "ultimate symbol of hope, inspiration, and the limitless potential of the human will and spirit to the American audiences"[14] before the PED scandal. The real and fallible Armstrong became lost to public adoration of an archetypal image.

---

[13]There is a long history of performance enhancing substance use in the Tour de France. In 1924, for example, riders used various pills, "cocaine for the eyes and chloroform for the gums." [Raphaël Massarelli and Thierry Terret, "The Paradise Lost? Mythological Aspects of Modern Sport," *Sport, Ethics and Philosophy* 5, no. 4 (2011): 405.]

[14]Kyle Kusz, *Revolt of the White Athlete: Race, Media and the Emergence of Extreme Athletes in America* (New York: Peter Lang Publishing, 2007)139.

When he confessed his substance use and cover-up, he tumbled from his pedestal, but dedicated fans did not lose him entirely as a source of hope. When Armstrong appeared in a few televised moments as truly contrite, some people were still willing to embrace him as the imperfect human who, regardless of cheating, was still a great athlete. In some ways this humbled Armstrong was someone with whom one could more easily identify.

However, there is still a loss and let down among fans especially since Armstrong personified the dream of succeeding against the odds. So, too, with Pistorius, who succeeded despite missing both lower legs. After Pistorius's arrest for the murder of his girlfriend Reeva Steenkamp, the South African media reported that Pistorius was regarded as "a hero by both blacks and whites, transcending the racial divide of the country."[15] This loss, and numerous others including baseball's Barry Bonds and Jose Canseco, track and field's Marion Jones, and cycling's Floyd Landis, profoundly disappointed fans even though it is not rational to expect athletes to be morally better than anyone else.

Athletes know that much is expected of them. Many enjoy the public adoration and want to maintain their star status. Most try to hide the things they know will be seen as moral failures. Tiger Woods knew that his sexual affairs would not be well regarded and if known about would affect public regard for him, not to mention his huge endorsement contracts. Similarly, athletes who use banned substances can feel ashamed when exposed, knowing their behavior had defied the spirit and/or the rules of the sport.[16]

Preliminary qualitative research on a small sample of elite athletes who admitted using banned substances indicates that athletes experience guilt and shame as consequences of doping. Moreover, this same qualitative study suggests that the predominant motive for doping by elite athletes may not be to win but "*to stay in the sport for as long as possible.*" These findings are consistent with the theory that hope and human fulfillment are significant to

---

[15]Wire Services, "Murder or Accident?" *Kingston Whig-Standard* (Kingston, ON, 23 February 2013) 18.

[16]Kate Kirby, Aidan Moran, and Suzanne Guerin, "A Qualitative Analysis of the Experiences of Elite Athletes Who Have Admitted to Doping for Performance Enhancement," *International Journal of Sport Policy and Politics* 3, no. 2 (2011): 205–24.

the meaning of sport. Hope is built partly on notions of purity that include conforming to moral norms and maintaining bodily] purity. When athletes break the rules and transgress sporting ideals, likely they are conflicted. The high value placed on winning can put athletes in a bind: if they use banned substances they are bad, but if they fail to win, they are also bad.

In some ways, the expectations associated with star status are unreasonable. But athletes know that followers may seek to emulate them, and so their duty goes beyond an extreme individualism that says "I can do as I like, as long as I accept the consequences." The moral obligations of doing good and avoiding harm are at least as important as the assertion of individual choice.

Why would anyone want the to be a star athlete given the moral responsibility included in that status? Some reasons include: wanting to be the best, enjoying the adoration, realizing one's dreams, setting new goals, and achieving immortality. Star athletes, like most of us, want to be remembered and make a lasting—immortal—mark. Such desires are part of human vulnerability. Vulnerability and fragility in athletes affects the relationship with their fans. When fans are disappointed, they may distance themselves, but when star athletes are injured or suffer a loss, fans can be drawn closer. Theologically, superb performances by our star athletes inspire fans with the suggestion that many things are possible, but just as importantly, losses, injuries, and even the moral failures of our heroes and heroines serve as reminders of human frailty, and human fallibility. This vulnerability is part of the redemptive process because it underscores our need for each other, creation, and the transcendent.

Perfect Moments

Witnessing a perfect athletic moment is a liminal experience in which we engage with the Other as athletes touch what seems to be another world. The issue of perfection in athletic competition arises with regularity in literature on sport, religion, and spirituality.

A fundamental component of hope is the human quest for fulfillment, meaning, and happiness. Price reflects on the connection between perfect athletic moments and this quest for fulfillment: "[e]ven when the pursuit of a perfect performance in sport becomes corrupted or distorted—when it moves toward selfish goals rather than the joy and disclosive possibilities of play itself—it still manifests a fundamental human desire for fulfillment."[17] This desire for fulfillment is related to a yearning for the sacred. As theologian Gerald May asserts, "all humans have an inborn desire for God. Whether we are consciously religious or not, this desire is our deepest longing.... It gives us meaning....[W]e may experience it in different ways—as a longing for wholeness, completion, or fulfillment."[18]

Moments of perfection are part of the human experience. These moments can be fleeting but memorable and can inspire continued reaching toward perfection. Think of a hole-in-one in which the golfer's stroke seems almost effortless and time pauses before the ball clinks into the cup. Or the flawless ice-skating program by Jayne Torvill and Christopher Dean at the 1984 Winter Olympics. Or Mark Spitz's performance at the 1972 Olympics where, in the seven events in which he competed, he won seven gold medals and set seven world records. These are inspiring moments of athletic perfection that break expectations and fill the spectator with awe.

It might be said that true perfection is impossible, that it exists only in the realm of the imagination and with God. One of the reasons why the notion of human moments of perfection sometimes is resisted is the theological claim that only God is perfect; thus to claim perfection apart from that possessed by God would be to commit a Promethean sin showing disrespect for God. The meanings of human perfection and God's perfection are not clear, but there is no reason to assume that they are the same. Just as we are created in the image of God, and so have a glimmer of God within us, it may well be that we have perfect *moments* and that these moments are glimmers of God's perfection.

Perceptions of perfect moments are related to the eschatology debate: is all of the eschaton reserved for the end times when God has righted the world, or are there moments of realized eschatology in the here and now, as God's redemptive work is done with the participation of humanity. Theologies of the marginalized tend to favor the latter interpretation,

---

[17] Price, "An American Apotheosis: Sport as Popular Religion," 211.

[18] Gerald May quoted in Howard Clinebell, *Understanding and Counselling Persons with Alcohol, Drug, and Behavioral Addictions* (Nashville, TN: Abingdon, 1998) 272.

believing that God not only makes just relationship possible but requires human participation. Moreover, glimpses of perfection in the here and now empower and stimulate this participation in God's work. Moments of raw beauty that in some ways seem trivial, shine through as signifiers that we are capable of much more than we might think.

This search for perfect athletic moments does not preclude the recognition of human limits and fallibility. Rather, it assumes these limits and fallibility, which is why these few moments stand out as exceptional and so are celebrated: "For the immediate human existence sport is today the 'most important minor concern in the world,' offering endless possibilities for human happiness. These signs are better understood when one becomes aware of the imperfection of these moments of apex and one longs for an agglutination of the immediate with the definitive." [19] Perfect athletic moments offer hope that the almost unimaginable, never-before-done, is possible. Jürgen Moltmann sees Olympia, in its best form, as the expression of protest against barriers, divisiveness and oppression: "Olympia will be 'a symbol of hope' if its character as protest, as alternative, and as the prelude to freedom is stressed, in its contrast to burdened everyday life in the economic, political and social world. This is a primal human longing."[20]

Perfect athletic moments are mixed moments. As Michael Grimshaw suggests, they are instances of the sacred breaking into the profane[21]— moments of the "imperfect performer" bridging the gap between the transcendent and immanent, challenging their imagined bifurcation: Dick Fosbury's remarkable high jump, Nadia Comaneci's perfect ten in the 1976 Olympic gymnastics, Paul Henderson's stunning goal in 1972 Canada-Russia ice hockey series, and the list goes on.

A relentless demand, not quest, for perfection can be antithetical to the Christian message. A human understanding of perfection is distinct from God's perfection since humanity does not know perfection in the same way

---

[19]Dietmar Mieth, "A Christian Vision of Sport" in *Sport and Christianity: A Sign of the Times in the Light of Faith*, eds. Kevin L.C. Lixey, Christoph Hubenthal, Dietmar Mieth, and Norbert Muller (Washington, DC: Catholic University of America Press, 2012) 185.

[20]Jürgen Moltmann, "Olympia Between Politics and Religion," in *Sport*, eds. Gregory Baum and John Coleman (Edinburgh, UK: T & T Clark, 1989) 107.

[21]Grimshaw, "I Can't Believe My Eyes," 87.

as God. For example, we often prize wealth, status, and cultural beauty norms more than compassion, justice, and love. We can only glimpse God's perfection but this glimpse gives us opportunity to move closer to an eschatological vision. But because values other than compassion, justice, and love influence the world, human quests for perfection have yielded many tragedies and injustice.

An athlete's quest for perfection can include self-violence ranging from the muscle fiber tears needed to build muscular strength, to excessive thinness, to high risk-taking in extreme sports such as snowboarding and whitewater rafting. As I have discussed elsewhere, the moral assessment of violence is complicated, but at some point the harms caused by violence outweigh benefits.[22] This complicated relationship between religion, sport, and violence is exacerbated by the growing availability of risky enhancement means. As Loland warns, the "logic of the record performance is that 'enough is never enough.'"[23]

Perfection is complicated. When perceived with appreciation and awe, moments of athletic perfection can be inspiring, compelling athletes and observers to believe that what seems impossible might be possible.

Relational Embodiment

By embodiment I refer to the physical body dimension of a person that is intertwined with everything else that makes one human. Our physical bodies mediate how we experience the world and how the world experiences us, in an immediate way. Personhood, including relationships with self, others, ecology, and the divine, cannot be understood apart from embodiment. Relational embodiment is a location of hope in sport that concerns: the diversity of embodied persons and spiritual experiences of flow. First, we will consider embodied diversity as a location of hope in sport.

---

[22] Tracy J. Trothen, "Holy Acceptable Violence?: Violence in Hockey and Christian Atonement Theories," *The Journal of Religion and Popular Culture* 21 (2009): 1–42.

[23] Sigmund Loland, "A Well Balanced Life Based on 'The Joy of Effort': Olympic Hype or a Meaningful Ideal?" *Sport, Ethics and Philosophy* 6, no. 2 (2012): 155–62.

Redemption is about right relationship with God, which entails right relationship with self, others, and all of creation. God, as trinitarian, is community within Godself. The concept of the Trinity reflects the conviction that God is experienced in three different ways by humanity: as God the Creator, Sustainer (Holy Spirit), and Redeemer (Jesus Christ), but is one substance. Trinitarian language, in its complexity, communicates the mystery of God who is understood as profoundly relational, united, and diverse. Mike W. Austin sees the possibility of a "faint" glimmer of trinitarian diversity and unity in sports teams; there can be "unity of purpose as well as mutual commitment and sacrifice in pursuit of a goal" and diversity since sports teams are comprised of distinct individuals.[24]

Through a common purpose and shared commitment, sport has the potential to celebrate and unite a confluence of people from diverse racial, ethnic, and socio-economic backgrounds. In this way sport can offer hope and impetus for social transformation towards justice. For example, in 1947 Jackie Robinson, as a star player and the first African American to play major league baseball in the modern era, contributed to the American civil rights movement. Also, the championship performances of athletes who possess physical disabilities, such as Oscar Pistorius, challenge assumptions about the meaning and perceived limitations of disability. On a more subtle level, team sports offer the opportunity to step "lightly" into another's shoes by playing different positions. The world looks very different when playing forward from playing goal. The experience of trading positions or "perspectives" has the potential to help me understand the Other.[25]

However, sport has also reinforced barriers against athletes on the basis of sex, gender, disability, race, ethnicity, age, and sexual orientation. For example, Hayley Wickenheiser and all the women Olympic hockey players have helped challenge gender stereotypes simply by playing such a high level of hockey. It has been thought that women are not able to play hockey well or, if they do, they must be very "masculine" women. Gender stereotypes persist (witness the example of Caster Semenya) but they continue to be challenged in some Olympic sports. Another example is Michael Sam who,

---

[24]Mike W. Austin, "Sports as Exercises in Spiritual Formation," *Journal of Spiritual Formation & Soul Care* 3, no. 1 (2010): 68.

[25]Price, *Rounding the Bases*, 211.

in 2014, became the first American football player to come out as gay before being drafted by the St. Louis Rams. Cut by the Rams at the end of training camp, Sam has since been signed by the Montreal Alouettes in the Canadian Football League. Sam will be the first openly gay player in the CFL. His courageous identification of his sexual orientation contributes to the combat of homophobia.[26] Elite athletes can challenge preconceived notions and stereotypes. Sadly, many would-be-athletes continue to be excluded, pushed out, threatened, and bullied, because of their marginalized status.

It may be that more could be done with flow experiences to help educate athletes and others regarding the value of diversity. Experiences of flow states may help to increase openness through the sense that all life is connected, but this is not guaranteed. The loss of individual ego and concomitant sense of connection that is characteristic of flow can provide the opportunity for one to see past the humanly constructed barriers that damage relationships. Or, the athlete can enjoy the flow moment but fail to connect it to everyday life. Flow represents possibility, not guarantee. Perhaps more intentional reflection on these qualities and insights in flow experiences could assist in dismantling prejudice.

The potential for flow experiences to generate surprising moments of athletic perfection also fosters hope. Flow experiences can encourage belief that the extraordinary and unexpected happen and are within reach. Wins and losses are not guaranteed. There is hope in this ambiguity. This lack of certainty means more anxiety and also can make victorious moments even more meaningful. Similar to Jewish and Christian beliefs, in sport the future is not closed; there are always opportunities and no record is guaranteed to last.

Sport offers the possibility of a relational and vibrant embodied life. Athletics can inspire one to feel strong, able, and confident enough to try things that one otherwise may not. Sport also reminds us that we are limited. We cannot do everything and we cannot always win. We lose. We

---

[26]Some studies suggest that diversity can be promoted effectively in recreational sport, combating societal prejudices [See, for example, William Bridel and Genevieve Rail, "Sport, Sexuality, and the Production of (Resistant) Bodies: De-/Re-Constructing the Meanings of Gay Male Marathon Corporeality," *Sociology of Sport Journal* 24 (2007): 127–44.]

get injured. Sport offers a glimmer of the power and limitations of being human. And there is hope in that.

Sport can correct the notion that we are made up of discreet parts: body, spirit, and mind. Particularly in a culture that undervalues the body and valorizes the rational mind, we need to be reminded that we are intertwined as embodied beings. And this complex unity makes us human. There is some knowledge that must be experienced physically to have meaning. Flow experiences illuminate that point and can increase awareness that the mind is not confined to the brain. The themes of diversity and unity are apparent in embodied humanity. We simply lack the words to explain adequately what it means to be embodied humans. And, we struggle with the interconnection and interdependence of all life in its diversity. The coexistence of diversity and unity is something that escapes many of us on a social and global level. Sport can help challenge the easy categorizing and bifurcations that separate us from ourselves, the cosmos, others, and the holy.

The capacity to take joy in being embodied persons with limitations and strengths can be encouraged in sport. Sport provides the opportunity to celebrate the power, possibilities, and struggles associated with being embodied persons. Sport does not allow one to forget one's body. And sport, when it is at its best, teaches participants that the person is a complex unity of body, spirit, and mind: no one part can or should be denied. It is the person as a whole who experiences flow states, hope, sadness, and all that comes with life.

In the final analysis, it is perhaps the mystery and the continuity in sport that lie at the root of hope. We don't know if our team will win or lose. We don't know when to expect the next perfect athletic moment. We don't know all the ingredients that make for a stunning performance. We don't know how morally upright our sports stars are. We see reason to hope and we see possibilities through witnessing the unexpected. We know there will be future opportunities.

When Hope Meets Techno-science

While it is difficult sometimes to discern good from evil or virtue from vice, we must try. The assessment of the use of techno-science creations in sport is complicated, and there is no single answer regarding how best to use these creations. However, there are several criteria that are used to evaluate the ethics of enhancement use in sport. I suggest that the recognition of the intersection of sport with religion adds an important dimension, reshaping this discussion.

In the secular religion of sport, meaning and that which is sacred are experienced in different ways for different people. Sport offers metaphorical responses to questions of meaning including why some win and some lose, even when all appear equal or when a losing team or athlete has evidenced repeatedly that they are "better": How can one persist in the face of very low odds or repeated failure? How can one negotiate relationships when one experiences enmity? How can one rise above one's perceived limit? And from where does that unexpected inspiration or propulsion come?

While this secular religion is not the same as traditional religions such as Christianity, Buddhism, Judaism, Taoism and others, the decline of religious affiliations and participation in the United States, the United Kingdom, and Canada has not meant that theological notions of the sacred, meaning, and hope have simply disappeared. Rather, people search for these elsewhere. Sport provides, perhaps even more than ever, a sense of the sacred, and a source of hope and meaning for many.

In considering the acceptability of techno-science options in sport, the function of sport as a source of hope must be prominent. Enhancement options are sure to interact with the sacred dimension of sport, and hope, as a spiritual quality, will be affected. An examination of the four main ethical approaches to the sportenhancement debate shows that the relevance of the religious dimension of sport to the use of techno-science in sport has not yet been considered. Techno-science choices have implications for the spiritual dimension of sport and particularly for hope. With the decline of mainstream religious affiliation, sport's spiritual dimension is becoming even more important to followers' well-being. A comprehensive approach to the techno-science sport debate must address this spiritual dimension and, particularly, hope.

Chapter 7

Approaches to the Enhancement Debate in Sport

There have been four main approaches to the sport enhancement ethics debate. These approaches have been limited by certain assumptions including the reduction of enhancements to doping or to added enhancements, a decisionist focus, and the acceptance of social and technological normative values.

Many ethicists have recognized that enhancements go beyond that which is considered "normal," and the general understanding of what counts as an enhancement has been expanding. However, most ethicists do not consider the use of science to reveal existing advantages as part of the enhancement debate. Particularly as germline genetic modification technologies emerge, the relevance of this dimension of the issue will grow. For example, if in the future someone uses a germline genetic modification technology to increase their oxygen carrying capacity, passes this enhancement onto their children, and one of these children becomes an Olympic marathoner, how should this enhancement be assessed? Currently, the use of science in, for example, gender testing or testing for other genetic anomalies is not usually (although it has been considered occasionally) considered to be directly relevant to the enhancement debate.

Part of the reason for this exclusion is the prevailing decisionist focus. As I discussed earlier, decisionist ethics are concerned with what to do in a situation, and the weighing of the possible outcomes of these choices. Decisionist approaches are action oriented and geared to an end. Principles, duties, and consequences are accorded varying degrees of importance in decisionist models. Regarding the sport enhancement issue, ethical analyses have focused on how to decide what should be banned and what should be permitted to enhance athletic performances. While this question is very important and pressing on a public policy level, it is important not to lose sight of virtue ethics questions that are not as concerned with decisions regarding the acceptability of enhancements but with character. Character includes questions of motivation and values. [1] What drives us to pursue enhancements? What do we believe makes us better? Why is sport valued so highly? Why does it attract so many followers and participants? These questions go to the heart of what we value and for what we long. A more conscious and critical understanding of the values and desires underlying the sport enhancement debate is necessary to well informed decision-making.

Although the development of effective policy is crucial, this need not preclude going beyond a decisionist focus to consider underlying values and epistemological issues, including the use of scientific knowledge to reveal existing advantages. Expanding the issue to address values and epistomology will not simplify the debate. However, it will help to clarify why this debate is so loaded; it has to do with much more than the development of a list of banned substances and paraphernalia versus acceptable enhancements.

Almost all ethical analyses of the use of technology and science in sport, and particularly in elite sports, have framed the issue in an exclusively decisionist manner that implicitly accepts normative values. I want an approach that questions the underlying normative values and epistemology issues such as embodiment categories and takes seriously sports' spiritual and religious dimensions.

I have distilled the main approaches to the sport enhancement debate into four categories: Those that are based on: 1. individual rights and potential physical harms; 2. conceptions of fairness in athletic competitions; 3. the internal goods of each particular sport or sports more generally; and 4. a distinction between therapy and enhancement. Recognizing that no one approach is going to address every concern, I will summarize and critique each. The spiritual and religious dimension of sport, as established earlier, will be considered in relation to these approaches.

Individual Rights and Potential Physical Harms

The strong emphasis on rights based arguments can make it appear that it is as simple as consenting adults making a choice to use enhancements or not. Proponents of athletes' access to enhancement techno-science usually appeal to the individual choice, making the case that athletes should have greater freedom to choose techno-science creations that

---

[1]See chapter two, pp. 33-34.

enhance their performance so long as these creations are available, not used for the purpose of gaining a covert competitive edge, and accessible to all competitors. The argument is usually as follows: If the use of these technologies or substances is transparent and if athletes consent to any risks or other potential consequences, then they ought to be free to make that choice. The only type of enhancing intervention that raises concerns for most proponents of individual choice are germline genetic technologies because future generations cannot consent to such interventions. In short, the argument centers on expressed individual desire and choice.

To question the authenticity of an athlete's desire (that informs a choice) is considered by some as not only paternalistic but dehumanizing. For example, sports philosopher Claudio Tamburruni and Torbjörn Tännsjö state that there is no reason to question the authenticity of athletes' desires to use an enhancing substance. To do so, they argue, would necessarily suggest that no athlete can have authentic desires.[2] And ethicist Andy Miah fleshes out his support for individual choice with the qualification that the decision to use enhancement technologies and particularly genetic modification technologies must be motivated not by a desire to enhance performance but by the desire to create a way of being human that is closer to one's authentic self.

Authenticity of desire and choice are difficult to unveil. This difficulty is at the core of the problem with most individual choice approaches. A liberal individualism does not probe the relevance of context and global relationships. It assumes that the individual is separate, and under no constraints that cannot be overcome through the exercise of will. Relational and gender theorists have shown that an understanding of process is necessary to an understanding of choice. In other words, as researcher Susan Sherwin reminds us, we do not arrive at our values, beliefs, and desires through a purely individual process. Rather we come to hold certain values through engagement with our socio-cultural contexts.[3] These values then

---

[2] Claudio Tamburruni and Torbjörn Tännsjö, "Enhanced Bodies," in *Enhancing Human Capacities*, eds. Julian Savulescu, Ruud ter Meulen, and Guy Kahane (Oxford, UK: Wiley-Blackwell, 2011) 274–90.

[3] Susan Sherwin, "Genetic Enhancement, Sports and Relational Autonomy," in *Sport, Ethics and Philosophy* 1, no. 2 (2007): 171–80.

contribute to our desires, which are connected to our hopes. If I want to teach well and to accumulate a healthy savings account, then as long as I have some reason that makes sense to me, I will hope to attain these things. These desires and hopes are informed by my values of stability, security, and achievement. Or it may be that I hope only to survive each day. My only desire is for my family and friends to find enough food and water to make it through another day, reflecting values of physical life, close relationships, and survival. Any additional hopes in this last scenario are reserved for another life after death.

Feminist relational theorists have shown that our values do not always support our best interests. Oppressive values can be internalized and serve to maintain conditions that are harmful to oneself and others.[4] These values are not freely chosen and do not reflect unfettered authentic desires, although they may appear to do so. Rather, they are embraced as part of a coping and survival mechanism. The meaningful question is not what one chooses but rather what processes have informed one's values, desires, and hopes.

Arguments based on individual choice do not account sufficiently for the complexities of content. Proponents of this approach do not typically give much weight to the processes that affect choice, including the culture of elite sports and other contextual factors. Context may be considered but is not seen as significantly affecting one's ability to make authentic choices. Additionally, possible effects of these decisions that go beyond that individual are not usually seen as important enough to modify the emphasis on choice.

Liberal individualism is only one way to understand autonomy and the exercise of choice. A relational understanding of autonomy is another way. This way supports individual rights, including the power to make choices, but limits these rights and identifies challenges to knowing one's values, desires, and hopes, as morally relevant. Choice has import beyond the individual making the choices. Systemic power imbalances including those between men and women, abled and disabled, rich and poor, different races

---

[4]See, for example, sociologist Gillian A. Walker's thorough study of abuse [*Family Violence and the Women's Movement: the Conceptual Politics of Struggle* (Toronto, ON: University of Toronto Press, 1990)].

and ethnicities, mean that some have greater capacity to choose "freely" and act on these choices than do others.

Not only is power unequally distributed, there are also strong, value-laden messages that influence what come to feel like our values, authentic desires, and hopes. A liberal individualism has become normal in the West. So, too, have become the technologically driven values of efficiency and utility. This emphasis on liberal individualism, efficiency, and utility exaggerates the importance of an ends focused approach to elite sport: individual winning performances have always been important, but now efforts towards this goal have expanded to full-time work and the engagement of the most advanced scientific knowledge and technologies. In turn, this exaggerated value placed on winning shapes the desire to use enhancement options.

Having established that context and values influence how one understands autonomy and what one desires, we will examine common objections to freedom of choice arguments. These objections are: there is undue (if not coercive) pressure on elite athletes to choose enhancements that are used by their peers; not every athlete has equal access to enhancement technologies; there are significant potential harms associated with some enhancements; and athletes, as role models, have a moral duty to avoid using any enhancing substances that are perceived as dope. These objections, respectively, are countered by proponents of liberal individual choice as: paternalistic and/or inconsistent with the nature of sport; temporary; and inappropriate or insignificant. I will consider each objection and counter argument.

Consent, some argue, is compromised in elite sports by the extreme pressure to win or be ranked competitively. If other athletes in a particular sport are using an enhancing technique or substance, then the use of the enhancement typically spreads. The 1998 Tour de France is viewed often as an infamous example of this dynamic wherein more than fifty riders either admitted to, or tested as, having used banned substances to enhance their performance. Athletes may be faced with choosing between using the enhancements or no longer being competitive.

Complicating the matter, not all athletes or aspiring athletes would have access to the same range of enhancing options; not all competitors would be able to make the same choices. For example, the more recent

FINA-approved super swimsuits such as Speedo's LZR Elite Recordbreaker Kneeskin 2 sold for about $330 (US) in 2014. This swimsuit is 100 percent textile and is legitimate for competitive use. Unfortunately, the suits seem to last for only three to five races. It would be particularly difficult for an up-and-coming swimmer who did not yet have sponsors to afford the cost of this enhancing swimsuit. The suit is said to improve times by 2 to 3 percent, which can be significant in a close competition.

Allowing athletes to use enhancing technologies such as cutting-edge swimsuits or currently banned substances such as ephedrine is seen by some ethicists as unacceptable, even if not quite coercive, since it can mean choosing between being competitive or not. Indeed, sport's nutritionist Kate Kirby's small qualitative study suggests that elite athletes who "dope" do so to a significant degree because of a desire to stay in the game.[5] When the desire to stay in the game is so strong, it is not surprising that some and perhaps many athletes would choose using an enhancement—banned or not, expensive or affordable, safe or risky—over no longer playing. It is reasonable to expect that most elite athletes' "desires" will conform to the normative expectations of elite sport, systemic dynamics, and their particular contexts.

Freedom of choice proponents point out that the undue pressure argument is inconsistent. Pressure is accepted when it comes to intensive training regimens, or the use of equipment such as hypobaric chambers that are permitted in particular sports. If athletes want to stay in the game and be competitive, they must abide by their coaches and the training developed for them. Perhaps the issue of choice begs more of a cultural critique—both within sport and more broadly—than mere agreement or disagreement. It may be that there is a problem with the pressure within sports to conform to all training expectations and to use accepted enhancements.

A liberal individualism fails to ask about the processes that influence one's values and desires, i.e., the factors that constrain and empower decision making. Athletes are pressured often to follow the training program set out by the coaching team, or to follow a particular nutritional program. Because

---

[5]Kate Kirby, Aidan Moran, and Suzanne Guerin, "A Qualitative Analysis of the Experiences of Elite Athletes Who Have Admitted to Doping for Performance Enhancement," *International Journal of Sport Policy and Politics* 3, no. 2 (2011): 221.

it appears that the ethical reasoning is inconsistent (pressure within some parameters of sport is acceptable whereas it would not be acceptable regarding the use of what are currently banned enhancements), the conclusion is that the argument must be correct: athletes should be able to choose any enhancement that they desire and they are able to make that choice freely. A better approach would be to note that on one level the objections to individual choice are illogical, and then to ask what is behind this illogic. Maybe the objections to enhancements are based on repugnance and/or a legalistic approach that reflects the current rules. Or maybe objections stem from a more substantive awareness of the causal dynamics that shape desire and hope.

Another facet of the objection to individual choice concerns potential physical harms: athletes must be protected not so much from their own risky choices but particularly from others who might impose these risks on them if there were open access to enhancements. There are at least two initial questions that are asked of this objection. One, how serious are such health risks? And second, how are these risks any different from the risks already accepted by elite athletes?

Some argue there are minimal health risks associated with most currently banned enhancing substances. As Verner Møller points out, "the substances that athletes dope themselves with are forms of medicine developed to *improve* human health."[6] But the fact that these substances are derived from medicines that are used to improve health does not mean there are *no* risks associated with the use of these substances. EPO use, for example, has a risk of blood clotting and sudden death. Other substances such as ephedrine would have to be consumed in extremely high doses (beyond that which would be performance enhancing) to pose any health risk. Little is known about possible side effects of many predicted enhancement technologies, such as genetic modification technologies, and it seems reasonable to expect that even when such technologies become approved for use by health agencies, there may be additional unknown risks.

The second critique of the possible harms objection is similar to that regarding the undue pressure objection: the argument is inconsistent.

---

[6]Verner Møller, *The Ethics of Doping and Anti-Doping: Redeeming the Soul of Sport?* (New York: Routledge, 2010) 8.

Because athletes accept the risk of injury and potentially even death while engaging in their sport, and the choice of whether or not to assume this risk is left to the athlete, some reason that—to be consistent—athletes should also be permitted to make their own choices regarding the use of risky enhancements. Not all proponents of individual choice reject concerns about health risks, and advocate free usage of any enhancing substance simply because athletes are willing to take risks that are associated with their sport.[7] Some supporters of choice argue that athletes should not be able to choose enhancements until they are proven medically safe. Others argue that as long as information regarding the risks is clear, athletes should be able to choose the enhancement just as they are able to choose their sport regardless of the risk level.

For many elite athletes physical safety, including health, is but one value and is not prioritized over other values such as finding a competitive advantage[8] or optimizing one's performance or staying competitive.[9] Competitive sports are risky by definition. Extreme sports such as aerial skiing, snowboarding, free solo climbing, and whitewater kayaking are particularly risky, and athletes are not prevented from choosing them. Even supposedly "mainstream" sports carry risks of serious injury or death. Hockey, for example, involves bodies traveling at high speeds with sharp blades. Particularly for female athletes, excessive thinness is a problem[10] as athletes aim for that perfect form or optimal weight for competitive weight categories or lifting in the case of pairs figure skating. Excessive thinness can cause health concerns including eating disorders, amenorrhea, and lower

---

[7]Andy Miah, "From Anti-Doping to a 'Performance Policy': Sport Technology, Being Human, and Doing Ethics," *European Journal of Sport Science* 5, no. 1 (2005): 52.

[8]Brent M. Kious, "Philosophy on Steroids: Why the Anti-Doping Position Could Use a Little Enhancement," *Theoretical Medicine and Bioethics* 29 (2008): 217.

[9]Kirby et al., "A Qualitative Analysis of the Experiences of Elite Athletes Who Have Admitted to Doping for Performance Enhancement" (2011): 220.

[10]Michelle M. Lelwica, "Losing Their Way to Salvation: Women, Weight Loss, and the Salvation Myth of Culture Lite," in *Religion and Popular Culture in America,* eds. Bruce David Forbes and Jeffrey H. Mahan (Berkeley: University of California Press, 2000) 180–200.

bone mineral content. Training itself poses health risks as athletes are pushed by themselves and their coaches to excel.

Clearly not all risks to physical well-being are bad. There is some degree of risk in everyday living for all of us. But where is the line between acceptable and unacceptable violence? From a relational autonomy perspective, the beginning point must be the investigation of factors that inform values and desires concerning violence to the self in sport. A thorough investigation would be far beyond the scope and intent of this chapter, but I do contend that there are systemic and epistemological factors that render the issue of choice far more complex than a simple individual yes or no. I will suggest that these factors relate to sport's spiritual dimension and, in particular, to the function of hope.

Many ingredients go into the construction of the sports hero. These ingredients include the willingness and capacity to endure physical pain, and the ability to overcome significant obstacles both in competition and more personally, e.g. debilitating injury, serious illness, harsh upbringing, and poverty. Fans tend to identify with their sports stars. Their humanity is like but not like mine. The theorized reasons for this identification vary. Some say that humanity has always needed scapegoats to redeem our purity and to be a link to God.[11] Sports stars can serve this purpose, and are often judged harshly as they inevitably fail to meet unrealistic expectations. Some critics take exception to this claim, contending that fans have become disillusioned and no longer see sports heroes and heroines as role models; rather, the only hope these heroes/heroines offer is the conviction that you too can become a sports star because the means to become so (doping) is "in everyone's reach."[12] However, most believe that star athletes continue to be perceived as not only role models but even as moral exemplars.[13] Most often, as Feezell notes, star athletes are only deserving of the assessment that they play their

---

[11] Half-human and half-divine scapegoats are able to bridge the perceived gap between humans and the gods. [See, for example, Raphaël Massarelli and Thierry Terret, "The Paradise Lost? Mythological Aspects of Modern Sport," *Sport, Ethics and Philosophy*, 5, no. 4 (2011): 403; and Carwyn Jones, "Drunken Role Models: Rescuing Our Sporting Exemplars" *Sport, Ethics and Philosophy* 5, no. 4: 422.

[12] Massarelli and Terret, "The Paradise Lost?" 396.

[13] Randolph Feezell, *Sport, Philosophy, and Good Lives* (Lincoln: University of Nebraska Press, 2013) 131–54.

sport very well. However, sometimes the athletic hero/ines are truly admirable people. I think of hockey legends Wayne Gretzky, Darryl Sittler, Haley Wickenheiser, or Paul Henderson, who have inspired countless followers to become better people and athletes. Of course, it is equally easy to think of bad examples, those who failed to live up to the moral expectations associated with their hero/ine status.

There is no rational reason to expect that someone is living a virtuous life because they play a sport exceptionally well. Yet these athletes are role models, whether they signed on for that or not, and are responsible for the power associated with that status, just as professionals in other disciplines like medicine or academia are responsible for the power that comes with those credentials and status.

Sports stars have the added dimension of demonstrated physical and mental capacity to withstand large amounts of physical duress. We admire them for overcoming pain and the fear of that pain. From where does this admiration of physical suffering and capacity to withstand pain come? Christian theologies that glorify purity, innocence, self-sacrifice, and physical suffering as salvific contribute to this admiration of the capacity to withstand pain. As I have argued elsewhere,[14] atonement theologies or interpretations of God's saving actions in the world through the crucifixion and resurrection of Jesus have contributed to the distorted belief that the endurance of physical pain is a moral good regardless of cause. Sports hero/ines are symbols of hope. And the meaning of hope is influenced by values promoted by culturally derived norms, including those informed by religion (whether or not one claims to be religious) and technology.

The capacities to endure pain and take risks are not the only elements needed to be a sports hero/ine. The hero/ine or role model must also live up to standards of purity and excellence. This combination of qualities can add up to a conundrum for the athlete, especially if enhancement use is left to individual "choice." First, the avoidance of using some enhancements on the basis of risk of pain would not be a sufficient reason since athletes are supposed to withstand pain and not complain. Second, purity prohibits the

---

[14]Tracy J. Trothen, "Holy Acceptable Violence?: Violence in Hockey and Christian Atonement Theories," *The Journal of Religion and Popular Culture*, 21 (2009): 1–42.

use of any technology or substance that would be perceived to alter or compromise the body and sport. Third, excellence requires that an athlete go to any length possible to optimize her or his performance but not to cheat.

The use of banned enhancements is, at least for now, associated with poor character. This association is due to at least two related assumptions. First the term "enhancements" has come to be equated, on a popular level, with banned substances and particularly "doping." Second, athletes who use banned substances are thought of as being no different from shallow stereotypes of people who use street drugs: they lie and cheat, and they deserve to be caught and punished. This reasoning ignores the complexities influencing the use of banned enhancing substances.

In addition to breaking notions of purity and stirring up stereotypes of drug users, is a deeper and more serious issue. I suspect that underlying strong reactions to star athletes who have been caught using prohibited substances is anger and dismay that they have tarnished what they represent to us: hope. If athletes' enhancement use may affect the hope that is so important to followers, this must be factored in to the enhancement debate. Although it seems that most fans' hope is resilient and persistent, we do not know at what point hope may be eroded.

Simple reasoning that it is up to each person to make good choices or bad choices and that is the end of it, is reassuring on the one hand. On the other, this approach denies the complexities of the processes through which values and desires are acquired, and the potential consequences of individual choices on others. While choice is an important factor, a more relational approach to autonomy is necessary in order to address the many factors that confront athletes and complicate the process of making choices.

The consideration of causal dynamics and potential consequences to others becomes even more complicated if the enhancement debate is broadened, as I argue it ought to be, to include the use of science to reveal existing advantages. If a criterion of individual choice is transparency of advantages (e.g., no covert advantages), then presumably all advantages, including existing advantages, would have to be disclosed. With the anticipated advent of Athletes' Biological Passports, much more will become known about each athlete's existing advantages. If this information were made transparent and thus available to anyone, it may have implications for the parameters of choice. Would athletes be able to choose hormonal enhancement if their competitors have higher levels, for example, of testosterone? On the basis of what criteria would some enhancements be prohibited from choice? Would the desire to win be the only factor informing athletes' choices?

Motive is very complex and impossible to know fully even within oneself. Motive to choose enhancements or not has to do with values and desires. I posit that authenticity requires the identification and examination of underlying factors that shape desires so that we more self-consciously understand what drives us and why. To know what counts as authentic desire—or desire that is truly our own—is an ongoing, incomplete process. The identification of authenticity is helpful in that it redirects attention back to the ontological issue of what it means to be human. I propose that hope, as a spiritual quality, is at the core of what it means to be human. And until we know more about what it is that we truly desire, we are doomed to remain unsatisfied, unfulfilled, caught in an endless spiral of wanting more.[15]

Individual choice will not address the self-awareness needed to understand the processes that have shaped our values and desires. Until we better understand these processes, individual choice is an insufficient criterion for making decisions about enhancement use by athletes. We need additional criteria to inform enhancement use.

Fairness

Most definitions of sport include mention of the spirit of sport, and this spirit includes fairness. For example, the World Anti-Doping Agency (WADA) explains that the "spirit of sport" is what is intrinsically valuable about sport. It is the "celebration of the human spirit, body and mind, and is characterized by the following values: Ethics, fair play and honesty; Health; Excellence in performance; Character and education; Fun and joy; Teamwork; Dedication and commitment; Respect for rules and laws; Respect for self and other *Participants*; Courage; Community and

---

[15]Patrick D. Hopkins, "A Salvation Paradox for Transhumanism: *Saving* You versus Saving *You*," in *Religion and Transhumanism: The Unknown Future of Human Enhancement*, eds. Calvin Mercer and Tracy J. Trothen (Westport, CT: Praeger, 2015) 71–82.

solidarity."[16] Detractors point out that the meanings of these values cannot be pinned down. Because the meanings of these values are not completely clear, the argument goes, the values and the use of the phrase "spirit of sport" are not helpful to the sport enhancement debate.

I disagree. While it is true that there is no consensus about what these values mean and even what elements characterize the spirit of sport,[17] there is a *general* sense that this spirit of sport is about human virtue in the context of physical challenge. While values and virtues are impossible to name definitively, attempts reflect general understandings of the positive features of athletics. Without normative attempts, such as that made by WADA, assumed values are reinforced. Regardless of the difficulties in defining values, it is important to recognize that sport can and does promote notions of virtue and what it means to be an admirable athlete and person. As a result, attempts to define the spirit of sport or sport's values are important as long as they are recognized as generalizations.

What I find more debatable is WADA's choice of values that are identified as intrinsic to the "spirit of sport," which is defined as "the celebration of human spirit, body and mind." While in many ways the list is quite comprehensive, it shies away from the spiritual dimension of sport in spite of recognizing the human spirit as part of sport. For example, "resilience and hope" could be added as values intrinsic to sport. Or, it may be that hope is not so much a value as a propositional attitude (e.g., a mental state) and is implicit in all of the values named. I see hope as more than that—it is a spiritual quality that has a shaping effect on values and, more generally, on how we live. Understood in this way, hope is implicit in the "spirit of sport" and threaded throughout the values listed. But because it is not common to talk about hope explicitly, we need words to remind us of the importance of hope in sport. Otherwise, hope is overlooked when we reflect on the meaning of sport, and ethical issues in sport.

---

[16] WADA 2009 "Fundamental Rationale for the World Anti-Doping Code" in World Anti-Doping Code, www.wada-ama.org/Documents/Anti-Doping_Community/WADA_Anti-Doping_CODE_2009_EN.pdf, 13.

[17] See Tara Magdalinski, *Sport, Technology and the Body: The Nature of Performance* (New York: Routledge, 2009) 17; and Møller, *The Ethics of Doping and Anti-Doping*, 14.

What if the spiritual dimension of sport was included in this list of values? How might this explicit inclusion reshape or influence the sport enhancement debate? One possibility is that a predominant concern about enhancement use would be how an enhancing technology might affect the spiritual dimension of sport.

As it is, fairness is the value at the crux of many discussions about sport enhancement. Fairness is also defined in ways that reflect normative Western secular faith claims including extreme individualism. Those who favor this approach to the sport enhancement debate are concerned primarily with undue advantages among competitors.

The most recent fairness based proposal for assessing whether or not an athlete has used banned substances is the concept of phenotypic plasticity. As previously discussed, the Athletic Biological Passport would allow for the fairness of advantages to be assessed on the basis of what is natural for each individual athlete. The concept of fairness is difficult to apply particularly given the roles of genetics and phenotypic plasticity in determining trainability as well as responsiveness to various enhancing agents. However, as discussed earlier, this solution cannot address the assessment of acceptable baseline "naturalness," i.e., how much of a genetic anomaly and which genetic anomalies are deemed acceptable? The phenotypic plasticity approach assumes that natural advantages are fair whereas procured advantages are not, posing an interesting conundrum in that what is average biologically among elite athletes is not average (or normal) among the general population. The passport would chart each individual athlete's baseline and could show any changes that occur within that individual. How and who interprets these baselines and any changes is key to the effectiveness of the passport.

Although many genetic anomalies are considered fair, some are not. Pistorius, born without lower fibulae, needed surgery and prosthetics to become mobile. In a sense, his cheetah legs are normal for him. However, there has been much concern expressed regarding the fairness of Pistorius's running blades. Noting that while other athletes with disabilities have competed successfully in the Olympics (for example, deaf athlete Jeff Float competed in 1984 and won a gold medal in swimming), Brendan Burkett, Mike McNamee and Wolfgang Potthast observe that, with one possible exception, these Olympians did not employ technologies that may have given them an edge. The exception was Neroli Fairhall who, in the 1984 Olympics, competed in archery events while in a wheelchair that some argue may have given her additional stability. In the end, Burkett and his colleagues conclude that Pistorius's prostheses give him an advantage in terms of greater efficiency.[18] But most importantly, they argue that fairness can distract attention from what they consider the more problematic issue (which is assessed on pp. 154-56): Does Pistorius actually "run"? Others remain committed to the criterion of unfair advantage, including major sports' regulating bodies such as WADA.[19]

It is important to ensure some degree of fairness in sports competitions. To do this, it has to be decided what fairness means generally and how it should be applied. "Fair play" is an expected and noble dimension of sport. Although the definition of fairness is not completely clear, there is a general sense that fairness has to do with equipment standards and compliance to rules. There is also the expectation that athletes bring different and often very beneficial physical characteristics to the game, and that these are fair because they are natural. A degree of physical diversity due to one's genetic make-up is expected and accepted as fair within certain sport-specific parameters.

Of course, even seemingly simple parameters like these are not simple at all. Caster Semenya, for example, disrupted expectations of acceptable limits even though her advantages (if there were any) were genetic and arguably "natural." Why have Semenya and Pistorius not been seen as natural models of ideal athletes and instead have attracted charges of unfair advantage? Connected to how we decide what constitutes an "enhancement" is how we decide what counts as an ideal embodiment characteristic instead of an undesirable embodiment characteristic.

---

[18] Brendan Burkett, Mike McNamee, and Wolfgang Potthast, "Shifting Boundaries in Sports Technology and Disability: Equal Rights or Unfair Advantage in the Case of Oscar Pistorius?," *Disability & Society* 26, no. 5 (August 2011): 643–54. See also Mark Sutcliffe, "Amputee Sprinter Treads Uneven Track," *The Ottawa Citizen* 13 January 2008, http://www2.canada.com.

[19] See for example, Sutcliffe "Amputee Sprinter Treads Uneven Track," 13 January 2008, http://www2.canada.com; and Tamburrini "What's Wrong With Genetic Inequality? The Impact of Genetic Technology on Elite Sports and Society."

Both Semenya and Pistorius visibly disrupt essentialised embodiment categories. Notions of fairness tend to assume a normative ordering of the world. Most obvious, in a normative ordering as it applies to sport, are embodiment features that are visible and that threaten expectations. Semenya's masculine physical characteristics attracted resistance and charges of unfair advantage. She looked too much like a man. Pistorius's prostheses are very visible and assessed as not normal or natural and therefore have generated suspicion. Is what he does on the track recognizable as running? More importantly, what if he can run faster than able-bodied athletes? In short, neither athlete fits into normative embodiment categories, and this lack of fit generates discomfort or sometimes, as professor of religious studies Don Braxton posits, disgust.[20]

Fairness is a matter of perspective. What is fair to the majority of athletes who appear to fit into these normative categories is likely not fair to those who are judged to fall outside of them. Yet, invisible (or barely visible) nonconformity to embodiment categories is often assumed acceptable. In fact, so long as these differences are mostly invisible few questions are raised beyond testing for banned substances. For example, although multi-gold medal winner swimmer Michael Phelps possesses some physical variance from the average male athlete's body, these differences are not judged significant. Often more problematic in terms of actual athletic advantage are invisible genetic anomalies, such as high hemoglobin levels or the capacity to respond at an unusually high level to training, that give an athlete a distinct advantage in competitions. These anomalies are often ignored. Some diversity is seen as enhancing while too much and especially very *visible* diversity is judged unfair or repulsive.

Perhaps fairness could be addressed by creating more categories within sport to better match competitors. The Paralympic Games, in which embodiment diversity is often much more visible, have numerous categories

---

[20]Donald M. Braxton, "Does Transhumanism Face an Uncanny Valley Among the Religious?" in *Religion and Transhumanism: The Unknown Future of Human Enhancement*, eds. Calvin Mercer and Tracy J. Trothen (Westport, CT: Praeger, 2015) 331–50.

in an attempt to more evenly match competitors.[21] Athletes are classified in different sports according to disability, size, sex, and age. But there are problems with this strategy. Why are basketball players not divided into categories by height? Why are there male and female divisions for archery?[22] And who gets to decide what differences are most significant? Ultimately, the argument is often made that we simply want to know who is best in a given sport regardless of congenital or acquired advantages.[23] As Ivo van Hilvoorde and Laurens Landeweerd note, this ongoing debate reflects the "'struggle' to find the right balance between a good competition based on differences in talent on the one hand and the demonstration of excellence within a group with relevant similar skills on the other."[24]

It is important to further unpack the meaning of fairness. Genetic anomalies and other advantages are pervasive in sport and the world. There is no true meritocracy in sport if meritocracy means that everyone has equal opportunity and advantage. Equality in opportunity and advantage is an illusion. Those who have been born with genes conducive to their chosen sport are very fortunate and athletically advantaged if they work hard, have "heart," and have access to money and other resources. What I call the "meritocracy illusion" remains tenacious regardless of knowledge to the contrary. Nowotny and Testa observe, "the more that equality turns out to be a fiction, the more it seems necessary to cling to it."[25] Witness the unreasonable and determined hope of many Canadian parents that their son will make the National Hockey League. Parents sacrifice money, time, and

---

[21]Thomas H. Murray, "Making Sense of Fairness in Sports," *The Hastings Center Report* 40, no. 2 (2010): 13–15.

[22]Sigmund Loland and Hans Hoppeler, "Justifying Anti-Doping: The Fair Opportunity Principle and the Biology of Performance Enhancement," *European Journal of Sport Science* 12, no. 4 (2012): 347–53.

[23]Kutte Jönsson, "Who's Afraid of Stella Walsh? On Gender, 'Gene Cheaters', and the Promise of Cyborg Athletes," *Sport, Ethics and Philosophy* 1, no. 2 (2007): 239–62.

[24]Ivo van Hilvoorde and Laurens Landeweerd, "Disability or Extraordinary Talent: Francesco Lentini (Three Legs) Versus Oscar Pistorius (No Legs)," *Sports, Ethics and Philosophy* 2, no. 2 (2008): 99.

[25]Helga Nowotny and Giuseppe Testa, *Naked Genes: Reinventing the Human in the Molecular Age,* trans. Mitch Cohen (Cambridge, UK: MIT Press, 2010) 20.

attention to what can become an all-consuming drive to have their son become the next Wayne Gretzky or Sydney Crosby. Children's well-being, happiness, and familial contentment can become low priorities compared to that next hockey performance.[26]

Connected to the "American dream" idea that anyone can "succeed" regardless of background or obstacles, the meritocracy illusion is so very important for sports followers likely because it represents hope and transcendence. Hope for what seems impossible—to transcend limitations of biology, class, or race, for example—is part of the human spiritual quest. But different values shape a deliberate spiritual quest as compared to quests driven primarily by the desire to win or even to remain competitive.

The hope that is part of sport for many followers and participants leads to what may be an even more powerful reason for the persistence of the meritocracy illusion: the thirst for mystery. Knowledge of physiological and genetic reasons behind an elite athlete's stellar gold medal performance threatens to remove some of the sense of awe and wonder generated by his or her performances. As well regarded medical ethicist Arthur L. Caplan theorizes, "Strangely, the greatest threat to the future of sport is not necessarily new drugs, gene therapy or better chemistry. The more knowledge we gain ... the greater the threat to our ability to value performance as the result of anything other than random luck.... Science does not destroy the possibility of effort but it may diminish our understanding of its role to the point where sport simply devolves into exhibition."[27] The suggestion that athletic accomplishments are reducible to mere biological or genetic luck may dampen or destroy the inspiration experienced in witnessing a perfect moment.

Some suggest that the increasing knowledge of biological diversity and advantages may not threaten the concept of meritocracy; instead it may provide the possibility of creating a truly level playing field. As science

---

[26]Charlie Gillis, "The Real Scandal in Hockey: Ken Campbell on the Problem With Canada's Obsession," *Maclean's*, 20 January 2013, http://www2.macleans.ca/2013/01/20/year-round-training-and-320000-wont-guarantee-an-nhl-career-or-even-a-future-fan/.

[27]Arthur L. Caplan, "Does the Biomedical Revolution Spell the End of Sport?" *British Journal of Sports Medicine* 42 (2008): 997.

unveils human diversity and as more enhancing technologies emerge, we could move closer to an even playing field by providing the same advantages to all athletes. Lance Armstrong's blood doping, seen through this lens, would simply be a way to allow all athletes to have the same advantage that some, such as Eero Mäntyranta, have due to a genetic anomaly. Already, surgical interventions, for example, are permitted in some sports that enhance an athlete beyond normal status, matching or exceeding the capacities of other exceptional athletes. Consider Major League Baseball's decisions to permit pitchers to replace a torn ulnar collateral ligament (UCL) in the elbow of their throwing arm with a longer tendon, and to allow players to enhance their eyesight beyond "normal" with laser therapy. As Tamburrini argues, enhancement technologies such as genetic modification could make competitions fairer by "level[ing] out differences in performance capacity established by birth."[28]

This strategy of using enhancement technologies to match the advantages among athletes is built on the presupposition that fairness requires sameness or as close to sameness as possible. But what counts as an enhancement: are enhancing technologies only the technologies that enable one to win? Is winning the only important good in sport? And who gets to decide the answers to these questions? As it is, athletes' diversity makes for compelling performances.

As more enhancement technologies are used the trans-athlete[29] will exhibit different qualities as will sport more generally. Enhanced athletes could change sport to be more like entertainment or "spectacle."[30] An elite

---

[28] Tamburrini, "What's Wrong With Genetic Inequality?" 234.

[29] "Transhumanism" refers to an intellectual and cultural movement that advocates the use of a variety of emerging technologies for human enhancement. The convergence of these technologies may make it possible to take control of human evolution, providing for the enhancement of human mental and physical abilities and the amelioration of aspects of the human condition regarded as undesirable. The "trans-athlete" is the athlete who makes use of human enhancement technologies with the goal of becoming "better" than ordinarily human.

[30] M. R. King, "A League of their Own? Evaluating Justifications for the Division of Sport into 'Enhanced' and 'Unenhanced' Leagues," *Sport, Ethics and Philosophy* 6, no. 10 (2012): 36.

sport competition would become, to use ethicist Robert L. Simon's terms, less of a "contest between persons" and more of a contest of "competing bodies." Simon's concern is that sport would devolve into a contest of whose body responds best to enhancing substances rather than a contest between whole persons--genes, physiology, phenotype, phenotypic plasticity, training, effort, and that elusive element we sometimes call spirit.[31]

The vulnerability of the athlete as the imperfect performer is a substantial ingredient in the attraction that sport holds for followers. Contrary to the theory held by both Tamburrini and Tännsjö,[32] an extreme distance between fans and athletes does not seem to be the draw. Rather, fans tend to identify with "their" teams and their players or athletes.[33] It is in the vulnerability or humanity that the connection between many fans and athletes is forged. Vulnerability is different from weakness. Vulnerability in athletes often helps fans appreciate their strength in that awareness of the vulnerability helps fans see how difficult it is for everyone to become the best that they can be. Vulnerability prompts empathy and identification. We all know what it is to be human and when our capacity to connect with another's struggle and interdependence is felt, we tend to pull for them.

Sport can provide that glimpse into an "anything's possible" reality. As Michael Grimshaw puts it, the most inspiring athletic performances are those the "'perfect moment[s]' accomplished by the 'imperfect performer'" bridging the transcendent and immanent for that brief time.[34]

---

[31]Robert L. Simon, "Good Competition and Drug-Enhanced Performance" in *Ethics in Sport*, eds. William J. Morgan, Klaus V. Meier, Angela J. Schneider (Champaign, IL: Human Kinetics, 2001) 119–29; and Nicholas Dixon, "Performance-Enhancing Drugs, Paternalism, Meritocracy, and Harm to Sport," *Journal of Social Philosophy* 39, no. 2 (2008): 246–68.

[32] See Tamburrini, "What's Wrong With Genetic Inequality?" 234; and Torbjörn Tännsjö, "Genetic Engineering and Elitism in Sport," in *Genetic Technology and Sport: Ethical Questions*, eds. Claudio Tamburrini and Torbjörn Tännsjö (London and New York: Routledge, 2005) 55–69.

[33]See, for example, Robert Ellis, "The Meaning of Sport: An Empirical Study into the Significance Attached to Sporting Participation and Spectating in the UK and US," *Practical Theology* 5, no. 2 (2012): 169–88.

[34]Michael Grimshaw, "I Can't Believe My Eyes: The Religious Ascetics of Sport as Post-Modern Salvific Moments," *Implicit Religion* 3, no. 2 (2000): 87.

For some it is more the moral judgment against "drugs" that fuels a resistance to enhancing substances, but for others it is the desire to witness the "real" thing in sports. Either way, for applied ethicist Nicholas Dixon is likely correct in his contention that if the public perceives that performance enhancing drugs (and, I would add, any technologies that are not considered normal or are banned) are shaping an athlete's performance, then they will likely "lose interest in the sports."[35] I suspect it is the "realness" that is perceived in sport that inspires hope that anything is possible, that barriers and limitations that constrain us can be overcome. The question is what limits do we see as undesirable and constraining. The response to this question is located in the worldview or faith that we choose. As theological ethicist Gerald McKenny notes, "The issue at stake is what constitutes or would constitute true fulfillment or flourishing."[36]

Accordingly, some have pondered the possibility of creating enhanced and unenhanced leagues as inequity grows between those who opt for enhancements and those who do not. That way, the competition would be more even and those who wanted to watch more of a spectacle could opt for the enhanced league games. But, as King notes, this does not solve the fairness problem. In particular, continuity issues would persist.[37] FINA's decision to ban super swimsuits was based partly on the performances of swimmers wearing the suits. Improved technology changed competitors' times so dramatically that one could not say if any athlete who won while wearing a polyurethane suit was better than past athletes competing in the same event.[38] And there would be the conceptual difficulty of distinguishing between performers that were enhanced and unenhanced (e.g., what is permitted and what is not). Further, the problem of athletes in both leagues-

---

[35] Dixon, "Performance-Enhancing Drugs, Paternalism, Meritocracy, and Harm to Sport," (2008): 262.

[36] Gerald P. McKenny, "Transcendence, Technological Enhancement, and Christian Theology" in *Transhumanism and Transcendence: Christian Hope in an Age of Technological Enhancement,* ed. Ronald Cole-Turner (Washington, DC: Georgetown University Press, 2011) 179.

[37] M. R. King, "A League of Their Own?" Evaluating Justifications for the Division of Sport into 'Enhanced' and 'Unenhanced' Leagues," (2012).

[38] See, for example, John Gleaves, "No Harm, No Foul? Justifying Bans of Safe Performance-Enhancing Drugs," *Sport, Ethics and Philosophy* 4, no. 3 (2010): 274.

-assuming there would be some kind of regulating terms—seeking unfair advantages remains.

Most importantly, the idea of enhanced and unenhanced leagues does not address underlying causal issues. As techno-science progresses athletes' use of at least some enhancements will become normalized. Fairness will be addressed through policies that allow these technologies. And there will always be debate around new technologies. The more significant question is how will the use of these technologies affect not only sport but the larger questions of meaning that are part of sport.

Internal Goods and the Nature of Sport

Increasing attention is being given to the meaning of sport as possibly a more important criterion than either individual choice or fairness, for assessing enhancements. I will briefly address two main issues: the particular question of what defines a sport and the more general question of internal goods in sport. Enhancement technologies will continue to affect both of these questions. The argument offered by some scholars is that the degree to which both the basic tests of sport and the internal goods of that sport are affected ought to be criteria for evaluating the acceptability of a given enhancement. Since these aspects are mutually dependent in many ways, I discuss them together.

The basic test of a sport defines the structure of that sport and the rules of competition. For example, FINA judged that the polyurethane swimsuits made the athletic test of swimming too easy. Because this basic test (e.g., swimming through water) was affected to the point of disrupting reasonable continuity with past performances, it was decided that these suits must be banned. In short, the super swimsuits were deemed enhancing to the point that swimming itself was changed.[39] One could theorize further that the suits diminished the distinctiveness of each athlete by making swimming too easy.[40]

Another example is Pistorius. Critics have charged that what he does is not running since he does not use two natural legs. In this case, the criticism

---

[39]Murray, "Making Sense of Fairness in Sports," 14.

[40] See Dixon's critique of sport becoming less meritocratic through the increased influence of PEDs and decreased influence of effort and skill. (258)

is not that he has an unfair advantage but that what he does is not running and so does not satisfy the basic test of this sport.[41]

The overall concern is that continued development and use of enhancements will change the nature of sports to the point that each sport is no longer recognizable. The basic test of a sport will be too easy (as in the case of polyurethane swimsuits) or inappropriate (as some argue regarding Pistorius).

The implications of these breaches are significant. If the test becomes too easy, then meaningful comparisons with past performances can no longer be made.[42] The sport will also lose its excitement. As professor emeritus of biomedical ethics Thomas Murray writes, "sports are about what can be accomplished under specific limitations."[43] If the limitations are removed or diminished to a significant degree, then the meaning of the sport is changed or lost. For example, philosopher of sport John Gleaves shows that baseball, like other sports, is very contextual: It is meaningful and therefore attractive only in particular cultural contexts. He outlines ways in which it is particularly suitable to the United States due to its mirroring of American values. For example, baseball depends on both "individual agency [e.g., a lone batter against a single pitcher] as well as cooperative agency [e.g., advancing of runners and sacrifices]" and, as such, while very popular in the United States is not as popular in some other countries.[44] If the challenge of achieving a homerun became mundane, easily achieved through the combination of enhanced eyesight and reflexes, then the sport would lose a significant element of its mystery and meaning. The basic tests of a sport

---

[41] Brendan Burkett, Mike McNamee, and Wolfgang Potthast, "Shifting Boundaries in Sports Technology and Disability: Equal Rights or Unfair Advantage in the Case of Oscar Pistorius?" *Disability & Society* 26, no. 5 (2011): 643–54.

[42] Gleaves, "No Harm, No Foul? Justifying Bans of Safe Performance-Enhancing Drugs" (2010): 276. While the ability to compare past records is not immediately essential to the nature of the sport, if one cannot make meaningful comparisons with past records, this suggests that something—and this something may be about the basic test(s) (and therefore about the nature of the sport) of the sport—has changed.

[43] Murray, "Making Sense of Fairness in Sports," 14.

[44] Gleaves, "No Harm, No Foul? Justifying Bans of Safe Performance-Enhancing Drugs," 273.

are, in other words, very much related to the goods and meaning derived from that sport.

WADA's list of values (e.g., "ethics, fair play and honesty; health; excellence in performance; character and education; fun and joy; teamwork; dedication and commitment; respect for rules and laws; respect for self and other participants; courage; community and solidarity")[45] is associated with both external and internal goods. External goods are objects of competition such as money, status, fame, and power. In contrast to internal goods, external goods are scarce and only available to a limited group of people. Internal goods are not scarce. They are available to anyone engaged in the sport and benefit not just one person but the whole community. Virtues help us to achieve internal goods.[46]

The internal goods, or group defined virtues, of a sport are specific to that particular sport, not taking exactly the same shape in any other sport. For example, excellence of performance is an internal good for all elite sport but is defined in a particular way for each sport. Excellence in rowing includes the achievement of a synchronized rowing rhythm. The attainment of this rhythm depends on the additional internal goods of communication and a sense of connection between the rowers. Excellence in weight lifting is more reliant on the internal goods of muscle development, strength, and disciplined lifting techniques. Internal goods are shared among the different sports but with varying priority. And the prioritizing of these internal goods also changes with the competitive level of the sport. For example, someone who engages in recreational distance running may see relaxation and improved health as significant internal goods in distance running. Olympic marathoners may instead identify speed and endurance as significant internal goods to the sport.

A focus on sport's internal goods moves the ethical discussion of sport enhancement technologies away from a decisionist focus to a virtue focus. "What sort of person should I be?" is the question, rather than the decisionist question of "What shall I do?" In a virtue ethics model, it is understood that decisions and actions will follow from an understanding of

---

[45]WADA, "Fundamental Rationale for the World Anti-Doping Code," 14.

[46]Alasdair MacIntyre, *After Virtue: A Study in Moral Theory*, 3rd ed. (Notre Dame, IN: University of Notre Dame Press, 2007) 191.

what kind of person one desires to be. A virtue model is an uncomfortable model particularly in a social context that prizes decisionist approaches that appear to be objective and value-neutral. This illusion of objectivity feeds the mistaken belief that it is possible and desirable to avoid influence from convictions, loyalties, experience or any other source of authority. These shaping influences must be recognized as they form our values. And values inform our desires and what we think we will find fulfilling. A critical approach to values can help expand our possibilities of fulfillment.

Internal goods of sport are "intrinsic satisfactions that come from meaningful engagement in them."[47] Internal goods are in the experiencing of the sport, by both fans and participants. These goods, unlike external goods, are not utility oriented. For example, to be a Cubs' fan is to pursue goods beyond winning. Rather, it is more about loyalty, persistence, and perhaps taking joy in those moments of achievement and beauty in a given ballpark regardless of final outcome. Of course, Cubs' fans (just as do Leafs' fans) wish very much for a championship win, but that hope is not the only thing that draws them again and again to the game. And even though we may be tempted to think of Frisbee golf or an afternoon run as extravagances, it is not uncommon to discover fun, meaningfulness, or even joy in these mundane moments. Internal goods are about the way in which the game is played or the sport experienced.

The attraction and pressures of external goods can compromise internal goods. The distinction between internal and external goods is important although blurry at times.[48] External goods include financial reward, advertising gigs, fame, status, medals and ribbons, and most obviously, winning. Performance enhancements may very well direct the athletes' attention even more toward external goods, and further undermine sport's internal goods. Technology's utility driven character sharpens the focus on efficiency and particularly on winning. These technological values combined with our societal focus on extreme individualism and the acquiring of possessions will

---

[47]William J. Morgan, *Why Sports Morally Matter* (New York, NY: Routledge, 2006) 249.

[48]Alasdair MacIntyre presents one of the finest discussions of internal and external goods [MacIntyre, *After Virtue: A Study in Moral Theory*, 187–91.

sharpen further the importance of winning. When winning is the preeminent good, other goods are disregarded or at least undervalued.

Because internal goods are the goods that benefit the game and the wider sports community, sports ethicist Dennis Hemphill argues that "[performance enhancing] drug use can undermine the significance attached to the spirit of sport and compromise the sport's ability to promote its internal goods" and therefore should not be permitted. He is concerned with the public perception that drug use is wrong and that those who are found to be using drugs are poor role models, reflecting badly on sports generally. Because sport does have so much to offer in terms of its internal goods, Hemphill reasons, anything that threatens the promotion of these goods ought to be prevented if possible.

Hemphill's is an interesting point that bears consideration. As discussed earlier, not all enhancing substances or technologies that are considered unacceptable or bad today will be considered in the same way in the future. Our conceptions of normal and acceptable evolve. Because the wish persists that sport represents the pure and natural, which are highly desirable, those things that represent the unnatural and morally bad, trigger disgust.[49] Another layer is added when the perceived "unnatural" disrupts normative embodiment categories. We search for order and will impose it to make sense of the world. In short, a sport community's reaction against violation of the rules and against particular enhancements (especially those called "drugs") is so strong because these violations "threaten ... the sport's constructed social order, one that supports athletes' identity and meaningful way of life."[50]

Some internal goods of sport are countercultural and some are not. And there is no consensus on these goods[51] except that they are intrinsically satisfying not merely utility driven. Internal goods are sport specific and shift in response to changing contexts and times. This dynamism does not mean there is no point to normative claims. Manifested in particular ways in each

---

[49] Braxton, "Does Transhumanism Face an Uncanny Valley Among the Religious?," 331–50.

[50] Dennis Hemphill, "Performance Enhancement and Drug Control in Sport: Ethical Considerations," *Sport in Society* 12, no. 3 (2009): 320.

[51] Ibid., 319.

sport, there are some internal goods that are common to most team sports, such as good communication between the athletes. Good communication (combined with skill) in hockey can mean seamless passing plays, while in pairs skating good communication (and skill) can mean a beautifully executed lift. Morgan proposes that "wholehearted engagement" also is an internal good.[52] Hemphill argues that "practice excellence" is the preeminent internal good and entails maximal effort and the upholding of shared "purposes and acceptable means in the sport practice community."[53] I suggest that the capacity to claim one's power also can be an internal good, particularly for many women and other marginalized people. All these internal goods of sport are related to what we think makes for a good life.

A good life, happiness, or in Feezell's terms, "the conditions of meaningful activities,"[54] are concepts important to an internal goods approach to the sport enhancement issue. The good life is not guaranteed by the achievement of external goods. External goods are defined more by utility and socially constructed meanings of success. Athletes and fans will often speak of success, happiness, and meaning in other terms. As mentioned earlier,[55] Jackson and Csikszenthmihalyi conclude that "... research shows that the most memorable and happy moments in people's lives usually involve a job well done that required skills and concentration or a struggle to overcome a difficult obstacle."[56]

The most important internal good of sport is, I submit, its spiritual and religious dimension. Most particularly, this internal good is the capacity of sport to inspire hope and, as part of hope, a sense of meaning. It is hope that spurs us on to overcome obstacles. Yet, this dimension rarely is identified in sport's literature as a normative good, outside of sources specific to the

---

[52]Morgan, *Why Sports Morally Matter*, 239–53.

[53]Hemphill, "Performance Enhancement and Drug Control in Sport: Ethical Considerations," 318.

[54]See, for example, Feezell, *Sport, Philosophy, and Good Lives*, 193; Morgan, *Why Sports Morally Matter*, 249; Hubert Dreyfuss and Sean Dorrance Kelly, *All Things Shining: Reading the Western Classics to Find Meaning in a Secular Age* (New York: Free Press, 2011).

[55]See chapter five.

[56]Susan Jackson and Mihalyi Csikszentmihalyi, *Flow in Sports: The Keys to Optimal Experiences and Performance* (Champaign, IL: Human Kinetics, 1999) 35.

relationship between sport and religion. And as we have seen, even in these sources the religious and spiritual dimension of sport is often seen as more suspect than satisfying in a good or spiritually adequate way.

Although not every subjective spiritual experience fits with every understanding of what constitutes a genuine spiritual experience, most seem to fit with Pargament's general definition of spirituality. Sport's spiritual and religious dimension provides a sense of the sacred and something more than the mundane that rises up over external goods and can foster a sense of meaning.

If this spiritual and religious dimension of sport is identified as an internal good, and if the increasing importance of secular religions including sport is recognized, how might these conditions reshape the sport enhancement debate? The question of how an enhancing technology might affect spiritual experiences and especially hope in sport would become important. The identification of the spiritual dimension of sport as an internal good would also shift the meaning of enhancement to include the increased frequency or deepening of spiritual experiences in sport as enhancing (something is only seen as enhancing if it amplifies something that is recognized as desirable). Also, a technology that limited or harmed this dimension would be seen as less desirable.

For example, flow experiences may be affected by enhancement technologies. If athletes' bodies are increasingly regarded as tools for achieving winning performances in sports contests, this valuing will affect the enhancements we engineer and choose. Likely, the capacity to withstand pain in order to achieve external goods will be privileged over flow experiences. As a way of experiencing deep connection, and unexpected sporting moments, flow may not be valued as much as enhancements that predictably increase an athlete's chances of winning. On the other hand, if research on happiness is taken seriously and happiness as an internal good is highly valued, the fact that flow is associated with happiness,[57] may result in efforts to enhance both fans' and athletes' experiences of flow. Further, if the spiritual dimension of sport is valued in itself, flow will also be valued as a spiritual experience.

---

[57]Ibid.

Therapy—Restoration—Enhancement

Most often, anti-doping policies rely on what has become known as the therapy-enhancement distinction in determining the acceptability of enhancing interventions. If an intervention is judged to fall within the therapeutic spectrum, it is acceptable. If it is enhancing, it is usually not permitted unless it is deemed normal or inconsequential. The middle zone of interventions that are not clearly either therapeutic or enhancing is more complex. Until recently, this approach has been referred to as the "therapy enhancement" continuum without explicitly naming a mid-zone.

This approach is particularly interesting in the context of elite sport since sport is intrinsically enhancing. Athletes, coaches, and fans are always seeking the next breakthrough that will help athletes to transcend limits in competition. One might expect that any method of enhancing would be desirable since that is what sport sometimes seems to be about. But, as we have seen, that is not *all* sport is about. Imagined as one of the last bastions of purity, morality, and drama, sport represents higher aspirations. For many, it is about hope, transcendence, and meaning. Yet this spiritual and religious dimension is typically unnamed and unaddressed.

Sport is about enhancing within certain parameters, and it is also about limits. The overcoming of constructed obstacles is at the heart of each sport. Excellent performance is not meant to be easy or predictable. That would obviate the purpose of the sport. Enhancements that are deemed natural or earned through effort are not seen as enhancements in this approach. Enhancements, rather, are artificial add-ons. The therapy-enhancement approach is helpful in evaluating added enhancements but not existing advantages.

This approach relies on the problematic concept of "normal" as the dividing line between therapy and enhancement.[58] It is also associated with constructed distinctions between natural (good and therapeutic) and artificial (bad and enhancing). We have to ask ourselves: At what point does a substance, for example, become artificial and no longer natural? Given that all substances available to us are at the least naturally derived, at what point does human manipulation of these natural substances render them

---

[58]See chapter two for more discussion of "normal" as a problematic concept.

unnatural. The list of banned substances is in flux, changing as some substances become normalized and accepted, new ones created, and others currently in use prove risky, undesirable, or unhealthy.

These complications have been cited as reasons for abandoning the therapy-enhancement approach. In spite of these limitations, the therapy-enhancement approach continues to be useful.[59] Although not every intervention can be easily judged, this difficulty is also a virtue of the approach. The lack of a clear dividing point on the therapy-enhancement continuum is a good thing in the sense that it reflects the complexity in assessing what it means to be human and what we might hope for humanity to become. Also, as ethicist Jim Parry points out, generalities are useful even though there are exceptions.[60]

The therapy-enhancement approach is grounded in a complicated continuum. I propose that it is not necessarily the case that a techno-science intervention is always unacceptable even if it is judged to be in the enhancement end of the continuum. Rather, it will be usually unacceptable and always requiring further deliberation before such an intervention is considered. Over time, it may become seen as more normal.[61] Particular performance-enhancing drugs include anabolic steroids at one end of the continuum due to their clear health risks, measurable effect on performance, and banned status. Typically, they are meant to serve one purpose, i.e., to increase the athlete's chances of winning and to do so covertly. At the other end of the continuum are therapeutic interventions such as ultrasound treatment for a soft tissue injury, or surgery to repair a torn ligament. Somewhere in the middle of the continuum is the use of hypobaric chambers to increase an athlete's oxygen capacity for endurance sports. This technique is often justified on the basis of fairness (other athletes who live in high altitudes get this benefit) and because it falls in the middle of this

---

[59]For example, Tamburrini and Tännsjö make a cautious distinction between therapy and enhancement [Tamburrini and Tännsjö, "Enhanced Bodies," 274.

[60] Jim Parry, "Must Scientists Think Philosophically About Science?" in *Philosophy and the Sciences of Exercise, Health and Sport: Critical Perspectives on Research Methods*, eds. Mike McNamee (New York: Routledge, 2005) 21–33.

[61]Complicating the issue is the intense attractiveness of enhancements in the western world; ours is an enhancement-junkie culture. So what becomes regarded as normal in this context must be regarded as suspect and part of our consumer culture.

continuum. While hypobaric training chambers are enhancing for athletes who do not live in high altitudes, the effect of these chambers could be considered on a par with those athletes who do live at high altitudes.

This middle zone has become acknowledged as including interventions that are neither only enhancing nor only therapeutic. These interventions have been described as restorative,[62] preventative,[63] or non-therapy,[64] and they are sometimes deemed acceptable in sport. As Magdalinski, Beamish, and others point out, there is no clear-cut distinction between restoration or recovery, and enhancement.[65]

Miah gives the example of laser eye surgery to provide someone with 20/20 vision. In the case of someone whose eyesight has deteriorated from its previously normal state, this intervention could be seen as restorative or perhaps therapeutic. But if this person never had average eyesight, would not this intervention be enhancing? Miah raises the question of how it is decided what is normal (and who decides) and, therefore, where the intervention is located along the continuum. Additionally, he points out that external and temporary sources of vision enhancement such as glasses, binoculars, and magnifying glasses are seen as therapeutic or helpful aids whereas surgery is more questioned. I suspect that this distinction has a lot to do with notions of naturalness versus artificiality, and harkens back to Magdalinski's point that temporary enhancements such as binoculars do not tend to elicit a disgust response, unlike permanent visible enhancements. Miah proposes that problematic interventions such as laser eye surgery that could be seen as

---

[62]See, for example, Magdalinski, *Sport, Technology and the Body*, 11; and Rob Beamish, *Steroids: A New Look at Performance-Enhancing Drugs* (Santa Barbara, CA: Praeger, 2011) 63.

[63]Preventative interventions are those designed to retain a "normal" state. Ronald Green, [*Babies By Design: The Ethics of Genetic Choice* (New Haven, CT: Yale University Press, 2007) 60] as referenced in a helpful article by Jacob L. Goodson, "The Quest for Perfection in the Sport of Baseball: The Magnanimous Individual or the Magnanimous Team?" in *Sports and Christianity: Historical and Contemporary Perspectives*, eds. Nick J. Watson and Andrew Parker (New York: Routledge 2013) 229.

[64]Andy Miah, "Towards the Transhuman Athlete: Therapy, Non-therapy and Enhancement," *Sport in Society* 13, no. 2 (2010): 221–33.

[65]See Magdalinski, *Sport, Technology and the Body*, 11; Beamish, *Steroids*, 63; and Miah, "Towards the Transhuman Athlete" 221–33.

therapeutic for one person and enhancing for another (depending upon each person's former normal vision) are more properly understood as non-therapy. This way of framing the issue avoids the problematics of the term "restorative." The intervention would be restorative for the person who previously had 20/20 vision but not for the person who never had 20/20 vision. However, the intervention could be called non-therapy for both since it brings both people's vision up to a level that is regarded as normal for most people.

Others, including me, prefer the term restorative, understanding it to mean either restoring an individual's previous level of functioning or restoration to a more general human state of normalcy.[66] The concept of restoration to a normal state raises the additional question of context: elite athletes have a different normal than the rest of the population. So what version of normal should be the baseline? To continue with the example of laser eye surgery, Major League Baseball permits laser eye surgery for its players and permits enhancement beyond the normal 20/20 state. Clearly, it is considered acceptable to seek eyesight improvement beyond what is normal for the average person.

Since the medical model does not embrace the same value set as the elite sport model, there are divergences of opinion regarding acceptable interventions. As discussed earlier, acceptable levels of self-violence are higher among elite athletes; the capacity to withstand physical pain is assumed to be a virtue—and often the greater the capacity, the better. This valuing means that it is more likely that treatment techniques will continue to improve and that athletes will continue to accept a significant degree of risk of physical harms in order to perform as well as possible.

Major League Baseball's decision to permit pitchers to replace a torn ulnar collateral ligament (UCL) in the elbow of their throwing arm with a longer tendon raises the normal "bar" for elite pitchers in at least one way. Their career can be lengthened with the opportunity to continue to throw after sustaining what, at one time, would have been a career ending injury. Some perceive the surgery as not mere replacement of what was inborn but

---

[66]Both non-therapy and restorative intervention then carry similar meanings when defined in these ways. But the term "restorative" suggests a *return* to an expected or accepted state.

possibly as enhancement of one's pitching. While this is disputed,[67] the belief that it may have an enhancing effect has resulted in enthusiastic parents asking for their aspiring healthy pitcher sons to receive the surgery.[68] With the raising of this bar may come increasing pressure for pitchers to take advantage of this opportunity to improve their throwing arms. Since Tommy John, the first ball player (in 1974) to have this surgery and the one after whom the procedure is named informally, there have been thirty-four players to receive this surgery as of May 2014. Overhand throwing stresses the UCL and can eventually result in a tear needing surgery. Is the answer to provide effective and maybe even enhancing surgery or to reevaluate the injury-causing potential of training and throwing techniques? Any serious reevaluating would require an increased valuing of the athlete's health and a concomitant willingness to reconsider allowable pitching forms. In short, this serious reevaluating is not likely to happen; it is far more likely that the surgical procedure will continue to improve (already it is very successful but there is risk to the ulnar nerve) perhaps to the point of clear enhancement. Already, Tommy John surgery is accepted as a therapeutic or restorative intervention in Major League Baseball.

On a more everyday level, training necessarily involves muscular micro-tears. As medical interventions develop that can speed healing and recovery from these tears, they are embraced. After all, more effective recovery reduces the chances of serious injury and allows a faster return to training). As a result, recovery interventions can be seen as more therapeutic than enhancing. While the availability of effective recovery interventions can increase willingness to over-train and self-harm, they can also be very helpful not only to elite athletes but to all of us who try to maintain a level of fitness. Overall, such techniques could improve quality of health and reduce healthcare costs. At the same time, caution should be raised regarding the motives to use such interventions and the possibilities of harm. The issue becomes more problematic when considering future scenarios of more extreme "recovery" techniques and technologies. As referred to earlier,

[67] Jonah Keri, "Interview With Dr. Frank Jobe," 13 September 2007, http://ESPN.com.

[68] Jere Longman, "Fit Young Pitchers See Elbow Repair as Cure-All," 20 July 2007, http://nytimes.com/2007/07/20/sports/baseball/20surgery.html.

possible genetic transfer technologies involving modulation of the DREAM gene may enable athletes to endure more self-inflicted pain that would theoretically lead to improved athletic performance.

The therapy-enhancement approach provides the opportunity to identify more questions such as these (about pain and the use of medical interventions to speed healing of soft-tissue) regarding underlying values that support the acceptance of or resistance to various techno-science interventions. This approach does not begin with one particular value as do the individual choice and fairness approaches. As a result, the therapy-enhancement approach is more open to alternative values as criteria for evaluating enhancements.

Concluding Comment

The sport enhancement debate needs to be reshaped for three overlapping reasons: First, and most importantly, the function of sport as a popular secular religion with a spiritual dimension has not been considered in approaches to the debate. Second, in assuming a decisionist focus, the current approaches often fail to question critically the values informing the debate. Third, many current approaches do not draw explicit connections to evaluations of existing advantages possessed by athletes. Even so, there are very valuable facets of each of the four approaches that ought to be maintained in a reshaped approach to techno-science usage in elite sport.

In the next chapter I will discuss the relevance of techno-science usage to the locations of hope in sport. Building on this discussion, I suggest the reshaping and deepening of these four approaches to the sport enhancement debate based on the moral relevance of sport's spiritual dimension.

Chapter 8

Hope and Reshaping the Enhancement Debate:
A Christian Theological Reflection

Scholarly examinations of the relationship between sport and religion posit diverse conclusions but tend to agree that there is a relationship.[1] At the very least, sport possesses parallels to some aspects of institutional religion. The most significant debate regarding this relationship seems to be whether or not sport adequately addresses life's big questions such as: Why am I here? What makes life meaningful? What happens after death? Why does suffering happen? Joan Chandler is partially correct in saying that sport fails to address these questions and thus is not a religion. She correctly observes that sport neither doctrinally nor directly wrestles with these questions. Yet sport does address these questions metaphorically, as suggested by scholars including Michael Novak, Charles S. Prebish, Joseph L. Price and, in some ways, Randolph Feezell. Whether or not this metaphorical engagement is sufficient is a different issue. Nonetheless, since sport is functioning as a popular, secular religion, sport's spiritual dimension needs to be considered in the enhancement debate.

To understand something of the function of this spiritual dimension, sport proponents, teachers, policy makers, administrators, and other leaders can gain insights into the meaning and value of sport from traditional institutional religions that do wrestle with these questions—in particular, the question of what it means to be human and to yearn for the sacred is important as we explore the meaning of hope in sport. Not only can established religious traditions shed light on alternative constructions of hope and meaning, they also demonstrate the persistence of the human desire for something more than material goods or winning alone. This is

---

[1]See chapters four and five.

spirituality; a "yearning for the sacred."[2] The sacred is about the desire for hope, including meaning and fulfillment.

Hope: Sport and Techno-science

There are four main locations of hope in sport: winning, losing, and anticipation; star athletes; perfect moments; and relational embodiment. In this chapter, I will revisit these locations, considering each as it might intersect with techno-science, and offering Christian theological reflection. I will then identify features of each of the four approaches to the sport enhancement issue that, when combined with insights regarding hope in sport, would deepen understandings of the enhancement issue.

Winning, Losing, and Anticipation. Of course, not all fans or athletes celebrate winning graciously and afford dignity to the losing competitors. And not all fans and athletes consciously understand or have deliberately reflected on the value of losing, winning, and anticipating as these relate to the larger issue of hope. And some refuse even to see that losing is an important part of winning; after all, it is not possible to have one without the other in our current paradigm—someone must lose if someone wins. How participants experience winning and losing says a lot about how hope is experienced.

Non-rational persistence, anticipation, and intense investment in one's team or athlete or even oneself are hallmarks of the hope related to winning. Regardless of how it is expressed, this quest for fulfillment is indicative of human spiritual desire for the sacred. There is an expectation that the elusive win will lift us to new heights, infusing us with celebration and inspiration, and satisfying our desires. Yet without learning to discern what is authentically sacred, these desires cannot be satisfied in any lasting way. A win is wonderful and can be basked in for a while but the next competition often comes quickly.

If the desire for fulfillment is associated only with the external good of winning, we are left wanting more. When the focus is exclusively or almost

---

[2]Kenneth I Pargament, "Searching for the Sacred: Toward a Non-Reductionist Theory of Spirituality," in *APA Handbooks in Psychology, Religion, and Spirituality: Vol. 1 Context, Theory, and Research*, eds. K. I. Pargament, J. J. Exline, and J. Jones (Washington, DC: American Psychological Association, 2013) 258.

exclusively on winning, this goal takes on idolatrous dimensions. Winning becomes the only image of the transcendent and the only manifestation of fulfillment. From a Christian perspective, this means cutting God out and investing exclusively in the idol of the gold medal, the cup, or blue ribbon. From a secular religious perspective, it means flattening sport to one dimension, squeezing out other internal goods that contribute to a more robust hope.

The reduction of the quest for fulfillment to the acquisition of external goods is hopeless; the quest becomes self-defeating since no thing provides lasting satisfaction.[3] The human spiritual quest—which includes the quest for fulfillment—is about the search for the sacred, as Pargament reminds us. And the sacred is not found in the sheer acquisition of record performances and wins. Rather the sacred supersedes normative values and objects, and is about that which holds lasting meaning that is of and not of this world.

As more human enhancement technologies are developed and used, proponents of radical human enhancement see greater possibility for overcoming human limits and even, perhaps, achieving immortality.[4] Patrick Hopkins contends that it is precisely because of the impossibility of fully satisfying human desires through acquisition and improvement that ultimately transhumanism will not be able to provide any real form of salvation to human persons as long as we remain human.[5] Our desires will not be sated by technology no matter how strong, smart, beautiful, in control, or long living we make ourselves. We will always want more. Rather, we will always want something that cannot be captured in normative terms.

---

[3] For example, see Patrick D. Hopkins, "A Salvation Paradox for Transhumanism: *Saving* You Versus Saving *You*," in *Religion and Transhumanism: The Unknown Future of Human Enhancement*, eds. Calvin Mercer and Tracy J. Trothen (Westport, CT: Praeger, 2015) 71–82, for an analysis of desire and satisfaction, and Susan Jackson and Mihalyi Csikszentmihalyi, *Flow in Sports: The Keys to Optimal Experiences and Performance* (Champaign, IL: Human Kinetics, 1999) 35, regarding happiness.

[4] Derek F. Maher and Calvin Mercer, eds., *Religion and the Implications of Radical Life Extension* (New York: Palgrave Macmillan, 2009).

[5] Hopkins, "A Salvation Paradox for Transhumanism: *Saving* You Versus Saving *You*," (2015) 71–82.

Hope in sport is different in some ways from these acquisitive desires. The very temporality, uncertainty, and limited nature of sport draws people. Both wins and losses are temporary. No one athlete can always perform perfectly no matter how good they are. No season lasts forever. No Olympic Games will repeat in exactly the same way. No team stays constant. So the challenge and the hope in sport are ongoing; sport is a process involving loyalty, commitment, perseverance, and determination.

Enhancement technologies could change these conditions and so change the meaning of hope that is found in winning. Most obviously, winning could become too easy. Homeruns in baseball or hat-tricks in hockey could become so common that they are no longer viewed as achievements or worthy of attention. Or athletes could become much more evenly matched through enhancements that permit all to rise to the same level of oxygen-carrying capacity, visual acuity, muscle strength, or perhaps even emotional stability. It could be that human emotional variance becomes controllable or minimized through the blocking of feelings of guilt, empathy, loyalty, or other human characteristics (including the experience of physical pain) that might moderate a win at any cost mentality.

On the other hand, maybe enhancements will be developed that increase the hope of winning and this increase may help some athletes to claim their power and celebrate their human abilities and limitations.[6] Believing that one has the capacity to achieve a dream—to win the medal, to persist and not give up, to shoot high and maybe even get there, and to feel self-worth regardless of winning—is a redemptive mark of a lasting hope.

Both science and technology in elite sports will continue to be developed and used for the purpose of winning so long as winning is the normative value and most prized good in elite sports. Science will continue to reveal existing advantages. Likely we will continue to evaluate these advantages according to embodiment norms and prejudices. As more invisible advantages are made visible, the temptation to reduce the athletic person to a series of parts probably will grow. Hope in sport has proven tenacious but the reduction of the athlete to physical advantages and

---

[6]Reiterating this point from previous chapters, sin is not only excessive pride and undue will-to-power. Sin can also take the form of a lack of self-love, denial of one's power, and therefore the inability to assume appropriate responsibility.

disadvantages threatens to dampen the mystery of athletic excellence. Genetic determinism may grow with the development of techno-science usage in sport. The questions we must address include: How far will we go with the enhancement project and will-to-win? What might be sacrificed? What values will inform these decisions?

Star Athletes

Elite athletes, particularly winning Olympic athletes, are regarded as role models, idols, and icons. Winners often are assumed to be exemplary human beings on all levels.[7] Indeed, they take on almost god-like dimensions. The questions of who and what we admire are related to the values we hold. When we admire elite winning athletes (and A-list Hollywood actors) as representatives of ideal humanity, we are saying something about the values we hold and the desires we harbor.

Elite sports culture is characterized by conflicting values, with winning topping this value set. Because of these conflicts, there is much confusion regarding what is acceptable within competitive sports. This confusion about values shapes approaches to the sport enhancement issue. On the one hand, we want our athletes to be natural and pure, all about human effort, training, and heart. On the other, we typically admire only the winners. And we want and expect records to be broken endlessly without the use of performance enhancing technologies. It is hardly surprising that elite athletes who are caught intentionally using banned substances report feelings of shame and humiliation; it is not usually possible to live up to both standards.[8]

Further, we admire athletes even more who win while competing with serious injuries such Bobby Baun who in the 1964 Stanley Cup finals scored the game winning goal while skating on a fractured ankle. Yet, we also see elite athletes as paragons of health. We do not tend to applaud athletes for removing themselves from competition because they are injured. Sydney

---

[7] See chapter six for a more in-depth discussion of athletes as role-models and moral exemplars.

[8] Kate Kirby, Aidan Moran, and Suzanne Guerin, "A Qualitative Analysis of the experiences of Elite Athlete Who Have Admitted to Doping for Performance Enhancement," *International Journal of Sport Policy and Politics* 3, no. 2 (2011): 220.

Crosby had to endure many concussions before he was encouraged to take time to heal.

The theological claims that the body is good and physical healing desirable, have implications for sport including, perhaps particularly, star athletes. The cultural glorification of violence (to which Christian theological interpretations have contributed) and ability to withstand pain puts athletes at risk. The pressure to maintain star status may increase an athlete's willingness to take unnecessary risks. It is possible that future interventions that reduce pain from injuries and shorten recovery time may justify increased self-violence.

There are redemptive possibilities in the model of elite athletes as imperfect performers who sometimes perform perfectly. Athletes can be testimony to the hope that all manner of obstacles can be overcome if only for brief moments, which can have lasting inspirational effects.

But from a Christian theological perspective, the hope that is located in star athletes must be deemed problematic, particularly in terms of its possible implications for the use of techno-science in sport. On the plus side, effort, dedication, perseverance, and commitment are qualities worthy of admiration. Additionally, respect for the dignity and creativity of the human person as created in the image of God can be consistent with the athletic quest to realize one's potential.

Also, the pressure on star athletes to be "pure" as role models could help to safeguard against going so far with human enhancement that humanity as we now know it is lost. But likely records will not be broken indefinitely unless athletes are enhanced to the point of becoming trans- or post-human.[9] But the notion of purity is misplaced to the degree that it assumes conformity to human constructed values such as gender categories and other embodiment norms. The paradoxical pressure to conform to an impossible notion of purity and also to win at any cost can put athletes in an impossible position. Of course, even this pressure does not remove athletes' responsibility for their choices. But it broadens the scope of who shares this responsibility. Communities are responsible for an ethos. Increasing

---

[9] It is important to note that there is no clear demarcation between being human and transhuman; by some accounts we are already cyborgs given our relationship with technology as a built-in part of life.

enhancement options will play into the illusion that records can continue to be broken by equally human athletes. Part of the choice that we face is whether elite sports contests ought to be entertaining spectacles, or competitions between imperfect humans with whom fans can identify.

The human struggle with mortality complicates the relationship between star athletes and the use of enhancing interventions. The desire to be remembered and to be held in esteem may add to the pleasure of athletic success but it may also add to the pressure to achieve more star performances. The risky use of enhancing interventions may become more tempting the more one wins.[10]

If deliberate choices are not made regarding values and desires, and the question of what is most likely to bring us a sense of fulfillment is not considered, techno-science will continue to be used and developed for purposes that align with winning at any cost while trying to maintain the illusions of purity and well-being. A likely outcome is that elite athletes become more distanced as enhanced entertainers instead of sources of inspiration and hope with whom we can, in some way, identify.

Perfect Moments

The perfect moment by the imperfect performer confronts us with the mixture of sacred and profane. These perfect moments only hold meaning in light of our finitude and imperfection, just as winning only holds meaning if losing is a possibility. That perfect moments are rare makes them more special and more inspiring. If athletes become enhanced to the point of making these moments commonplace, not only would these moments become lackluster, but identification of the human spectator with the not-so-human athlete would disappear. The perfect moment would no longer be perfect; instead it would be a spectacular display or entertaining moment.

---

[10]The need to cope with our finitude is part of the human spiritual quest. One way of coping with this limit is to seek to overcome mortality through re-fashioning ourselves so that we might radically extend our lifespan or even try to live forever. As pointed out by Ronald Cole-Turner, at some point all life will end regardless of technological abilities to enhance [Cole-Turner, "Extreme Longevity Research: A Progressive Protestant Perspective," in *Religion and the Implications of Radical Life Extension*, eds. Derek F. Maher and Calvin Mercer (New York: Palgrave Macmillan, 2009) 53].

Identification and human limitation are necessary factors to this location of hope. We need to see the athlete as connected to us in some way. We can then believe (and it is a matter of belief) that we too have the potential to transform and touch perfection. And because humans are limited and are aware of at least some of these limitations, we can experience awe when we witness a moment that feels like perfection.

Care must be taken, however, not to confuse human ideas of perfection with God's perfection. Maintaining an awareness of this distinction is difficult since the only way we know is through our human experiences. But there are hints in scripture of what is meant by God's perfection. This perfection is not an overcoming of *all* limits but, almost perversely to many of us, a rejoicing in human interdependence[11] and the development of our abilities to be all that we can. These two are to go hand-in-hand, with the hoped for result that we inspire and create just and caring relationships. This includes the capacity to appreciate and create beauty. Perfection is in God, and humanity as created in God's image can perhaps become closer to God through becoming more fully human.

As embodied creatures, we find multiple ways to experience moments of perfection, including athletic moments. Although we cannot know for sure if these are moments in which we catch more of a glimpse of God, we do know that feelings of awe that stun us into a pause and pull us fully into such moments can evoke spiritual descriptions.

Whether or not an athletic performance has anything to do with God's providence is in some ways moot. As Peter Hopsicker argues regarding the perception of miracles in sports, thin theology underlies such claims but nonetheless there is value in these perceptions of God's work. The value is that claims of miracles can help inspire openness to the transcendent, or, in theistic terms, God.[12]

Sin can distort the perfect moment: for example, we can fail to recognize perfection, or we can try to possess it. Or, the moment can be

---

[11]Perfection may be found most in the very fragility and vulnerability that many of us try to overcome. It is this fragility and vulnerability that can help us to recognize our interdependence with all life and our need for relationship.

[12]Peter M. Hopsicker, "Miracles in Sport: Finding the 'Ears to Hear' and the 'Eyes to See'," *Sport, Ethics and Philosophy* 3, no. 1 (2009): 75–93.

redemptive and inspirational. With regard to the use of techno-science enhancements in sport, one question is, will we continue to experience these awe-inspiring moments or will technology eventually make these moments uninspiring? If spiritual hunger is confused with self-mastery, winning at any cost, and the re-making of ourselves in our own image, then there may be little left to experience other than entertainment and unsatisfied desire. Or it may be that we choose to use techno-science in ways that perhaps enhance these perfect moments by making us more attentive or empathetic. If we choose to value sport's spiritual dimension, relationship, human diversity, well-being, and mystery, then these values will shape approaches to the sport enhancement issue.

Relational Embodiment

The final location of hope in elite sport that I have identified is what I have termed relational embodiment. This location of hope concerns (1) the diversity of embodied persons made in the image of God for relationship with God, self, others, and creation, and (2) spiritual experiences of flow that are grounded in embodiment. The intersection of techno-science with this location of hope has significant implications for the meaning of sport.

The Christian doctrine of the *imago Dei* is critical to theological reflection on embodiment diversity and hope. The *imago Dei* doctrine demands the honoring of self and other; it is a statement about the sanctity and dignity of every person and is at the core of a Christian understanding of what it means to be human.

An evolutionary understanding of the *imago Dei* must be dynamic since humanity "is a relatively recent development within the 13.9 billion years of God's naturally evolving cosmic creation."[13] Since humans as a species were not in existence at the time of Earth's creation and since Christians still claim that humans are made in God's image, is it not reasonable to claim also that the other hominids were made in God's image? Who counts as being made in the image of God? Would a cloned person count? What

---

[13] Mathew Zaro Fisher, "More Human than the Human? Toward a 'Transhumanist' Christian Theological Anthropology," in *Religion and Transhumanism: The Unknown Future of Human Enhancement*, eds. Calvin Mercer and Tracy J. Trothen (Westport, CT: Praeger, 2015) 29.

about people who are conceived through in-vitro fertilization? Would an uploaded mind count? How enhanced is too enhanced to count? Do animals count?

Joshua Moritz and Celia Deane-Drummond argue that scientific research yields nothing that makes human qualitatively unique among animals. As a result, it may be, as Deane-Drummond proposes, that animals share in the *likeness* of God but not the *imago Dei* as that is the realm only of humans and angels.[14] Moritz opts to maintain a belief in the restriction of the *imago Dei* to humans not on the basis of science but on the basis of his theology of election in which humans are "called and chosen as God's image."[15] However, he stands by the argument that, in keeping with Darwinian science, there is no adequate scientific basis on which to claim that humans are a unique species with qualitatively distinct qualities related to freedom, lack of innate instincts, self-consciousness and self-awareness, culture, rationality, or moral behavior.[16]

If one can mount the argument that there is no scientific basis for claims of human qualitative uniqueness, then there seems little scientific reason to think that extremely altered humans would be made any less in God's image. But, as Moritz points out, this claim is not consistent with the theological tradition that affirms the particularity of humans and the relationship between humans and God. The consideration of the challenges that science presents to claims of human uniqueness may also help us to think more critically about the wider question of what it means to be human and what characterizes the relationship between God and humans.

Traditionally, Christian theological interpretations of the *imago Dei* have tended to privilege reason, or rational thought, in defining what it means to be human.[17] Feminist theologians have rejected this privileging for

---

[14]Celia Deane-Drummond, "God's Image and Likeness in Humans and Other Animals: Performative Soul-Making and Graced Nature," *Zygon* 47, no. 4 (December 2012) 934–48.

[15]Joshua M. Moritz, "Evolution, the End of Human Uniqueness, and the Election of the *Imago Dei*," *Theology and Science*, 9, no. 3 (2011): 330.

[16]Ibid., 312–13.

[17]For a more in-depth discussion of reason and interpretations of the *imago Dei*, see, for example, Trothen, "Redefining Human, Redefining Sport: The *Imago Dei* and Genetic Modification Technologies," in *The Image of God in the Human*

two main reasons. First, embodiment is necessarily woven into human identity. We are not disparate parts; the body, spirit, and mind are not separate. Our identities are formed through our particular embodied experiences. We cannot know what we know apart from our embodiment.

Second, reason has been used historically to persecute marginalized groups on the supposed basis that they do not possess enough rational capacity to deserve full participation. One need only consider the relatively recent decisions to allow women and African Americans to vote. There are numerous more appalling examples of people being killed, tortured, or enslaved because they have been judged to be lesser.

How decisions are made about what constitutes human beings and who is deserving of dignity or, from a Christian perspective, who is made in God's image are key concerns for the sport techno-science discussion regarding both existing advantages and added enhancements. As science reveals more genetic and other anomalies possessed by elite athletes, the mystery behind some measure of their success is revealed. Not only are these advantages discovered, they are then assessed for acceptability. Some of these anomalies are and will be acceptable while others not, as may have been the case for Semenya. As we have seen, much of the assessment depends on societal values and norms.

This aspect of the techno-science issue raises the question of embodiment categories in sport. On a practical level, how ought we decide which existing advantages are acceptable, and who qualifies to compete in particular events? Or do we need to reconfigure the competitive categories? If there are to continue to be separate male and female competitions in most sports, where should line that distinguishes males from females be drawn? Perhaps competitive categories should be at least partially decided based on how the athletes self-identify rather than purely on hormonal and other physical characteristics. Of course this would be problematic, too: would anyone lie to gain an advantage? How much weight would we give to self-identification? And, importantly, from a theological perspective, the question of whom we believe to be made in God's image must be asked. If it is generally agreed that diverse people are made in God's image, regardless of

Body: Essays on Christianity and Sports, eds. Donald R. Deardorff and John White (New York: Edwin Mellen Press, 2008) 217–34.

their capacity to fit in normative embodiment categories, what implications does this claim have for elite sport?

A theological assessment of what counts as an unfair advantage needs to consider human diversity and the reality that, in this diversity, people do not all fall into neatly defined categories. The *imago Dei* suggests that a glimmer of God can be discerned in this very diversity. Evolutionary science tells us there is no one universal "human nature." Humans are more than the product of their genes, and more also than the product of their environments; spirit—or however we may name this quality that adds to human unpredictability and desire for fulfillment, even if it is part of our genetic make-up—adds to this diversity.[18] The theological claim that diverse humanity, if not other animal species and other hominids as well, is made in God's image, conveys an intractable dignity and sacredness to each person. In this view, existing embodiment anomalies are suggestive of God and reflect God's diversity.

The question of added enhancements is problematized by the *imago Dei*. At what point, if any, do we compromise valuable dimensions of being human such as vulnerability and fragility?[19] Christian doctrines of creation, Incarnation, and the resurrection of the body all underscore the goodness of the body. Embracing embodiment is, on the one hand, part of and necessary to sport. Sport is about the limits and the potential of bodily glory. In theory, sport is about realizing all that one can be through dedication, training, and negotiating obstacles. In many ways, the popular secular religion of sport does a far better job of celebrating the goodness of embodiment than do many reformed Protestant churches. However, elite sports can go beyond the celebration of the body and the actualization of athletic potential to

---

[18]See, for example, Robert Song, "Knowing There is No God, Still We Should Not Play God? Habermas on the Future of Human Nature," *Ecotheology* 11, no. 2 (2006): 191; Joshua M. Moritz, "Natures, Human Nature, Genes and Souls: Reclaiming Theological Anthropology Through Biological Structuralism," *Dialog: A Journal of Theology* 46, no. 3 (2007): 266; and Ted Peters, *Playing God? Genetic Determinism and Human Freedom*, 2nd ed. (New York: Routledge, 2003).

[19]Erik Parens, "The Goodness of Fragility: On the Prospect of Genetic Technologies Aimed at the Enhancement of Human Capacities," in *Contemporary Issues in Bioethics*, 5th ed., eds. Tom L. Beachamp and LeRoy Walters (Belmont, CA: Wadsworth Publishing, 1999) 596–602.

inflicting undue harm and, potentially, enhancing the body in ways that take athletes away from their embodied humanities. I am concerned with the power that the desire to win can have over all other values, including the value of being human.

Values influence the enhancements we create and the ways in which they are used. Some enhancements means may help us to realize human potential, and some may inadvertently limit or harm this potential. The future use of IGF-1 genetic modification technologies will help to increase muscular strength. The DREAM gene potentially will help us to suppress pain. But these technologies will not be used only to facilitate healing and a better quality of life. As long as winning is the preeminent value in sport, anything that helps athletes to win will be attractive for use. Little thought may be given to other implications of using enhancing means for the purpose of winning, including potential effects on sport's spiritual dimension.

One part of sport's spiritual dimension that may be affected by enhancements is flow. Flow experiences are grounded in the embodied person. As it stands, flow cannot be engineered; some conditions necessary to flow experiences can be cultivated but even these do not guarantee a flow experience. There is always the possibility that technology could be created to enhance flow experiences, but this seems unlikely as flow is not seen as a winning technique in elite sport but as a phenomenon that might occur and might help a performance. Flow is unpredictable both in its occurrence and its precise effect on athletic performance. Flow can inspire unexpected and awe-inspiring performances, but does not always. Technology is used to facilitate efficiency, not uncontrollable and unpredictable bursts of athletic perfection.

Although technological enhancements undoubtedly will increase athletes' strength, endurance, ability to withstand pain, and other physical functions, the question of how these enhancements will affect the embodied spiritual person, and particularly the human quest for hope and meaning, has not been adequately considered. While greater efficiency and strength can be gained from techno-science interventions, much stands to be lost if we are not attentive to values other than winning.

A Hope-centered Approach to the Sport Enhancement Debate

The use of techno-science in sport concerns a complex set of issues and questions with few straightforward answers. Responses to the use of techno-science must consider the complicated questions of what it means to be human and what it means to be virtuous humans. Spirituality must be part of this conversation especially since sport functions as a popular secular religion for many fans and athletes.

To reiterate, I am convinced that it is necessary first to widen the discussion regarding the values and assumptions that undergird the enhancement debate in sport if the question of what enhancements are acceptable is to be addressed adequately. In particular, attention must be paid to sport's spiritual dimension and especially the locations of hope in sport if we are to apprehend the implications of techno-science choices. In short, one of my goals has been to specify problems in the athletic enhancement debate by showing that the spiritual dimension of sport is morally relevant to this debate and has been neglected or forgotten.

Some of the points I have made regarding approaches to this question of techno-science usage in sport are important to recall. First, techno-science, religion, play, and sport are not all good or all bad. There is redemptive potential as well as the potential for harm in each of these. Second, there are a variety of intersections between elite sport and techno-science, including the increased visibility of existing advantages amongst athletes and added enhancements. Third, sport is a secular religion and has a spiritual function for many followers and participants. Fourth, hope is part of this function and there are at least four identifiable locations of hope in elite sport (e.g., winning, losing, and anticipating; perfect moments; star athletes; and relational embodiment). Fifth, techno-science use in elite sport affects these locations of hope. And sixth, there are four main approaches to the ethical discussion regarding enhancements and sport, none of which adequately address the spiritual dimension of elite sports.

Based on these established points, I will summarize and suggest some ways in which aspects of each of the four approaches to the sport enhancement debate may be reshaped through a consideration of sport's spiritual dimension of hope. Each of the four approaches has important components that ought to be retained in some measure and sometimes reshaped in light of sport's spiritual dimension.

Relational Autonomy and Well-being. There are very important elements in the first approach that was presented in chapter seven titled, "Individual Rights and Potential Physical Harms." By renaming this approach as "Relational Autonomy and Well-Being," I intend two shifts: 1) to expand attention to a broader understanding of autonomy that includes rights but extends beyond individual desires; and 2) to foster an understanding of well-being that includes avoidance of physical harm (non-maleficence), and expands to include beneficence (doing good).

An explicit relational understanding of autonomy helps to correct against myopic vision by drawing attention to how choices affect others and how systemic power imbalances affect global well-being. Political philosopher Michael Sandel cautions against what he calls a kind of "hyperagency" that is a Promethean desire to recreate human nature to satisfy only our immediate desires.[20] Without the ability to see beyond our current state and imagine a world more just and loving, we are doomed to social division, ecological disaster, and a lack of fulfillment. We hope for things that do not, in the end, satisfy our yearnings, and that often fail to benefit others and the environment.

In such a scenario, technology will be used not to meet our authentic selves and God—whoever God may be for us—but, as Cole-Turner writes, "to see ourselves in a new way, as our own projects for improvement."[21] This utility driven approach fails to take into account a larger vision for the world and people as dignified agents instead of as tools that can be improved and used. From a Christian viewpoint being human is more than the capacity to

---

[20] Michael Sandel, "The Case Against Perfection: What's Wrong With Designer Children, Bionic Athletes, and Genetic Engineering," in *Human Enhancement*, eds. Julian Salvescu and Nick Bostrom (Oxford, UK: Oxford University Press, 2009) 78.

[21] Ronald Cole-Turner, "Introduction: The Transhumanist Challenge," in *Transhumanism and Transcendence: Christian Hope in an Age of Technological Enhancement*, eds. Ronald Cole-Turner (Washington, DC: Georgetown University Press, 2011) 7.

make choices about what we want to possess; it is the capacity to make choices that contribute to communal dignity and overall well-being.[22]

Dignity-based arguments have been mounted against doping to enhance performance. But these arguments are critiqued on the basis that they prioritize particular values and thus take away the right of individuals to choose their values. However, this critique assumes that individual choice is the preeminent right. It may indeed be that some individuals genuinely prioritize conditional values such as fame, money, status, or victory over unconditional values such as health and well-being.[23] But what such critiques of dignity-based arguments miss, in addition to assuming the preeminence of individual choice, is the possibility that our capacity to identify our desires is molded to a large extent by a culture increasingly driven by technology and acquisition. We have a conundrum; the right to choose is important, but this right may not supersede all rights, and values and desires are not unencumbered.[24] We need to attend to the processes by which we come to choose these values and desires if we are to make more fully informed choices. We also need to explore what additional rights are important to human flourishing. In so doing, the possibility of a more fulfilling life increases.

---

[22] Karen Lebacqz, "Dignity and Enhancement in the Holy City," in *Transhumanism and Transcendence: Christian Hope in an Age of Technological Enhancement,* eds. Ronald Cole-Turner (Washington, DC: Georgetown University Press, 2011) 51–62. To experience self and others as created in God's image includes the capacity for awe, wonder, and respect for the dignity of diversely embodied others. This is no easy task in a culture that privileges individual gain and acquisition. As Richard Rohr and Andreas Ebert [Rohr and Ebert, *The Enneagram: A Christian Perspective* (New York: Crossroad Publishing, 2001), 21] insightfully ask: "Why in our encounter with life do we humans so often keep running up against ourselves instead of making a breakthrough to God, to the Totally Other?" If we cannot meet the Other, then we have lost the ability to experience transcendence. Instead, we will strive to re-create ourselves in our own image, and we will do so at the expense of fulfillment and a durable hopefulness.

[23] Brent M. Kious, "Philosophy on Steroids: Why the Anti-Doping Position Could Use a Little Enhancement," *Theoretical Medicine and Bioethics* 29 (2008): 223.

[24] Susan Sherwin, "Genetic Enhancement, Sports and Relational Autonomy," *Sport, Ethics and Philosophy* 1, no. 2 (2007): 171–80.

If well-being—and not merely avoidance of harm—is a criterion for the assessment of techno-science usage in elite sport, then the whole person must be considered. On a practical level, the consideration of all aspects of a person is impossible to do perfectly. While the well-being of the whole person does not translate well directly into policy regarding which enhancements are acceptable, it can draw attention to the multifaceted potential effects of techno-science on the athlete and athletic performances and, eventually, influence policy decisions. If embodiment, for example, is assumed to be good (as per the creation story and *imago Dei*) and if the body is healthy, then there may be little cause to change the embodied person through "enhancing" means. However, if well-being is compromised and techno-science could in some way increase well-being, then the use of enhancements may be warranted from this perspective.

For example, if an athlete sustains a soft tissue injury that could be healed more effectively or more quickly by a techno-science intervention that does not cause other harms, and if the athlete chooses it, there could be a case made to support the choice. Of course, it becomes more complicated when one considers choices that increase chances of injury, disability, or death. The glorification of bodily suffering and pain does not enhance well-being regardless of the distorted message that the capacity to withstand pain is indicative of a heroic disposition.

The question of what is meant by enhancement must also be addressed if the concept of well-being is taken seriously. To enhance means to make better but how do we know what better is? Again, the meaning of "better" has much to do with values. On the one hand, better is shaped by an extreme individualism that believes that acquisition, winning, and status will bring fulfillment and meaning. To an extent, they do—at least momentarily. On the other hand, the capacity of sport to inspire hope seems to be something to which many people turn repeatedly and refuse to give up easily. Part of hope, as has been discussed, is relationship and connection with others, including those who inspire us. Given current normative values, we may fail to recognize the meaningfulness of creaturely conditions of imperfection and vulnerability (including losing), interdependence, and even mortality.

The possible implications of techno-science usage for hope warrant careful consideration. Many people follow and/or participate in sport for reasons that relate to hope. Reliance on individual choice can mean the neglect of relevant systemic issues such as the distribution of power, the impact of an individual's choice on others, and the processes that form desire and choice. Unintentionally, choice to use enhancements may cause broader harms including damage to sport's spiritual dimension.

Fairness, Diversity, and Justice. I have reimagined the fairness approach as "fairness, diversity, and justice." This revision is meant to correct the mistaken equation of fairness with sameness. Much is made of the possibility of enhancing athletes to similar or same physical levels. There are three problematic assumptions associated with this goal: 1) by replicating physical advantages the athletes will have the same capacities; 2) we know many of these existing advantages and soon will be able to identify all of these advantages; and 3) athletic competition is ideally performed between people who are the same physically.

Theologian Ted Peters makes a persuasive case against both genetic and environmental determinism, arguing for a third factor, human spirit. An athlete excels not only because of his or her particular physical and genetic attributes, but environmental factors such as where and how one grows up, and human spirit, also influence athletic performance. As long as we remain human, and there is a "slippery slope" between enhanced human and trans-human,[25] there will be the gestalt mystery of the human person. We are more than the sum of our parts. Indeed, our "parts" cannot be neatly dissected and cannot make sense when regarded separately. We cannot be sure that even if a hockey player's cognitive ability to strategize were enhanced, that would help her become more like Hayley Wickenheiser or Wayne Gretzky. Even if all athletes shared the same physical advantages, the way in which these pieces come together within each person is different.

Not only do individuals actualize a combination of characteristics in many different ways, our wider contexts also effect the development of athletic abilities. These factors go beyond what coach an athlete has, and include systemic power issues. The uneven distribution of privilege is the

---

[25] Celia Deane-Drummond, "Re-Making Human Nature: Transhumanism, Theology and Creatureliness in Bioethical Controversies," in *Religion and Transhumanism: The Unknown Future of Human Enhancement*, eds. Calvin Mercer and Tracy J. Trothen (Westport, CT: Praeger, 2015) 251.

"playing field" that needs most attention and most "evening." Because of the global disparity of wealth, some budding athletes get the resources they need to develop professionally in their sport while others do not. And because some groups, most often able-bodied young males (and skin color is relevant to particular sports as well), are valued more than others, some get more resources than others. Even as I write this, male soccer players are being provided with superior grass playing fields while women players, at the same elite World Cup level, are being forced to use the less desirable artificial turf.[26] These same power dynamics affect who has access to enhancements and who does not.

While there is general agreement that effort and "heart" ought to be determining factors in athletic competitions and so one's capacity for effort should not be "artificially" altered, there are mood and psychological enhancers that are used regularly in training. Psychological techniques, music, and biofeedback, also are used to stimulate effort and improve focus. If physical enhancements such as genetic modification technologies become available and accepted, might not attempts be made to even the playing field regarding effort and heart? And what about cognitive abilities, such as the capacity to strategize quickly and creatively? But even if we were to create these enhancements and use them, would athletes then all be the same?

If they were, competitions would devolve into spectacles instead of human encounters in which there is a level of identification between fans and athletes. Without this sense of the imperfect performer sometimes having perfect moments, there would be no bridge that allows us to believe that anything is possible. There would be no inspiration, only entertainment. Sport hinges on the diversity of athletes. No one is the same in elite sports, but all possess exceptional qualities. Sometimes we see surprising performances because of the differences between athletes. For example, Gretzky's almost uncanny ability to predict where the puck and players will

---

[26] See, for example, Scott Stinson, "Complaint Over Artificial Turf at Women's World Cup Highlights Double Standard in Sports," (Toronto, ON) *National Post*, 15 October 2014, http://sports.nationalpost.com/2014/10/15/complaint-over-artificial-turf-at-womens-world-cup-highlights-double-standard-in-sports/?__federated=1.

be as a play unfolds, allowed him to stage some very strategic and beautiful goals.

I wonder if Gretzky would have been even better if he could have had greater muscle mass or oxygen-carrying capacity. Maybe he would been better. Or maybe there was a delicate balance of factors that he learned to put together in a unique way that might have been disrupted by an added enhancement. For fairness, likely he would not have received added enhancements but he may have been the benchmark for other players. Then one has to wonder what the effects would be if another forward who plays with a different style, received enhancements to make him or her more like Gretzky. These may work to improve their performance or, again, they may throw their style off or change them in ways that are not all desirable for their team. And what if the confluence of factors that make up an athlete interact with an enhancement in unexpected ways? Or, what if we ended up with a team of Wayne Gretzky's?

Techno-science may be used in ways that help us to see that athletes are even more diverse than meets the eye, and this diversity makes sport captivating. This increased visibility may help us to develop a greater appreciation of human diversity. Or, greater efforts will be made to flatten the diversity. The meanings of fairness and acceptable advantages will affect the use of enhancements in sport. Hopefully, the beauty of diversity will gain appreciation. If it does not, we risk losing unexpected athletes who can do amazing things.

Goods and the Nature of Sport. An approach that focuses on the goods and nature of sport is perhaps the most promising of the approaches to the sport enhancement debate. It may have the most potential for including sport's spiritual dimension as morally relevant.

The basic test of each sport is necessary to the identity of that sport. The question of how to define precisely each basic test is part of the key, in this approach, to deciding which enhancements might be unacceptable. The protection of sport's basic goods is the other part of the key.

Complications arise when an enhancement seems to change the sport's basic test. For example, does Pistorius run with cheetah legs or is it something else that he does? Does he satisfy the basic test of track competition? The governing bodies decided that he did as signaled by the decision to allow Pistorius to compete in Olympic running events. What about super swimsuits? Do they violate the basic test of swimming? Although FINA banned the suits, this decision seems based more on a discontinuity with past competitors than on a violation of swimming's basic test. The enhancing qualities of the suit were seen as too significant in increasing swimmers' speeds, but most would agree that the wearers were still swimming. A question that arises is how much increased buoyancy or streamlining would be too much for the motion of the competitor to be called swimming.

It is even more difficult to identify and agree on what goods characterize a sport than it is to identify the basic test with precision. Both internal and external goods are important to sports and, as Alasdair MacIntyre points out, the pursuit of neither is necessarily bad or unhealthy unless the acquisition of external goods supersedes the value placed on internal goods. As those aspects of sport that benefit the "whole community who participates in the practice,"[27] internal goods do not require winners and losers since they are not limited to winning participants.

I want to include hope as an internal good, along with confidence, empowerment, teamwork, joy, and others. External goods are ends such as fame, status, money, and victory that are restricted to the winners. External goods are typically more temporary and not experienced every time one plays. Internal goods go beyond external ones in terms of longevity and availability.

Regarding hope as a spiritual internal good of sport, the extended sports community includes fans; fans share in the benefits of hope in sport. In elite level sports, there are a significant number of people who persist in cheering for and investing in their team(s); who almost never give up hope; and who rejoice and despair in the human mystery that can lead to surprising victory, extraordinary beauty, and shocking defeat. All share in the internal goods of sport.

How will techno-science affect elite sports' locations of hope? The sense of meaning and fulfillment derived by fans and athletes in competition is connected to this persistent hope. If mystery is removed increasingly from sports performances, if competitions become more of a display than an

---

[27] Alasdair MacIntyre, *After Virtue: A Study in Moral Theory*, 3rd ed. (Notre Dame, IN: University of Notre Dame Press, 2007) 190–91.

opportunity for exercise of human excellence, this secular religion will lose its heart. At what point will such a configuration of elite sports cease to attract the best athletes and the committed fans? This spiritual dimension of sport is perhaps the preeminent internal good.

Therapy-Restoration-Enhancement. While having limited value because of the conceptual difficulties associated with line-drawing, the therapy-restoration-enhancement approach nonetheless has helpful aspects that ought to be maintained.

As stated earlier, generalizations are helpful as long as it is clear that there are exceptions. The intent of this approach is to rule out technologies that enhance athletes beyond what is considered "normal." The meaning of normal varies; for example, normal vision in Major League Baseball is higher than 20/20, which is considered normal for the rest of the population. Heart surgery was not normal in the 1960s, but it is today. A normal training regimen today for an Olympic weight lifter was not normal decades ago.

In this approach, technologies falling clearly in the enhancement zone are not acceptable, while those in the therapeutic zone are not only acceptable but are often ethically obligatory. Interventions falling in the middle zone of restoration, non-therapy, or prevention, may be acceptable. Consideration of these middle zone interventions is complicated and interesting. This middle zone includes interventions that prevent deterioration from what might be considered a "normal" state, interventions that are not therapeutic but do not enhance past "normal," and interventions that can restore one to a normal state.

Christianity understands humanity's prelapsarian (before the Fall) state as the state intended for humanity. The promise of resuming this state is God's future gift. It is part of salvation. In the eschaton, it is believed that God will give us transformed, new bodies and a new earth, through God's grace. Humans are extolled to suspend disbelief and to trust in God since it is only through God that this new life can be found. Humans can and ought to work towards right relationship and flourishing but ultimately a divine source is needed; we cannot re-discover a prelapsarian state without God.

Similarly, when we look to sport for moments of perfection and persistent, indeed insistent hope, we are looking for the sacred. We participate as we can in the work of redemption, knowing that we fall short but also knowing that we do have moments, fleeting though they are, of realized perfection (or, in Christian terms, realized eschatology). These moments, however trivial they seem, are meaningful in the ways that they inspire and insist that there are always possibilities. In short, co-creating human well-being and experiencing that well-being to the fullest extent are parts of redemptive work.

Therapeutic and most restorative interventions are used with the intent to heal and sustain life. Assessments of interventions in the complicated zone between therapy and enhancement must consider motive. For example, in the case of the pitcher who undergoes ulnar collateral ligament reconstruction (Tommy John surgery), is his or her intent to heal or to become better than he or she was before the injury? If it is to heal, then the intervention is theoretically justifiable but if the motive is only to enhance, then the surgery is not necessary. Unless the intent is to heal an injury, the risks and potential harms of the procedure are not justifiable. In this approach, one might hope that one's arm becomes even better than it was previously, but the main intent must be therapeutic to justify the potential harms.

Potential harms are not limited to immediate physical consequences. These harms can extend beyond the individual athlete and include distributive justice issues and implications for what it means to be human. The intent to become better humans or even, more simply, athletes, is fraught with challenges and risks. The meaning of "better" changes with context and is conditional upon normative values. Because I want something, it does not mean it will bring me fulfillment or meaning. The locations of hope in sport suggest that what humans long for is not primarily about becoming faster, stronger, or higher than what our humanness permits, but it is more the overcoming of difficult challenges and living into our potential that enhances happiness.

The problem with the enhancement end of the continuum is that we really do not know what enhancements would be fulfilling and make life more meaningful. To choose to construct ourselves or elite athletes in ways that we now think are improved may be getting ahead of ourselves.

Authenticity is about more than individual desire. The most important theological dictum relating to the sport enhancement debate may not be the Promethean precaution to avoid thinking of ourselves as divine, but the proactionary exhortation to become as fully human as possible. The avoidance of hubris is part of becoming more fully human, as is the claiming of one's power and voice. Without more voices weighing in on the sport enhancement debate, we will not get a fuller picture of what is at stake and what the possibilities might include.

As with traditional organized religions, sport can distort the very things that make it shine. Even with these distortions, sport inspires hope and brings out some of the best qualities we have to offer. Techno-science developments are changing the way we live, including sport. These changes are complicated and decisions regarding how best to use science and enhancing technologies in sport are becoming more challenging. But one thing is certain, sport's spiritual dimension includes hope, and the locations of hope in sport are morally relevant to the sport enhancement discussion.

Bibliography

Albanese, Catherine. *America: Religions and Religion*. Belmont, CA: Wadsworth, 1982.

Anderson, W. French. "Human Gene Therapy." In *Contemporary Issues in Bioethics*, 5th ed., edited by Tom L. Beauchamp and Leroy Walters, 581–85. Belmont, CA: Wadsworth Publishing, 1999.

Andreano, Ralph. "The Affluent Baseball Player." In *Games, Sport and Power*, edited by Gregory P. Stone, 117–26. New Brunswick, NJ: Rutgers University, 1972.

Aschwandan, Christie. "The Future of Cheating in Sports." *The Smithsonian Magazine*, July 2012. http://www.smithsonianmag.com/science-nature/The-Future-of-Cheating-in-Sports-160285295.html.

Aschwanden, Christie. "'Gene Cheats', Drug Scandals in Sport Would be Nothing Compared to the Potential for Genetic Engineering to Create 'Super Athletes.'" *New Scientist*, no. 2221 (15 January, 2000): 24–29.

Austin, Mike W. "Sports as Exercises in Spiritual Formation." *Journal of Spiritual Formation & Soul Care* 3, no. 1 (2010): 66–78.

Bain-Selbo, Eric. "Ecstasy, Joy, and Sorrow: the Religious Experience of Southern College Football." *Journal of Religion and Popular Culture* 20 (Fall 2008): 1–12.

———. *Game Day and God: Football, Faith, and Politics in the American South*. Macon, GA: Mercer University Press, 2009.

Baker, William J. "Religion." In *Routledge Companion to Sports History*, edited by S.W. Pope and John Nauright, 216–28. London and New York: Routledge, 2010.

Baum, Gregory. "Editorial: Sport, Society and Religion." In *Sport*, edited by Gregory Baum and John Coleman, 3–8. Edinburgh, UK: T&T Clark, 1989.

Beamish, Rob. *Steroids: A New Look at Performance-Enhancing Drugs*. Santa Barbara, CA: Praeger, 2011.

Bellah, Robert N. "Civil Religion in America." In *Religion in America*, edited by W.G. McLoughlin and R.N. Bellah, 3–23. Boston: Houghton Mifflin, 1967.

Birrel, Susan, and Diana M. Richter. "Is a Diamond Forever? Feminist Transformations of Sport." In *Women, Sport and Culture*, edited by Susan Birrell and Cheryl L. Cole, 221–44. Windsor, ON: Human Kinetics, 1994.

Blazer, Annie. "Religion and Sports in America." *Religion Compass* 6, no. 5 (2012): 287–97.

Bouchard, C. "Genetics and Sports Performance." Paper presented at the International Convention on Science, Education and Medicine in Sport, Glasgow, United Kingdom, 20 July 2012.

Braxton, Donald M. "Does Transhumanism Face an Uncanny Valley Among the Religious?" In *Religion and Transhumanism: The Unknown Future of Human Enhancement*, edited by Calvin Mercer and Tracy J. Trothen, 331–50. Westport, CT: Praeger, 2015.

Bridel, William and Genevieve Rail. "Sport, Sexuality, and the Production of (Resistant) Bodies: De-/Re-Constructing the Meanings of Gay Male Marathon Corporeality." *Sociology of Sport Journal* 24 (2007): 127–44.

Brioux, Bill. "TV Ratings for Olympics Down, Digital Viewing Soars." In *The* (Halifax) *Chronicle Herald*, 25 February 2014. www.thechronicleherald.ca>News>Sochi.

Brock, Rita Nakashima. "And a Little Child Will Lead Us: Christianity and Child Abuse." In *Christianity, Patriarchy and Abuse: A Feminist Critique*, edited by Joanne Carlson Brown and Carole R. Bohn, 42–61. New York: Pilgrim Press, 1989.

Brownlee, Christen. "Gene Doping: Will Athletes Go for the Ultimate High?" *Science News* 166, no. 18 (October 2004): 280–81.

Burkett, Brendan, Mike McNamee, and Wolfgang Potthast. "Shifting Boundaries in Sports Technology and Disability: Equal Rights or Unfair Advantage in the Case of Oscar Pistorius?" *Disability & Society* 26, no. 5 (2011): 643–54.

Caplan, A. L. "Does the Biomedical Revolution Spell the End of Sport?" *British Journal of Sports Medicine* 42 (2008): 996–97.

Cavar, Mike, Damir Sekulic, and Zoran Culjak. "Complex Interaction of Religiousness with other Factors in Relation to Substance Use and Misuse Among Female Athletes." *Journal of Religious Health* 51 (2012): 381–89.

Carmody, Denise Larner. "Big-time Spectator Sports: A Feminist Christian Perspective." *New Catholic World* (July/August 1986): 173–77.

Chadwick, Ruth. "Nutrigenomics, Individualism and Sports." In *Genetic Technology and Sport: Ethical Questions*, edited by Claudio Marcello Tamburrini and Torbjörn Tännsjö, 126–35. London: Routledge, 2005.

Chandler, Joan M. "Sport is Not a Religion." In *Sport and Religion*, edited by Shirl J. Hoffman, 55–61. Champaign, IL: Human Kinetics Books, 1992.

Chapman, Audrey. "Religious Perspectives on Human Germ Line Modifications." In *Beyond Cloning*, edited by Ronald Cole Turner, 64–76. Harrisburg, PA: Trinity Press International, 2001.

Chidester, David. "The Church of Baseball, the Fetish of Coca-Cola, and the Potlatch of Rock 'n' Roll." In *Religion and Popular Culture in America*, edited by Bruce David Forbes and Jeffrey H. Mahan, 219–38. Berkeley: University of California Press, 2000.

Cipriani, Roberto. "Sport as (Spi)rituality." *Implicit Religion* 15, no. 2 (2012): 139-51.

Clinebell, Howard. *Understanding and Counselling Persons with Alcohol, Drug, and Behavioral Addictions*. Nashville, TN: Abingdon, 1998.

Cole, David R. "The Genome and the Human Genome Project." In *Genetics: Issues of Social Justice*, edited by Ted Peters, 49–70. Cleveland, OH: Pilgrim Press, 1998.

Cole-Turner, Ronald. "Extreme Longevity Research: A Progressive Protestant Perspective." In *Religion and the Implications of Radical Life Extension*, edited by Derek F. Maher and Calvin Mercer, 51–61. New York: Palgrave Macmillan, 2009.

———. "Introduction: The Transhumanist Challenge." In *Transhumanism and Transcendence—Christian Hope in an Age of Technological Enhancement*, edited by Ronald Cole-Turner, 1–18. Washington, DC: Georgetown University Press, 2011.

———. "Transhumanism and Christianity." In *Transhumanism and Transcendence— Christian Hope in an Age of Technological Enhancement*, edited by Ronald Cole-Turner, 193–204. Washington, DC: Georgetown University Press, 2011.

———, ed. *Transhumanism and Transcendence: Christian Hope in an Age of Technological Enhancement*. Washington, DC: Georgetown University, 2011.

Collins, Francis S. "Human Genetics." In *Cutting-Edge Bioethics—A Christian Exploration of Technologies and Trends*, edited by John F. Kilner, C. Christopher Hook, and Diann B. Uustal, 3–17. Grand Rapids, MI: Eerdmans Publishing, 2002.

Csikszentmihalyi, Mihalyi. *Beyond Boredom and Anxiety*. San Francisco: Jossey-Blass, 1975.

———. "The Concept of Flow." In *Play and Learning*, edited by Brian Sutton-Smith, 257–74. New York: Gardner Press, 1979.

Csikszentmihalyi, Mihalyi, and Giovanni B. Moneta. "Models of Concentration in Natural Environments: A Comparative Approach Based on Streams of Experiential Data." *Social Behavior and Personality* 27, no. 6 (1999): 603–38.

Culbertson, Leon. "Pandora Logic; Rules, Moral Judgment and the Fundamental Principles of Olympism." *Sport, Ethics and Philosophy* 6, no. 2 (2012): 195–210.

Cumming-Long, Grace D. *Passion & Reason: Women Views of Christian Life*. Louisville, KY: Westminster/John Knox Press, 1993.

Daly, Mary. "Theology After the Demise of God the Father: A Call for the Castration of Sexist Religion." In *Sexist Religion: Women in the Church*, edited by Alice L. Hageman, 125–42. New York: Association Press, 1974.

Davancy, Sheila Greeve. "Theology and the Turn to Cultural Analysis." In *Converging on Culture: Theologians in Dialogue With Cultural Analysis and Criticism*, edited by Delwin Brown, Sheila Greeve Davaney, and Kathryn Tanner, 3–16. Oxford, UK: Oxford University Press, 2001.

Davies, Gareth A. "London 2012 Olympics: double amputee Oscar Pistorius makes 400m qualifying time." London Telegraph, 24 March 2011. www.telegraph.co.uk/sport/othersports/olympics/8403343/London-2012-Olympics-double-amputee-Oscar-Pistorius-makes-400m-qualifying-time.html

Deane-Drummond, Celia. "God's Image and Likeness in Humans and Other Animals: Performative Soul-Making and Graced Nature." *Zygon* 47, no. 4 (December 2012): 934–48.

———. "Re-Making Human Nature: Transhumanism, Theology and Creatureliness in Bioethical Controversies." In *Religion and Transhumanism: The Unknown Future of Human Enhancement*, edited by Calvin Mercer and Tracy J. Trothen, 245–254. Westport, CT: Praeger, 2015.

DeFrantz, Anita. "An Open Letter: Sport Belongs To Us All." *Journal of Women and Religion* 18 (2000): 13–14.

Dillon, Kathleen M., and Tait, Jennifer L. "Spirituality and Being in the Zone in Team Sports: A Relationship?" *Journal of Sport Behavior* 23, no. 2 (2000): 91–100.

Dixon, Nicholas. "Performance-Enhancing Drugs, Paternalism, Meritocracy, and Harm to Sport." *Journal of Social Philosophy* 39, no. 2 (2008): 246–68.

Doehring, Carrie. *The Practice of Pastoral Care: A Postmodern Approach*. Louisville, KY: The Westminster John Knox Press, 2006.

Dreyfuss, Hubert, and Sean Dorrance Kelly. *All Things Shining—Reading the Western Classics to Find Meaning in a Secular Age*. New York: Free Press, 2011.

Durkheim, Émile. *The Elementary Forms of the Religious Life*. New York: Free Press, 1965 [1912].

Dvorsky, George. "Michael Phelps: 'Naturally' Transhuman." *The Institute for Ethics and Emerging Technologies*, 19 August 2008. http://ieet.org/index.php/IEET/print/2575/.

Eassom, Simon. Head of Sports Studies at De Montfort University. Interview by Amanda Smith, *Sports Factor, ABC*, United Kingdom 2001, www.abc.net.au/rn/talks/8.30/sportsf/stories/s435073.htm

Edwards, Lisa, and Carwyn Jones. "Postmodernism, Queer Theory and Moral Judgment in Sport." *International Review for the Sociology of Sport* 44, no. 4 (2009): 331–44.

Elkington, Sam. "Articulating a Systematic Phenomenology of Flow: An Experience-Process Perspective." *Leisure/Loisir* 34, no. 3 (2010): 327–60.

Ellis, Robert. "'Faster, Higher, Stronger': Sport and the Point of It All." *Anvil* 28, no. 1 (2012): 5–13.

———. "The Meaning of Sport: An Empirical Study into the Significance Attached to Sporting Participation and Spectating in the UK and US." *Practical Theology* 5, no. 2 (2012)" 169–188.

Evans, Christopher H., and William R. Herzog II, eds. *The Faith of 50 Million: Baseball, Religion, and American Culture*. Louisville, KY: Westminster John Knox Press, 2002.

Fagg, Lawrence W. "Are There Intimations of Divine Transcendence in the Physical World?" *Zygon* 38, no. 3 (September 2003): 559–72.

Feezell, Randolph. *Sport, Philosophy, and Good Lives*. Lincoln: University of Nebraska Press, 2013.

———. "Sport, Religious Belief and Religious Diversity." *Journal of the Philosophy of Sport* 40, no. 1 (May 2013): 135–63.

Feschuk, Dave. "Canadian Speed Skater Gilmore Junio Gives Up His Spot to Denny Morrison." In *The Toronto Star*, 11 February 2014. www.thestar.com.

Fisher, Mathew Zaro. "More Human than the Human? Toward A 'Transhumanist' Christian Theological Anthropology." In *Religion and Transhumanism: The Unknown Future of Human Enhancement*, edited by Calvin Mercer and Tracy J. Trothen, 23–38. Westport, CT: Praeger, 2015.

Foer, Franklin. *How Football Explains the World*. London: Arrow Books, 2004.

Foucault, Michel. *Technologies of the Self*. Boston: University of Massachusetts Press, 1988.

Frey, Rodney E. "Another Look at Technology and Science." *Journal of Technology Education* 3, no. 1 (2011): 1–12. www.scholar.lib.vt.edu/ejournals/JTE/v3n1/pdf/frey.pdf.

Friedmann, Theodore, Olivier Rabin, and Mark S. Frankel. "Gene Doping and Sport." *Science* 327 (2013): 647–48.

Garcia, Tamara, and Ronald L. Sandler. "Enhancing Justice." In *Ethics and Emerging Technologies*, edited by Ronald L. Sandler, 252–56. London: Palgrave MacMillan, 2013.

Garner, Stephen. "Christian Theology and Transhumanism: The 'Created Co-Creator' and Bioethical Principles." In *Religion and Transhumanism, Religion and Transhumanism: The Unknown Future of Human Enhancement*, edited by Calvin Mercer and Tracy J. Trothen, 229–44. Westport, CT: Praeger, 2015.

Garratt, Dean. "'Sporting Citizenship': the Rebirth of Religion?" *Pedagogy, Culture & Society* 18, no. 2 (2010): 123–43.

Gaudard, A., M.E. Varlet, F. Bressolle, et al., "Drugs for Increasing Oxygen and Their Potential Use in Doping: A Review." *Sports Medicine* 33, no. 3 (2003): 187–212.

Gebara, Ivone. *Out of the Depths: Women's Experience of Evil and Salvation*. Minneapolis: Fortress Press, 2002.

Gillis, Charlie. "The Real Scandal in Hockey: Ken Campbell on the Problem With Canada's Obsession." *Maclean's*, 20 January 2013. http://www2.macleans.ca/2013/01/20/year-round-training-and-320000-wont-guarantee-an-nhl-career-or-even-a-future-fan/.

Gleaves, John. "No Harm, No Foul? Justifying Bans of Safe Performance-Enhancing Drugs." *Sport, Ethics and Philosophy* 4, no. 3 (2010): 270–83.

Goodson, Jacob L. "The Quest for Perfection in the Sport of Baseball: The Magnanimous Individual or the Magnanimous Team?" In *Sports and Christianity: Historical and Contemporary Perspectives*, edited by Nick J. Watson and Andrew Parker, 225–49. New York: Routledge, 2013.

Gotz, Igancio L. "Spirituality and the Body." *Religious Education* 96, no. 1 (2001): 2–19.

Green, Ronald. *Babies By Design: The Ethics of Genetic Choice*. New Haven, CT: Yale University Press, 2007.

Grimshaw, Michael. "I Can't Believe My Eyes: The Religious Ascetics of Sport as Post-Modern Salvific Moments." *Implicit Religion* 3, no. 2 (2002): 87–99.

Guttman, Allen. *From Ritual to Record: The Nature of Modern Sports*. New York: Columbia University Press, 1978.

Habermas, Jürgen. *Knowledge and Human Interest*. Boston: Beacon Press, 1971.

Harvey, Lincoln. "Towards a Theology of Sport: A Proposal." *Anvil* 28, no. 1 (2012): 5–15.

Hefner, Philip. "The Animal that Aspires to be an Angel: The Challenge of Transhumanism." *Dialog: A Journal of Theology* 48, no. 2 (June 2009): 158–67.

Herrigel, Eugen. *Zen in the Art of Archery*. New York: Random House, 1999/1971.

Hemphill, Dennis. "Performance Enhancement and Drug Control in Sport: Ethical Considerations." *Sport in Society* 12, no. 3 (2009): 313–26.

Higgs, Robert J. *God in the Stadium: Sports and Religion in America*. Lexington: University Press of Kentucky, 1995.

Higgs, Robert J. "Muscular Christianity, Holy Play, and Spiritual Exercises: Confusion About Christ in Sports and Religion." In *Sport and Religion*, edited by Shirl J Hoffman, 89–103. Champaign, IL: Human Kinetics Books, 1992.

Higgs, Robert J., and M.C. Braswell. *An Unholy Alliance: The Sacred and Modern Sports*. Macon, GA: Mercer University Press, 2004.

Hoffman, Shirl J. *Good Game: Christianity and the Culture of Sports*. Waco, TX: Baylor University Press, 2010.

———. "Recovering a Sense of the Sacred in Sport." In *Sport and Religion*, edited by Shirl J Hoffman, 153–59. Champaign, IL: Human Kinetics Books, 1992.

———. "The Sanctification of Sport: Can the Mind of Christ Coexist with the Killer Instinct?" *Christianity Today* 30, no. 6 (April 1984): 17–21.

———. *Sport and Religion*. Champaign, IL: Human Kinetics Books, 1992.

————. "Whatever Happened To Play?" *Christianity Today* 54, no. 2 (February 2010): 21–25.

Hopkins, Patrick D. "A Salvation Paradox for Transhumanism: *Saving* You versus Saving *You.*" In *Religion and Transhumanism: The Unknown Future of Human Enhancement*, edited by Calvin Mercer and Tracy J. Trothen, 71–82. Westport, CT: Praeger, 2015.

Hopsicker, Peter M. "Miracles in Sport: Finding the 'Ears to Hear' and the 'Eyes to See'." *Sport, Ethics and Philosophy* 3, no. 1 (2009): 75–93.

House of Commons, Science and Technology Committee. "Human Enhancement Technologies in Sport: Second Report of Session 2006–07." 7 February 2007, London England.

House of Commons, Science and Technology Committee, "Memorandum from Professor Julian Savulescu" in "Human Enhancement Technologies in Sport: Second Report of Session 2006–07." 7 February 2007, London, England.

Householder, Mark, Benjamin J. Chase, and Ted Kluck. "Are Sports the Problem? Three Views." *Christianity Today* 54, no. 2 (2010): 26–27.

Huizinga, Johan. *Homo Ludens: A Study of the Play Element in Culture.* Boston: Beacon Press, 1955.

Jackson, Susan, and Mihalyi Csikszentmihalyi. *Flow in Sports: The Keys to Optimal Experiences and Performance.* Champaign, IL: Human Kinetics, 1999.

Johnson, Elizabeth A. *She Who Is: The Mystery of God in Feminist Theological Discourse.* New York: Crossroad, 1992.

Joisten, Karen. "Man, Mortality, and the Athletic Hero: Yesterday and Today." In *Sport and Christianity: A Sign of the Times in the Light of Faith*, edited by Kevin L.C. Lixey, Christoph Hubenthal, Dietmar Meith, and Norbert Muller, 15–38. Washington DC: The Catholic University of America Press, 2012.

Jönsson, Kutte. "Who's Afraid of Stella Walsh? On Gender, 'Gene Cheaters', and the Promise of Cyborg Athletes." *Sport, Ethics and Philosophy* 1, no. 2 (2007): 239–62.

Kahane, Guy. "Mastery Without Mystery: Why There is No Promethean Sin in Enhancement." *Journal of Applied Philosophy* 28, no. 4 (2011): 355–68.

Kambouris, M., F. Ntalouka, G. Ziogas, and N. Maffuli. "Predictive Genomics DNA Profiling for Athletic Performance." *Recent Patents on DNA & Gene Sequences* 6, no. 3 (2012): 229–39.

Kelly, Patrick. "Flow, Sport and the Spiritual Life." In *Theology, Ethics and Transcendence in Sports,* edited by J. Parry, M. Nesti and N. Watson, 163–77. London: Routledge, 2011.

Keri, Jonah "Interview With Dr. Frank Jobe." ESPN.com. 13 September 2007.

King M.R. "A League of their Own? Evaluating Justifications for the Division of Sport into 'Enhanced' and 'Unenhanced' Leagues." *Sport, Ethics and Philosophy*, 6, no. 10 (2012): 31–45.

Kious, Brent M. "Philosophy on Steroids: Why the Anti-Doping Position Could Use a Little Enhancement." *Theoretical Medicine and Bioethics* 29 (2008): 213–34.

Kirby, Kate, Aidan Moran, and Suzanne Guerin. "A Qualitative Analysis of the Experiences of Elite Athletes Who Have Admitted to Doping for Performance

Enhancement." *International Journal of Sport Policy and Politics* 3, no. 2 (2011): 205–24.

Kirby, Sandra, Lorraine Greaves, and Olena Hankivsky. Th*e Dome of Silence: Sexual Harassment and Abuse in Sport.* Halifax, NS: Fernwood, 2002.

Kretschmann, Rolf, and Caroline Benz. "Morality of Christian Athletes in Competitive Sports: A Review." *Sports Science Review* 21, nos. 1–2 (2002): 5–20.

Kretchmar, R. Scott. "The Normative Heights and Depths of Play." *Journal of the Philosophy of Sport* 34, no. 1 (2007): 1–12.

Kretchmar, Scott. "Why Dichotomies Make it Difficult to See Games as Gifts of God." In *Theology, Ethics and Transcendence in Sports,* edited by Jim Parry, Mark Nesti, and Nick Watson, 185–200. London: Routledge, 2011.

Kuhn, Thomas S. *The Structure of Scientific Revolutions,* 2nd ed. Chicago: University of Chicago Press, 1970.

Kusz, Kyle. *Revolt of the White Athlete: Race, Media and the Emergence of Extreme Athletes in America.* New York: Peter Lang Publishing, 2007.

Ladd, Tony, and James A. Mathisen. *Muscular Christianity: Evangelical Protestants and the Development of American Sport.* Grand Rapids, MI: Baker Books, 1999.

Lebacqz, Karen. "Dignity and Enhancement in the Holy City." In *Transhumanism and Transcendence: Christian Hope in an Age of Technological Enhancement,* edited by Ronald Cole-Turner, 51–62. Washington, DC: Georgetown University Press, 2011.

Lelwica, Michelle M. "Losing Their Way to Salvation: Women, Weight Loss, and the Salvation Myth of Culture Lite." In *Religion and Popular Culture in America,* edited by Bruce David Forbes, and Jeffrey H. Mahan, 180–200. Berkeley: University of California Press, 2000.

Levinas, Emmanuel. *Humanism of the Other.* Champaign, IL: University of Illinois Press, 2006.

Loland, Sigmund. "A Well Balanced Life Based on 'The Joy of Effort': Olympic Hype or a Meaningful Ideal?" *Sport, Ethics and Philosophy* 6, no. 2 (2012): 155–65.

Loland, Sigmund, and Hans Hoppeler. "Justifying Anti-Doping: The Fair Opportunity Principle and the Biology of Performance Enhancement." *European Journal of Sport Science* 12, no. 4 (2012): 347–53.

Longman, Jere. "Fit Young Pitchers See Elbow Repair as Cure-All." *New York Times* (20 July 2007). http://newyorktimes.com/2007/07/20/sports/baseball/20surgery.html.

Lowenthal, K.M. *Religion, Culture and Mental Health.* Cambridge, UK: Cambridge University Press, 2007.

MacIntyre, Alasdair. *After Virtue: A Study in Moral Theory* [1981, 1984]. 3rd ed. Notre Dame, IN: University of Notre Dame Press, 2007.

Macur, Juliet. "Rule Jostles Runners Who Race to their Own Tune." *New York Times* (1 November 2007). http://www.nytimes.com/2007/11/01/sports/othersports/01marathon.html?_r=2&.

Magdalinski, Tara. "Performance Technologies: Drugs and Fastskin at the Sydney 2000 Olympics." *Media International Australia* 97 (2000): 59–69.

———. *Sport, Technology and the Body: The Nature of Performance.* New York: Routledge, 2009.

Magdalinski, Tara, and Timothy J. L. Chandler, eds. *With God on their Side*. London, Routledge, 2002.

Maher, Derek F., and Calvin Mercer, eds. *Religion and the Implications of Radical Life Extension*. New York: Palgrave Macmillan, 2009.

Maravelias, C., A. Dona, M. Stefanidou, and C. Spiliopoulou. "Adverse Effects of Anabolic Steroids in Athletes: A Constant Threat." *ScienceDirect* 158, no. 3 (2005): 167–75.

Marcuse, Herbert. *One Dimensional Man: Studies in the Ideology of Advanced Industrial Society*. Boston: Beacon Press, 1964.

Markovits, Andrei S., and Emily K. Albertson. *Sportista: Female Fandom in the United States*. Philadelphia: Temple University Press, 2012.

Maslow, Abraham H. *Toward a Psychology of Being*. Princeton, NJ: Van Nostrand, 1962.

Massarelli, Raphaël, and Thierry Terret. "The Paradise Lost? Mythological Aspects of Modern Sport." *Sport, Ethics and Philosophy* 5, no. 4 (2011): 396–413.

Mathisen, James. "From Civil Religion to Folk Religion: The Case of American Sport." In *Sport and Religion*, edited by Shirl J. Hoffman, 17–33. Champaign, IL: Human Kinetics Books, 1992.

McCarroll, Pamela R. *The End of Hope—The Beginning: Narratives of Hope in the Face of Death and Trauma*. Minneapolis: Fortress Press, 2014.

McCrory, Paul. "Super Athletes or Gene Cheats?" *British Journal of Sports Medicine London*. 37, no. 3 (2003): 192–93.

McKenny, Gerald P. "Transcendence, Technological Enhancement, and Christian Theology." In *Transhumanism and Transcendence: Christian Hope in an Age of Technological Enhancement*, edited by Ronald Cole-Turner, 177–92. Washington, DC: Georgetown University Press, 2011.

Mechikoff, R.A., and S.G. Estes. *A History and Philosophy of Sport and Physical Education*. 4th ed. New York: McGraw-Hill, 2005.

Mieth, Dietmar. "A Christian Vision of Sport." In *Sport and Christianity: A Sign of the Times in the Light of Faith,* edited by Kevin L.C. Lixey, Christoph Hubenthal, Dietmar Meith, and Norbert Muller, 156–85. Washington, DC: Catholic University of America Press, 2012.

———. "The Ethics of Sport." In *Sport*, edited by Gregory Baum and John Coleman. Edinburgh, UK: T&T Clark, 1989.

Mercer, Calvin, and Tracy J. Trothen, eds. *Religion and Transhumanism: The Unknown Future of Human Enhancement*. Westport, CT: Praeger, 2015.

Miah, Andy. "The DREAM Gene for the Posthuman Athlete: Reducing Exercise-Induced Pain Sensations Using Gene Transfer." In *The Anthropology of Sport and Human Movement: A Biocultural Perspective*, edited by Robert R. Sands and Linda R. Sands, 327–41. Plymouth, UK: Lexington Books, 2010.

———. "From Anti-Doping to a 'Performance Policy': Sport Technology, Being Human, and Doing Ethics." *European Journal of Sport Science* 5, no. 1 (2005): 51–57.

———. *Genetically Modified Athletes: Biomedical Ethics, Gene Doping, and Sport*. New York: Routledge, 2004.

———. "Towards the Transhuman Athlete: Therapy, Non-Therapy and Enhancement." *Sport in Society* 13, no. 2 (2010): 221–33.

Michaelson, Valerie, Tracy Trothen , Frank Elgar, and William Pickett. "Eucharistic Eating, Family Meals and the Health of Adolescent Girls: A Canadian Study." *Practical Theology* 7, no. 2 (2014): 125–43.

Møller, Verner. *The Ethics of Doping and Anti-Doping: Redeeming the Soul of Sport?* New York: Routledge, 2010.

Moltmann, Jürgen. *God in Creation: A New Theology of Creation and the Spirit of God.* Translated by Margaret Kohl. San Francisco: Harper & Row, 1985.

———. "Olympia Between Politics and Religion." In *Sport*, edited by Gregory Baum and John Coleman, 101–09. Edinburgh, UK: T&T Clark, 1989.

———. *The Spirit of Life: A Universal Affirmation.* Translated by Margaret Kohl. Minneapolis: Fortress Press, 1992.

Morgan, William J. *Why Sports Morally Matter.* New York: Routledge, 2006.

Moritz, Joshua M. "Evolution, the End of Human Uniqueness, and the Election of the *Imago Dei.*" *Theology and Science* 9, no. 3 (2011): 307–39.

———. "Natures, Human Nature, Genes and Souls: Reclaiming Theological Anthropology Through Biological Structuralism." *Dialog: A Journal of Theology* 46, no. 3 (2007): 263–80.

Munro, M. "Dressing for Success at the Olympics; Is it 'Doping on a Hangar' or Is it Just a Swimsuit? Either Way, Canada is Hoping that a Little Technology Will Lead to a Gold Strike in Beijing." *The Gazette* (27 July 2008). http://search.proquest.com/docview/434667680?accountid=6180.

Murray, Thomas H. "Making Sense of Fairness in Sports." *The Hastings Center Report* 40, no. 2 (2010): 13–15.

Murphy, Michael, and Rhea A. White. *In the Zone: Transcendent Experience in Sports.* New York: Open Road Integrated Media, 1978.

Neal, Wes. *Total Release Performance: A New Concept in Winning.* Grand Island, NE: Cross Training Publishing, 2000.

Novak, Michael. "The Joy of Sports." In *Religion and Sport: The Meeting of Sacred and Profane*, edited by Charles S. Prebish, 151–72. Westport, CT: Greenwood Press, 1993.

———. *The Joy of Sports: End Zones, Bases, Baskets, Balls and Consecration of the American Spirit.* New York: Basic Books, 1967/1994.

Nowotny, Helga, and Giuseppe Testa. *Naked Genes: Reinventing the Human in the Molecular Age.* Translated by Mitch Cohen. Cambridge, MA: MIT Press, 2010.

O'Connor, Lanty M., and John A. Vozenilek. "Is It the Athlete or the Equipment? An Analysis of the Top Swim Performances from 1990 to 2010." *Journal of Strength and Conditioning Research* 25, no. 12 (2011): 3239–41.

O'Gorman, Kevin. *Saving Sport: Sport, Society and Spirituality.* Dublin, UK: Columbia Press, 2010.

Overman, Steven J. *The Influence of the Protestant Ethic on Sport and Recreation.* Aldershot, UK: Avebury Ashgate Publishing, 1997.

Parens, Erik. "The Goodness of Fragility: On the Prospect of Genetic Technologies Aimed at the Enhancement of Human Capacities." In *Contemporary Issues in*

Bioethics, 5th ed., edited by Tom L. Beachamp and LeRoy Walters, 596–602. Belmont, CA: Wadsworth Publishing, 1999.

Pargament, Kenneth I. "The Pursuit of False Gods: Addressing the Spiritual Dimension of Addictions in Counseling." In *Psychotherapy as Cure of the Soul*, edited by Thomas St. James O'Connor, Kristine Lund, and Patricia Berendsen, 245–54. Waterloo, ON: Waterloo Lutheran Seminary Press, 2014.

———. "Searching for the Sacred: Toward a Non-Reductionist Theory of Spirituality." In *APA Handbooks in Psychology, Religion, and Spirituality: Vol. 1 Context, Theory, and Research*, edited by K.I. Pargament, J.J. Exline, and J. Jones, 257–74. Washington, DC: American Psychological Association, 2013.

———. "Spirituality as an Irreducible Human Motivation and Process." *International Journal For The Psychology Of Religion* 23, no. 4 (1 October 2013): 271–81.

Parry, Jim. "Must Scientists think Philosophically about Science?" In *Philosophy and the Sciences of Exercise, Health and Sport: Critical Perspectives on Research Methods*, edited by Mike McNamee, 20–31. New York: Routledge, 2005.

Partridge, Brad. "Fairness and Performance-Enhancing Swimsuits at the 2009 Swimming World Championships: the 'Asterisk' Championships." *Sport, Ethics and Philosophy* 5, no. 1 (2011): 63–74.

Peace, Thomas G.M. "Journeying by Canoe: Reflections on the Canoe and Spirituality." *Leisure/Loisir* 33, no. 1 (2009): 217–39.

Pengelley, Richard. "Sport and Spirituality: an Ancient Connection for Our Modern Times." *Dialogue Australasia* 20 (October 2008): 1–9.

Percy, Martyn, and Rogan Taylor. "Something for the Weekend, Sir? Leisure, Ecstasy and Identity in Football and Contemporary Religion." *Leisure Studies* 16 (1997): 37–49.

Peters, Ted. *God—The World's Future: Systematic Theology for a New Era*, 2nd ed. Minneapolis: Fortress Press, 2000.

Peters, Ted. *Playing God? Genetic Determinism and Human Freedom*, 2nd ed. New York: Routledge, 2003.

Peters, Ted. "Progress and Provolution: Will Transhumanism Leave Sin Behind?" In *Transhumanism and Transcendence: Christian Hope in an Age of Technological Enhancement*, edited by Ronald Cole-Turner, 63–86. Washington, DC: Georgetown University Press, 2011.

Prebish, Charles S. *Religion and Sport: The Meeting of Sacred and Profane*. Westport, CT: Greenwood Press, 1993.

Price, Joseph L. "An American Apotheosis: Sport as Popular Religion." In *Religion and Popular Culture in America*, edited by Bruce David Forbes and Jeffrey H. Mahan, 195–212. Berkeley: University of California Press, 2000.

Price, Joseph L. "Here I Cheer: Conversion Narratives of Baseball Fans." *Criterion* 42, no. 2 (Spring 2003): 12–19.

Price, Joseph L. *Rounding the Bases: Baseball and Religion in America*. Macon, GA: Mercer University Press, 2006.

Ratele, Kopano. "Looks: Subjectivity as Commodity." *Agenda* 90, no. 25 (2011): 92–103.

Reyser, Stephen. "Secular Versus Religious Fans: Are They Different?: An Empirical Examination." *Journal of Religion and Popular Culture*. 12 (Spring 2006): 1–11.

Rivera, Mayra. *The Touch of Transcendence*. London, UK: Westminster John Knox Press, 2007.

Robinson, Laura. *Crossing the Line: Violence and Sexual Assault in Canada's National Sport*. Toronto, ON: McClelland & Stewart, 1998.

Robinson, Simon. "The Spiritual Journey." In *Sport and Spirituality: An Introduction*, edited by J. Parry, S. Robinson, N. Watson, and M. Nesti, 38–58. London, UK: Routledge, 2007.

Rohr, Richard, and Andreas Ebert. *The Enneagram: A Christian Perspective*. New York: Crossroad Publishing, 2001.

Saiving, Valerie. "The Human Situation: A Feminine View." *Journal of Religion* 40 (April 1960): 100–12.

Sandel, Michael. "The Case Against Perfection: What's Wrong With Designer Children, Bionic Athletes, and Genetic Engineering." In *Human Enhancement*, edited by Julian Salvescu and Nick Bostrom, 93–104. Oxford, UK: Oxford University Press, 2009.

Sanford, A. Whitney. "Pinned on Karma Rock: Whitewater Kayaking as Religious Experience." *Journal of the American Academy of Religion* 75, no. 4 (2007): 875–95.

Santana, Richard W. and Gregory Erickson. *Religion and Popular Culture: Rescripting the Sacred*. Jefferson, NC: McFarland & Co., 2008.

Scarpa, Stefano, and Attilio Nicola Carraro. "Does Christianity Demean the Body and Deny the Value of Sport?: A Provocative Thesis." *Sport, Ethics and Philosophy* 5, no. 2 (2011): 110–23.

Schilbrack, Kevin. "What Isn't a Religion." *The Journal of Religion* 93, no 3 (July 2013): 291–318.

Schjerling, Peter. "The Basics of Gene Doping." In *Genetic Technology and Sport: Ethical Questions*, edited by Claudio Tamburrini and Torbjörn Tännsjö, 19–31. London and New York: Routledge, 2005.

Schneider, Angela J., Matthew N. Fedoruk, and Jim L. Rupert. "Human Genetic Variation: New Challenges and Opportunities for Doping Control." *Journal of Sports Sciences* 30, no. 11 (2012): 1117–29.

Scholes, Jeffrey. "Professional Baseball and Fan Disillusionment: A Religious Ritual Analysis." *Journal of Religion and Popular Culture* 7 (Summer 2014): 1–14.

Sherwin, Susan. "Genetic Enhancement, Sports and Relational Autonomy." *Sport, Ethics and Philosophy* 1, no. 2 (2007): 171–80.

Shogan, Debra. *The Making of High-Performance Athletics: Discipline, Diversity, and Ethics*. Toronto, ON: University of Toronto Press, 1999.

Simon, Robert L. *Fair Play: The Ethics of Sport*. 2nd ed. Boulder, CO: Westview Press, 2004.

———. "Good Competition and Drug-Enhanced Performance." In *Ethics in Sport*, edited by William J. Morgan, Klaus V. Meier, and Angela J. Schneider, 119–29. Champaign, IL: Human Kinetics, 2001.

Sinclair-Faulkner, Tom. "A Puckish Reflection on Religion in Canada." In *Religion and Culture in Canada/Religion et Culture au Canada*, edited by Peter Slater, 383–405. Ottawa, ON: Wilfrid Laurier University Press, 1977.

Sinden, Jane Lee. "The Elite Sport and Christianity Debate: Shifting Focus from Normative Values to the Conscious Disregard for Health." *Journal for Religious Health* 52 (2012): 335–49.

Slusher, Howard. "Sport and the Religious." In *Religion and Sport: The Meeting of Sacred and Profane*, edited by Charles S. Prebish, 173–96. Westport, CT: Greenwood Press, 1993.

Song, Robert. "Knowing There is No God, Still We Should Not Play God? Habermas on the Future of Human Nature." *Ecotheology* 11, no. 2 (2006): 191–211.

Sottas, Pierre-Edouard, Neil Robinson, Oliver Rabin, and Martial Saugy. "The Athlete Biological Passport." *Clinical Chemistry* 57, no. 7 (2011): 969–76.

Kaji, Keisuke, Katherine Norrby, Agnieszka Paca, Maria Mileikovsky, Paria Mohensi, and Knut Woltjen. "Virus-free induction of pluripotency and subsequent excision of reprogramming factors." *Nature: International Weekly Journal of Science* 458 (1 March 2009): 771–75.
http://www.nature.com/nature/journal/vaop/ncurrent/full/nature07864.html

Stebner, Eleanor J., and Tracy J. Trothen. "A Diamond Is Forever? Women, Baseball and a Pitch for a Radically Inclusive Community." In *The Faith of 50 Million: Baseball, Religion, and American Culture*, edited by Christopher H. Evans and William R. Herzog II, 167–86. Louisville, KY: Westminster John Knox Press, 2002.

Steffensmeier, Timothy R. "Sacred Saturdays: College Football and Local Identity." In *Sporting Rhetoric: Performance, Games, and Politics*, edited by Barry Brummett, 218–34. New York: Peter Lang, 2009.

Stevenson, Christopher. "Christian Athletes and the Culture of Elite Sport: Dilemmas and Solutions." *Sociology of Sport Journal* 14 (1997): 241–62.

Stinson, Scott. "Complaint Over Artificial Turf at Women's World Cup Highlights Double Standard in Sports." (Toronto) *National Post*, 15 October 2014.
http://sports.nationalpost.com/2014/10/15/complaint-over-artificial-turf-at-womens-world-cup-highlights-double-standard-in-sports/?__federated=1.

Sullivan, Sean P. "God in My Sporting: a Justification for Christian Experience in Sport." *Journal of the Christian Society for Kinesiology and Leisure Studies* 1, no. 1 (2010): 9–17.

Sutcliffe, Mark. "Amputee Sprinter Treads Uneven Track." *The Ottawa Citizen*, 13 January 2008. http://www2.canada.com.

Swartz, Leslie, and Brian Watermeyer. "Cyborg Anxiety: Oscar Pistorius and the Boundaries of What it Means to be Human." *Disability & Society* 23, no. 2 (2008): 187–90.

Sweeney H., Lee. "Gene Doping." *Scientific American*, July 2004.
http://www.sciam.com/article.cfm?id=gene-doping.

Swift, E. M., and Don Yaeger. "Unnatural Selection." *Sports Illustrated.* 94, no. 20 (2001): 86.

Takefive, Webinar. "The Marketing Muscle of Sports." Com Cast spotlight. 13 March 2013. Speakers: John Miller, Stephen Master, Mike Wall.

Tamburrini, Claudio, and Torbjörn Tännsjö. "Enhanced Bodies." In *Enhancing Human Capacities*, edited by Julian Savulescu, Ruud ter Meulen, and Guy Kahane, 274–90. Oxford, UK: Wiley-Blackwell, 2011.

Tamburrini, Claudio M. "What's Wrong With Genetic Inequality? The Impact of Genetic Technology on Elite Sports and Society." *Sport, Ethics and Philosophy* 1, no. 2 (2007): 229–38.

Tännsjö, Torbjörn. "Genetic Engineering and Elitism in Sport." In *Genetic Technology and Sport: Ethical Questions*, edited by Claudio Tamburrini and Torbjörn Tännsjö, 55–69. London and New York: Routledge, 2005.

Trothen, Tracy J. "Hockey: A Divine Sport?: Canada's National Sport in Relation to Embodiment, Community, and Hope." *Studies in Religion/Sciences Religieuses* 35, no. 2 (2006): 291–305.

———. "Holy Acceptable Violence?: Violence in Hockey and Christian Atonement Theories." *The Journal of Religion and Popular Culture*, Special Edition—Religion and Popular Culture in Canada 21 (2009): 1–42. utpjournals.metapress.com/index/U926307K42351742.pdf.

———. "Redefining Human, Redefining Sport: The *Imago Dei* and Genetic Modification Technologies." In *The Image of God in the Human Body: Essays on Christianity and Sports*, edited by Donald R. Deardorff and John White, 217–34. New York: Edwin Mellen Press, 2008.

———. "Sport, Religion, and Genetic Modification: An Ethical Analysis of Gene Doping." *The International Journal of Religion and Sport* 1, no. 1 (2009): 1–20.

Twietmeyer, Gregg. "A Theology of Inferiority: Is Christianity the Source of Kinesiology's Second-Class Status in the Academy?" *Quest* 60 (2008): 452–66.

Unal, Mehmet, and Durisehvar Ozer Unal. "Gene Doping in Sports." *Sports Medicine* 34, no. 6 (2004): 358–59.

Van Hilvoorde, Ivo, and Laurens Landeweerd. "Disability or Extraordinary Talent: Francesco Lentini (Three Legs) Versus Oscar Pistorius (No Legs)." *Sports, Ethics and Philosophy* 2, no. 2 (2008): 97–111.

Van Hilvoorde, Ivo, Rein Vos, and Guido de Wert. "Flopping, Klapping and Gene Doping: Dichotomies Between 'Natural' and 'Artificial' in Elite Sport." *Social Studies of Science* 37, no. 2 (2007): 173–200.

Vannini, April, and Barbara Fornssler. "Girl, Interrupted: Interpreting Semenya's Body, Gender Verification Testing, and Public Discourse." *Cultural Studies Critical Methodologies*, 11, no. 3 (2010): 243–57.

Vondey, Wolfgang. "Christian Enthusiasm: Can the Olympic Flame Kindle the Fire of Christianity?" *Word & World* 23, no. 3 (Summer 2003): 312–20.

Wire Services. "Murder or Accident?" *Kingston Whig-Standard* (Kingston, ON, 23 February 2013) 18.

World Anti-Doping Agency (WADA). http://www.wada-ama.org/rtecontent/document/code_v3.pdf (accessed 5 August 2013) 3.

———. "Blood Doping." (2014) https://www.wada-ama.org/en/questions-answers/blood-doping.

————. "WADA Gene Doping Symposium Calls for Greater Awareness, Strengthened Action against Potential Gene Transfer Misuse in Sport" (June 2008). http://www.wada-ama.org/en/newsarticle.ch2?articleId=3115626.

————. "Fundamental Rationale for the World Anti-Doping Code" (2009). http://www.wada-ama.org/Documents/Anti-Doping_Community/WADA_Anti-Doping_CODE_2009_EN.pdf.

Walker, Gillian A. *Family Violence and the Women's Movement: The Conceptual Politics of Struggle.* Toronto: University of Toronto Press, 1990.

Walton, Heather. "The Gender of the Cyborg." *Theology & Sexuality* 10, no. 2 (2004): 33–44.

Ward, Graham. "A Question of Sport and Incarnational Theology." *Studies in Christian Ethics* 25, no. 1 (2012): 49–64.

Waters, Brent. *From Human to Posthuman: Christian Theology and Technology in a Postmodern World.* Surrey, UK: Ashgate Publishing, 2006.

Watson, Nick J., and Mark Nesti. "The Role of Spirituality in Sport Psychology Consulting: An Analysis and Integrative Review of Literature." *Journal of Applied Sport Psychology* 17, no. 3 (2005): 228–39.

Watson, Nick J., and Andrew Parker, editors. *Sports and Christianity: Historical and Contemporary Perspectives.* New York: Routledge, 2013.

Watson, Nick J., and Andrew Parker, "Sports and Christianity: Mapping the Field." In *Sports and Christianity: Historical and Contemporary Perspectives*, edited by Nick J. Watson and Andrew Parker, 9–88. New York: Routledge, 2013.

White, John. "The Enduring Problem of Dualism: Christianity and Sports." *Implicit Religion* 15, no. 2 (2012): 225–41.

Woods, Ronald B. *Social Issues in Sport.* Champaign, IL: Human Kinetics, 2007.

Young, Pamela Dickey, Heather Shipley, and Tracy J. Trothen, eds. *Religion and Sexuality: Diversity and the Limits of Tolerance.* Vancouver, BC: UBC Press, 2015.

Zhou, S., J. E. Murphy, and J.A. Escobedo et al., "Adeno-Associated Virus-Mediated Delivery of Erythropoietin." *Gene Therapy*, 5, no. 5 (1998): 665–70.

Index

Index

Index